# ROCK, ROLL & REMEMBER

# ROCK, ROLL
# & REMEMBER

## by Dick Clark
## and Richard Robinson

THOMAS Y. CROWELL COMPANY
New York / Established 1834

PHOTO CREDITS

Page 61 (all), courtesy of *TV Guide;* 78 (bottom), Robert Kelley, Time-Life Picture Agency © Time Inc.; 79 (top), courtesy of *16* magazine; 98, Time-Life Picture Agency © Time Inc.; 102, courtesy of *Cashbox* magazine; 103 (top), "Funky Winkerbean" by Tom Batiuk, courtesy of Field Enterprises, Inc.; 103 (middle), "B.C." by permission of John Hart and Field Enterprises, Inc.; 118 (top), *The Boston Globe;* 119 (top), Paul Schutzer, Time-Life Picture Agency © Time Inc.; 119 (bottom), John Loengard, Time-Life Picture Agency © Time Inc.; 120 (top and bottom), Robert Kelley, Time-Life Picture Agency © Time Inc.; 121 and 129 (bottom), Paul Schutzer, Time-Life Picture Agency © Time Inc.; 165 (bottom left and right), courtesy of *16* magazine; 211 (top left and right), photographs by United Press International.

Manufactured in the United States of America

Library of Congress Cataloging in Publication Data

Clark, Dick, 1929–
    Rock, roll & remember.

    1. Clark, Dick, 1929–    2. Rock music—United States—History and criticism.   I. Robinson, Richard, 1945–    joint author.   II. Title.
ML429.C55A3        784'.092'4        [B]        76-17606
ISBN 0-690-01184-9

10   9   8   7   6   5   4   3   2   1

# Acknowledgments

The authors are grateful for the kind assistance in gathering memories provided by the following individuals: Jay Acton, Barbara M. Barnard, Loretta Martin Clark, Richard A. Clark, Louis Heyward, Larry Klein, Fran La Maina, Bill Lee, Tony Mamarella, Kal Mann, Bob Marcucci, Dennis Mosher, Norm Nite, Judy Price, Lisa Robinson, Red Schwartz, Rex Sparger, Kari Wigton, John Zacherle, and Deane Zimmerman.

# Contents

# ROCK, ROLL
# & REMEMBER

# 1

## "They're Really Rockin' on 'Bandstand'"

August 5, 1957, was a hot, sticky Monday in Philadelphia. The humidity was near 90 percent and nobody at the WFIL-TV studios felt cool. Particularly me. I was soggy and on edge, but not just from the weather. At three o'clock that afternoon "Bandstand" would join the ABC-TV network for the first time. Sixty-seven stations coast to coast would pick it up live and I would become Dick Clark, host of "American Bandstand."

I'd hardly slept the night before, gotten to the station hours early, spent the morning nudging everyone, and by one o'clock had managed to drive them all out for a long lunch. I paced across the small office for a few minutes, checked my watch, and lifted the pile of thirty records off my desk and carried them across the hall to the control room.

"Going on early?" asked Frank Kern, the audio engineer. Taking the pile of records from me, he put them down next to the audio board.

I looked at my watch, it was 1:20. "No, I just want everything set. Have you got your copy of the play list?"

Frank sat down, stuck his pipe in his mouth, and looked at me quizzically. He was a heavyset, stodgy old fellow with gray hair and that great show-biz attitude where the world falls apart and he remains calm.

"Hmm?"

"The play list, have you got it?"

"I suppose I will by 2:45," he said. He turned to lean over the audio board and spin a dial. "I have every day for the past five years."

1

"Today is different. Don't you know . . ." My barking was interrupted as my producer, Tony Mamarella, stuck his head in the door.

"Dick, have you seen the records for the show? I could have sworn I left them on your desk."

"No records today. Dickie's gonna play harmonica," said Frank through his teeth while he kept them gripped around his pipe.

"Damn both of you," I muttered as I left the control room behind Tony. "Has Marlene typed the play list? I gave Frank the records."

"Marlene's at lunch at Singer's like she always is at this time. The list'll be ready. I think you'd better sit down. I'm ordering sandwiches from Herman's, want one?"

"No. Yes. Hell, I don't know. Order me something. Jesus, I'm glad we only go network once."

"*You're* glad!" said Tony. He laughed. "I'll order you a ham and Swiss cheese on a hard roll and a Coke."

"Maybe I should put on my suit?"

"Sure, why not. We'll have lunch formal."

I opened the broom closet at the end of the office where I kept my tape recorder, files, and my suit and extra shirt. Snapping on the overhead light, I stepped in and closed the door. Changing was no fun, but it was all I had as a dressing room. I had one leg in my suit pants when I heard the outer door of the office open.

"All set for the feed to New York?" It was Lew Klein, the TV program director at WFIL.

"Yeah," said Tony. "I'll check it again at three. Everything's fine except I'm not sure Dick is going to last the afternoon."

At that moment I stumbled pulling on the other pants leg and crashed against the closet door. I finished dressing to Tony and Klein's laughter.

Lunch arrived. I had a sip of the Coke, looked at the sandwich a couple of times, then started pacing the office.

"Why don't you do your makeup?" Tony growled.

"Good idea." Across the hall from the office was a men's room the size of a phone booth, the only one on the floor, where I did my makeup for the show. This consisted of smear-

2

ing my face with Max Factor's dark brown pancake makeup which I bought at Pop Singer's drugstore. As I dabbed my face and neck, my hand slipped and I left a brown streak across my blue shirt collar. I walked back across the hall and kicked open the office door.

Tony looked up in surprise and then laughed. "Got another shirt?"

At 2:30 I went into the men's room to comb my hair, and then I walked into Studio B.

ABC had sent a designer from New York to rework the set. The canvas record store backdrop was gone, replaced by a field of gold records hung in gold-trimmed frames from floor to ceiling. Nat Elkitz, WFIL's set man, was at the top of a stepladder affixing the last few records in the top row of frames. The crew, Pete Twaddle, Vince Gasbarro, Ralph Dicocco, and Bill Russell had pulled the pine bleachers out from the wall where they were stored between shows and were huffing and muttering as they pushed the podium Nat had designed up onto a riser. Hank Latvin was pasting glitter around the edges of a cutout map of the United States, though he had most of it on his gray janitorial uniform that WFIL supplied to the crews.

Nat looked around as I came in.

"How do you like it?" he asked as he climbed down the ladder.

"Looks great. What's that?" I pointed to a large, counter-length table off to one side.

"The new autograph table. I painted fake signatures of the stars all over the top of it so when they're sitting there signing autographs the cameras can pan down and get the signatures as a background." Nat touched the surface gingerly with his finger. "I hope they're dry by the time we go on the air."

I stepped up on the podium. The dance area was directly in front of me. To my right were the bleachers and autograph table, to my left the cutout map. Past the dance floor was the camera area where Hank and Pete were now fixing cables. I looked at the far wall of the studio. On the right were two windows, one above the other. The lower window was the control room, the one above where the sponsors watched. To

This picture was taken from the screen by a viewer. The award behind my left shoulder was given to me in 1957 by a group of Philadelphia promotion men. It's one of several hundred that I've received over the years, most of which are hanging in my offices on Sunset Boulevard.

Another fan photo taken from the screen in 1958 in front of the old Teen-age Top 10 Board we used on "The Dick Clark Saturday Night Show."

The familiar glitter cutout map of the United States. Our Philadelphia regulars used to dance behind it as we opened each show on ABC.

Bill Doggett, who had a hit with "Honky Tonk, Part II," came to visit us in October 1957, at Forty-sixth and Market streets, in Philadelphia.

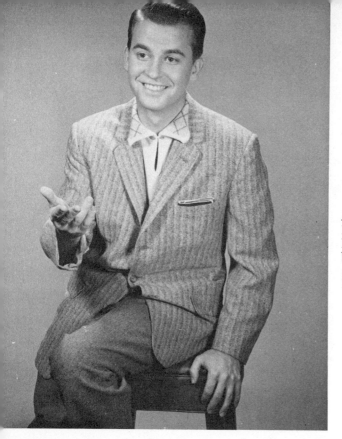

A publicity still in 1958. Don't you just love the "wet look"! That terrible greased-back look was achieved by applying pure lanolin to my hair every day.

In June 1956, Richard Widmark came by to promote his new picture. That's the old "Bandstand," pre-ABC network set, that Ralph Dicocco, our cameraman, was shooting.

In the early network days of "American Bandstand," our visitors were a mixture of pop stars and the new rock 'n' rollers. Frankie Laine was a guest in August 1958.

Behind me is our station affiliates map, and to the left the "Bandstand" bulletin board, with P.O. Box 6, Phila. 5 prominently displayed. That helped increase the mail flow in those days. Notice the viewer snapshots on the bulletin board.

the left of the sponsors' viewing booth was another window where the station executives looked into the studio from their offices. I checked the clock over the control room window. Half an hour to go.

On the podium was a folded note with my name scrawled on it. I opened it. "Don't be nervous, just the world and Alan Freed are watching." As I finished reading it, the crew burst into laughter.

"Don't worry, Dick, we love you," shouted Hank Latvin. "But don't you think you better pull up your fly?"

I reached down to check my fly; they were in hysterics. It was a little too much fun, I grinned nervously.

Marlene, my secretary, came in and handed me a telegram. It was from Army Grant, the head of daytime TV at the ABC network in New York, wishing me good luck.

I looked up to check the clock again. Fifteen minutes to go.

Eleanor Goldsmith, secretary to station manager Roger Clipp, waved from the executive viewing window. Ed Yates, the show's director, took a seat next to Frank Kern in the control room. He sat there chewing on his cigar, going over the play list with Kern. He caught my eye and winked at me.

Tony came in with the lists of records and commercials and the Cheerios cereal logo for their commercial. He handed them up to me.

"Don't forget, it's 'American Bandstand.' And the kids aren't supposed to say what high school, just their name and age, pretend the show isn't from Philly."

"Everything else set?"

Tony glanced around the studio. "The set's fine. The kids are lined up in the hall. They're more excited than we are. So it's up to you. Have you got the details straight on the Sal Mineo contest?"

"Yeah. I think it's all straight. I feel a little better. It's just that I've got only four weeks to prove it to ABC."

"We'll do it all right. You'll be the hottest twenty-six-year-old MC on the line." Tony grinned, then went to the door next to the control room to let the kids into the studio. I calmed down as they streamed in, pulling off their coats and dumping them along with school books and pocketbooks under the bleachers. It was just another day on "Bandstand," er "American Bandstand." The cameramen wandered in from their coffee break to take their positions. I saw Tony and Ed talking in the control room.

Little Roe, Barbara Marsden, Monte Montez, and a few other kids came up to the podium to wish me luck. I smiled at them. Bob and Justine, two regulars, joked with the cameramen, telling them to be sure to get some closeups.

There were no monitors facing me on the podium in the studio because we didn't want the kids to stand and watch themselves. I couldn't check to see if my tie was straight or my hair neat. I gave it all over to the fates.

"Okay," yelled Bill Russell, the floor manager, from behind the center of the three cameras. "As soon as you hear the music, start dancing." He raised his right arm above his head. The kids quieted down, some of them went to sit on the bleachers. "Stand by—five, four, three, two . . ." Bill swung his arm down to point at me. Les Elgart's "Bandstand Boogie" filled the studio. Ralph Dicocco brought the lights up on the grid above the dance floor, and the red tally light lit on top of camera number two. Near the bleachers, kids started dancing.

I took a deep breath. "Hi, I'm Dick Clark. Welcome to 'American Bandstand.' You and I have got an hour and a half to share together with some of my friends here, lots of good music, and our special guest stars." I smiled into the camera. It felt strange having to explain the show. I did fine though, until I blanked for a second. I glanced down at the play list where Tony had penciled in who the guests were. "With us today is the 'I'm-Gonna-Sit-Right-Down-and-Write-Myself-a-Letter' man, Billy Williams. The Chordettes will be here too. Right now, let's do a whole lotta shakin' with Jerry Lee Lewis."

The first record of the day was always a fast song. It got the kids moving. They came bounding down the bleachers, starting to dance as their feet hit the floor. A half-dozen girls danced with each other near the far left corner. Bob and Justine slid into position in front of the center camera. As Jerry Lee Lewis' chant rattled the studio speakers, the dance area filled up.

I looked up at the control room window. Ed nodded, smiling around his cigar. But Tony wasn't there. I picked up my phone on the podium. Ed answered. "Tony's in master control. The feed is fine, but we may have a problem in New York."

"What's wrong?"

"The union pulled a wildcat walkout . . . wait." Ed turned to speak to Tony as he came back into the control room. He handed Tony the phone.

"NABET just walked out in New York and Chicago because we're using a local crew here. They started the show with 'stand-by' signs."

"What's going to happen now?"

"Announce the next song, I'll let you know."

I dashed out into the hall, got a drink of water from the fountain, and was back at the podium as the first song ended. I announced the next record, Joni James's "Summer Love," a slow dance, and the cameras cut back to the kids.

I picked up the phone. Tony got it in the control room.

"We're back on the air, I think," he said.

"You sure? This is one hell of a way to start."

"Huh? Yeah. Just a second, I'll call you back." Dropping the phone, Tony ran out of the control room.

When the record ended I announced our Sal Mineo contest. Tony and I had come up with "Why I'd Like a Date with Sal Mineo" as a contest to draw mail to prove the show's strength to ABC. Sal was a big star coming off *Rebel Without a Cause;* he'd done the show when we were local a couple of times and had a Top 10 hit with "Start Movin'." As I gave the details of the contest I had a sinking feeling no one outside of Philadelphia was watching.

Billy Williams came on to do "I'm Gonna Sit Right Down and Write Myself a Letter." I sent him over to the autograph table while the kids lined up to get his signature.

Then I played a couple of fast songs. The cameras caught the kids doing the jitterbug and lindy. Watching the kids dance, I pondered what an ABC executive had said to me while we were getting the show ready to go network: "Does anybody really give a damn about watching kids dancing to rock 'n' roll in Philadelphia?"

The light went on on the podium phone. I picked it up.

Sal Mineo, during his visit in May 1957. He came by to promote his new record "Start Movin'." This was just one of many visits Sal made over the years.

"Everything's all right. NABET is up in arms, but we're on the air across the network. Give me a big smile and do the bit with the map." Tony pushed at the corners of his mouth with his fingers, leering through the control room window.

I smiled back. I walked over to the phony map of the United States we'd come up with, reeled off the call letters of a TV station that was taking the show from the network, and announced the next song. "The top tune in New Haven on WNHC is The Coasters with 'Searchin'.' Here it is."

From the control room window I saw Tony motioning for me to pick up the podium phone.

"What now?" I said, making a mental note to rip out the phone after the show if things kept up like this.

"You won't believe this. We caught you on-camera talking on the phone before. Well, the phone just rang in here. Somebody wanted to talk to you. I took the call. This kid gets on and says, 'I want to talk to Dick Clark.' 'He's on the air,' I said. The kid says, 'I know, but he's got a phone up there.' The kid was calling from St. Louis!"

I laughed. It looked like "American Bandstand" was going to work out fine.

We ran a roll call in the final 20 minutes of the show. During

The studio view of "American Bandstand."

a commercial I reminded the kids how it would work. When we were local they would say, "Mary Jones, South Philadelphia" —their name and their school. Now they had to say their name and age, breaking a four-year habit. But after the first few weeks we stuck to it as it turned out the viewers were interested in the kids on the show and how old they were.

The show ended that day with everything back to normal. When I got back to the office Tony was on the phone. He waved at me to pick up the extension quietly. It was Ted Fetter, director of programs at ABC in New York. He was telling Tony he thought the show had gone well.

"Tell me one thing," said Fetter. "Why do you keep shooting the kids' feet?"

"Teaches the other kids how to dance."

"Hmm, yes," said Fetter. "Okay, but why don't the kids smile more?"

I was so drained from the show I thought I'd start to giggle. Putting the phone down, I loosened my tie and lit a cigarette. Tony continued to take calls. A kid watching on WFAA in Dallas called to ask us to dedicate a song to Harold in Pasadena, a Dallas suburb. A New York record promo man called to say I should get some sharper clothes.

The door opened in the outer office and George Koehler, WFIL's general manager, walked in.

"I'm glad I'm not on your party line. I've been trying to call you guys for the last five minutes," he said, sitting on the corner of my desk. "Good show, Dick. Fetter called me after he talked with Tony. He says ABC estimates an audience of 20 million a week. I don't think there's any question about it. They want this show."

"What about NABET?" asked Tony.

"That'll be over by tomorrow. Although Lawrence Welk is going to have some unkind words for you rock 'n' rollers."

"Lawrence Welk!" Tony and I cried in unison.

Koehler nodded. "Fetter got it from one of the union people. In retaliation for 'Bandstand' not using a NABET crew, at eight o'clock tonight all the NABET crews across the country will walk out for an hour to write letters of protest about 'Bandstand.' So Welk gets the ax. Maybe you can slip in a couple of polkas tomorrow as a gesture of goodwill."

## "Wouldn't this be a great way to make a living?"

The week he graduated from high school in June 1943, my older brother, Bradley, enlisted in the Air Force. I was playing with my Lionel trains on the floor in the bedroom we shared when he came in and closed the door behind him.

"I got it!" he said excitedly as he flopped down on his bed. He pulled an envelope out of his pants pocket and tossed it at me. "They accepted me. I'm in," he said, lying back on the bed and swinging his arms in the air.

I left the trains on the floor and picked up the envelope where it had landed on my bed. It looked very official to my fourteen-year-old eyes. It had been ripped open; I pulled out the letter and unfolded it. I didn't know what to make of it, something about Bradley Clark being accepted by the Air Force. It scared me. I looked at Brad.

"Hey, what's the matter? Don't you understand?" He sat up and took the letter. "I got accepted into the Pilot Training Program of the United States Air Force!"

"What's that mean?"

"Means that without college, the Air Force is gonna teach me how to fly. Not many guys get that kind of a break."

"Do mom and dad know?"

"I haven't told them yet." Bradley put the letter back in the envelope. "I'll tell them tonight, at supper. You keep quiet about it."

Brad was my hero. He was tall, good-looking, and an excellent athlete. He made the varsity football team in high school. I was at the bony, awkward stage, with a face covered with

*Left:* From left to right, a seven- or eight-year-old Dick Clark, my cousin Betty Barnard, and my brother, Brad. That wooden sled at my feet was a museum piece from my grandmother's attic.

*Right:* I'm posing in front of a gigantic weeping willow tree at 2 Park Lane, Mount Vernon, New York. My family spent over twenty happy years on this site on the Barnum estate.

pimples. Though he was five years older, Brad often included me in his plans; we had a very close relationship.

His decision to enlist in the Air Force dismayed me. He would have been drafted in any case, but that afternoon, as he told me about the acceptance letter, I didn't understand. I sat on my bed in the room we shared and I sulked. It was like he was deliberately deserting me.

After he left for training, I was lonely. We lived in Mount Vernon, New York, in an apartment building at 2 Park Lane, located on the former Bailey (of Barnum & Bailey) estate. Brad and I had spent hours playing in the fields that surrounded the building. With him gone I spent more and more time in my room. My mother let us do whatever we wanted with the room; it was our private reserve. One wall was covered with stars and moons pasted on a blue background, another wall had dozens of photos and autographs of Hollywood stars I'd written away for—Edward G. Robinson, Shirley Temple, Humphrey Bogart. Hanging from the ceiling were model planes and a giant cardboard fan we'd installed to swing over our twin beds.

That summer I did little more than hang around the house.

I went outside only when my mother had had enough of me and wanted the house to herself for a few hours. In the evenings and on weekends I helped my father work on a little square of land behind the building that he'd designated as our "victory garden." We'd plant, hoe, water, and wait for mom to call us in for supper. We talked about Brad, where he was, and how the war was going. Brad had been offered a post as a flight instructor, but refused it. In September he was sent to Europe to fly fighter missions. That fall he sent home a photo of himself in uniform standing in front of a P-47. I took the photo and showed it to the kids in school.

I started reading the newspaper every day to find out how the war was going. Picking up the paper in the lobby on the way in from school, I would scan the headlines on the way up to the apartment.

I was in the lobby, shortly after Christmas 1944, excited that I had a week off from school. I'd picked up our paper off the pile, tucked it under my arm, and was waiting for the elevator.

Mr. Lindblum, the building superintendent, came in. He was an old friend who sometimes let me run the elevator and use his workshop in the basement. He stopped by the telephone switchboard when he saw me.

"Dickie, I'm sorry. You know how I felt about Brad. I don't know what to say."

I stood there, staring at him. He didn't realize he was the first to tell me that Brad was dead. I took the newspaper from under my arm, opened it up, and held it in front of my face, pretending to read it. I didn't say anything. I kept turning the pages.

I got in the elevator and Mr. Lindblum took me up to the second floor. I opened the door to our apartment. Mother was on the sofa, her face buried in the pillows, sobbing. It was the first time I ever saw her cry.

Our landlady, Ethel Payne, sat with her. Ethel waved me into my bedroom.

When dad came home, it was the same. We went through the motions of sitting down to dinner, though no one ate anything. After dinner we sat in the living room; the silence was

*Left:* A very young Dick Clark.

*Right:* Dick Clark all dressed up for a school portrait, age nine.

*Left:* Like the boy in the short pants, circa 1933?

*Right:* In the old days, there was always a guy with a pony upon which you had your portrait taken. You can see how thrilled I was at the prospect.

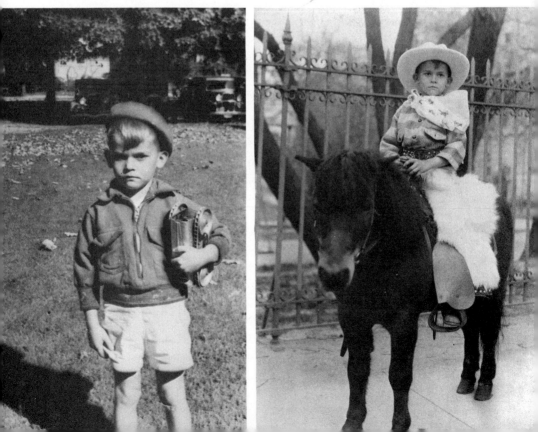

At A. B. Davis High School in Mount Vernon, New York, I belonged to Alpha Iota Epsilon High School Fraternity. I shared the cover of the March 1947 newsletter with two of my fraternity brothers.

awful. My father turned to me. "Dickie, I want you to go to bed now. We'll talk in the morning."

I went into the bedroom and looked at the walls with the pennants of Brad's team, our blue wall of pasted-up stars, the planes hanging from the ceiling. I undressed. Opening the closet to put my clothes away, I saw one of his sport jackets. That did it. I dropped down on the floor and cried uncontrollably.

A few days later, we got a letter from Brad's commanding officer. Brad had been a fighter pilot in the 371st Fighter Group. He'd volunteered for a mission during the Battle of the Bulge. He took off in the morning of December 23, in stormy weather; his plane was disabled and crashed.

Having served through World War I, my father was probably the most fatalistic about Brad's death. My mother was in shock. I don't think she ever had a day when she wasn't distracted by memories of Brad. For almost a year, I dealt with it by eliminating the outside world as much as possible.

By my sophomore year at A. B. Davis High School in Mount Vernon, I realized I had to come to grips with myself, so I ran my 128 pounds out to the scrimmage field to try out for football. I wound up on the ninth team, stayed around long enough to get the daylights kicked out of me, and then, mercifully, got scratched for good. I tried out for the swimming and track teams, but didn't make them either. I eventually saw a little glory by setting the school record for push-ups. It was obvious that varsity sports weren't for me. I guess I was trying to fill Brad's shoes.

About this time I discovered the magic world of the radio. In my room was a large Philco radio with a separate speaker that hung on the wall. In the afternoons before supper and in the evening when I finished my homework, I'd sit, twisting the dial, finding an escape in the disembodied fantasy world that came out of the speaker.

One of the first shows to catch my imagination was Martin Block's "Make-Believe Ballroom" on WNEW, broadcast from New York City. It was a wonderful show. Block played uninterrupted 15-minute segments of different singers. Before he'd spin the records he'd talk to his listeners as if he were the host at an imaginary nightclub in the sky. "Up there, on our stage, with the purple lights casting dazzling reflections on his face, is Perry Como," he'd say. Lying on my bed, my eyes closed, listening to Block, Perry Como really would be stepping up to the mike among the purple spotlights.

Another of my favorites on WNEW was Art Ford with his all-night show, the "Milkman's Matinee." I took the speaker off the wall, moved it to the nightstand next to my bed, and listened to Ford in the wee hours after my parents were asleep. It seemed so romantic to stay up all night and play records and get paid for it. I always wanted to be a midnight disc jockey. It was the only job in radio I never had.

Down the dial from WNEW was WMCA, which had "Battle of the Baritones" with singers like Frank Sinatra, Dick Haymes, and Andy Russell. Years later I borrowed that idea for "Bandstand" with our "Battle of the Songs" and "Battle of the Bands."

Of everything I heard on the radio, I liked the talkers most. Arthur Godfrey, Garry Moore, Steve Allen, and Dave Garroway became my idols—especially Arthur Godfrey. He was the first to realize that a radio announcer does *not* talk to "those of you out there in radio land"; a radio announcer talks to *me* as an individual. Godfrey knew that people listened to the radio one to one, so that was the way he treated his listeners.

I loved the fantasy world radio created. One night my parents took me into New York to see a live radio broadcast. It was the "Jimmy Durante–Garry Moore Show." I looked at the stars and the actors around them and thought, "Wouldn't this be a great way to make a living?" I saw the guy with the script in his hand waving to the audience to applaud. I saw the signals they used—*stretch* and *cut* arm motions. I peered through the double-glass partition into the control room where the engineers adjusted banks of dials. I sat spellbound as Moore and Durante romped through their bits around a big, stationary mike. I was hooked.

"Did you like it?" asked my mother on the train on the way home that night.

"That's what I want to do," I said. "When I write away for college catalogs, I'm going to find out which ones have a radio school."

My parents encouraged my dreams of a career in radio by suggesting I join the high school dramatic club. It proved a decisive step, giving me much-needed confidence. Not only did I join, I wound up president of the club. I gave speeches, went out of my way to make new friends, and acted my heart out whenever the opportunity presented itself.

I played the coward in *Submerged,* a play about six men trapped in a sunken submarine. In the last scene I was onstage alone, locked in the compartment by the rest of the crew. I banged on the compartment door, begging them to let me out. I really got into the role. At the first rehearsal I was on my knees, pounding on the door, screaming and sobbing for them to let me free. My cries echoed down the school corridors. By the time I finished the scene, half the school had run into the rehearsal room to see who was being murdered.

"On opening night, there wasn't a dry eye in the house," said Dorothy Feaster, my drama teacher.

With the Drama Club as my base, I forced myself out of my shell. I couldn't be the 90-pound weakling who developed into captain of the football team, but I was very much the guy who took piano lessons so they wouldn't laugh when he sat down to play. I amused my friends with imitations. I was an amateur hypnotist and at parties I never failed to have a few conjuring tricks in my pocket. I became a determined extrovert. In my senior year I was class president. I was also voted the "Man Most Likely to Sell the Brooklyn Bridge."

Meeting Barbara Mallery helped. Barbara was fourteen, I was fifteen at the time. I was still bashful with girls because my teen-age acne was slow in clearing up. I knew who Bobbie was and had a crush on her. She was a brunette, had blue eyes, and a great figure. She was part of what the boys at Davis referred to as "the rah-rah set" because she was a cheerleader.

In the late fall of my sophomore year, my best friend, Andy Grass, and I arranged a double date. My date was to be Diana Ruffalo, Andy's date was Bobbie. At the last minute Diana got sick. Andy told me to come along anyway. We went to the movies, then for sodas. Bobbie and I talked, liked each other, and were soon going steady. We went together from Halloween until Columbus Day of the following year.

Our teen-age romance was getting hot and heavy, and something told me that the situation was getting a little too serious. Our relationship was far from platonic. Perhaps I was afraid of the consequences. Maybe she was. In any case, Bobbie and I broke up and didn't see much of each other from that October until the next spring.

In May, a friend invited me to join a party of kids his parents were taking to the circus in New York City. No dates, just come and have a good time. I showed up at his house to find that Bobbie was one of the other guests. We went steady from then until I graduated.

# "I talked to the camera
# like it was a human being"

Just before I graduated from high school, my uncle Bradley Barnard, who owned the Rome *Sentinel* newspaper in Rome, New York, decided to open a radio station in the area. Late one Sunday night he called my father to offer him the job as sales manager of the new station. After twenty-six years in the cosmetics business, Dad gave his notice and we moved to Utica that spring.

I applied to and was accepted at nearby Syracuse University. When I asked my father for a summer job at WRUN, he thought it would be possible, but said he'd check with my Uncle Bradley first. A couple of days later, he told me I had the job.

I was tickled. "When do I start?" I demanded, certain it was only a matter of weeks before radio discovered I was the next Martin Block.

During my first week at WRUN I didn't even see a microphone. I was put in charge of the mimeograph machine. I cranked out hundreds of sales promotion flyers, got the mimeo ink in my hair and clothes, and didn't let on that this was hardly what I'd expected. The second week I was moved to the mailroom where I stuffed envelopes, took mail to the post office, and distributed interoffice memos. By the end of July I had made friends with everyone at the station and secretly confided to each of them my desire to be on the air. Mostly I demonstrated my enthusiasm for broadcasting by hustling through jobs that included emptying wastepaper baskets and running errands.

One afternoon dad came out of his office and told me I would pinch-hit for a vacationing FM announcer. In those days FM radio hardly existed; it wasn't much more than a noble experiment. I didn't care. This was my chance to get in front of the mike. I was ecstatic—Dick Clark was on the air.

I started out doing the weather forecast every hour on the FM rural network. My listeners couldn't have numbered more than seven or eight farmers, a couple of ducks, and a cow or two.

Before I left for the station the next morning I installed an FM radio in the kitchen so mom could listen to the debut of her son, the radio personality. She promised she wouldn't leave the house all day and that she wouldn't miss a word.

My first broadcast was the nine o'clock weather. I must have been a sight, a skinny teen-ager, holding the weather report off the news wire, waiting for my big moment. The news ended, the engineer pointed a finger at me, and I was on the air. I cupped my right hand around my ear, lowered my voice, and sounded as resonant as I possibly could. Father told me later it sounded more like Shakespeare than the weather.

By the end of the summer I surprised everyone with the professional style I developed. They let me do station breaks and the news on WRUN-AM—most of the day the station carried the ABC radio network with Don McNeil's "Breakfast Club," "School's Out," Don Gardiner and Paul Harvey with the news, Paul Whiteman, Mike and Buff Wallace, mystery shows, and very little music.

When September arrived I was off to school. In these early postwar years Syracuse University had 17,000 student in facilities built for 11,000. Many of the guys were back from the war to pick up at twenty-five or twenty-six where they'd left off. I was seventeen, floundering around, trying to drink my share of the beer and get used to mature life.

I majored in advertising, minored in radio. I studied a lot, getting a sound education in business administration. In an advertising course, I won a prize for writing the unforgettable slogan for Gem razor blades: "A man's best friend is a Gem."

The first semester I signed up for radio courses. My counselor told me I had to concentrate on my major and wait until I was a sophomore to start taking radio courses. After that first summer at WRUN I had radio in my blood, so when he told me I couldn't study radio, I searched out "Radio House," a three-studio student-run station on campus with the call letters WAER-FM. The station was located in a Quonset hut in the middle of the campus.

I walked into WAER and asked to see the student manager. He was a guy named Jerry Landay who went on to become a commentator for Westinghouse Broadcasting. I told him I'd had some experience. He agreed to an audition. I did my best low-voiced announcer imitation and was added to the program schedule.

The first show he gave me was a daily half-hour with foreign students, many of whom hardly spoke English. By my sophomore year I had a DJ hour, did newscasts, and ran my own version of the popular "Tex and Jinx" radio talk show.

When we moved to Utica and I began my first year at Syracuse, Bobbie finished high school and she, her mother, brother, and sister moved to Salisbury, Maryland, where Bobbie enrolled in the state teachers' college. Bobbie's father was dead and her mother worked. Her mother wanted to make sure Bobbie got a good education so she could support herself or help support a husband and family.

For the next three years we wrote each other torrid love letters. I made frequent runs from Syracuse to Salisbury in a 1934 Ford convertible I bought with my odd-jobs money. This was 1950, mind you. The car had no heater, so the seventeen-hour trip was murder in the winter. To keep warm I put on galoshes, wrapped my legs in blankets, wore as many sweaters as I could pull on, plus a coat, scarf, gloves, and earmuffs.

I dated a few other girls at Syracuse, but I always felt Bobbie and I were going steady. I dated one girl named Peggy. When she found out I was going with Bobbie, she stopped talking to me. Around my fraternity house she was referred to as "pissed-off Peg."

In my senior year, Bobbie's mother let her transfer to Oswego State College, only a few miles from Syracuse. She came to Syracuse every weekend from then on. We went to the movies, to dances, to Nickel Charlies with my fraternity brothers.

24

Buying trays full of beer at five cents a glass, we played chug-a-lug games; by the end of the evening we would leave the table-top covered with empty glasses. I presented Bobbie with my fraternity pin, and when we decided to get married I gave her an engagement ring that one of my friends persuaded his father to get me wholesale.

We agreed to wait until she graduated the following year before we got married. That would give me a year to get a good job to support her.

In January of my senior year at Syracuse I started applying for a job at the local radio stations. One of these was a peanut-whistle station, WOLF, in downtown Syracuse, owned by Sherman Marshall. Getting up my nerve, I called Marshall to make an appointment. His daughter, Pat, worked for him and took the call. She arranged an audition for me with Ham Woodle, WOLF's program director.

Woodle was a cigar-smoking, sharply dressed old radio pro. He scared the hell out of me at the audition, with his off-handed, no-nonsense manner that made me feel like I should apologize for wasting his time. However, I did the audition, reading the copy he gave me as well as possible, considering my hands were shaking.

"Not bad, kid," he said, blowing out a cloud of cigar smoke that engulfed me. "How many years of college you got left?"

I told him I graduated in June.

"Call me in May, we'll see what we can work out."

"Mr. Woodle, I need a job." I hesitated, then said in a rush, "Is there any possibility I could start sooner?"

To my surprise, Woodle didn't throw me out for being impertinent. He took the cigar out of his mouth and said, "Can you work weekends?"

"Yes sir."

"Come in this Saturday, you can do weekend relief."

Within a month I was working at WOLF fulltime and going to college. I worked thirty to forty hours a week for them. The pay was a dollar an hour.

I stayed with WOLF until July 1951, a couple of months after I graduated. Sherm had discovered something that Todd

Storz, who is known as the father of pop radio, discovered many years later—that people always ask for the same records. He ran a show called "The Sandman Serenade" in the evening. Kids from the university would call in their requests, and Sherm hired college kids to sit by the phones and take down the requests. Of course we never played the requests, but by the end of the night we could see that the same forty or fifty records were asked for over and over. That was our play list. Storz later learned the same thing when he watched people in a bar play the records they liked over and over on the jukebox, and he turned this observation into the "Top 40" records format of radio.

I did newscasts at WOLF and announced a show called "The WOLF Buckaroos." I played records by "Eddy Arnold, the Tennessee plowboy" and "Gene Autry, the million-dollar cowboy." I guess I was a country music disc jockey before I played any other kind of music.

I was anxious to get on with my career, but not as a hillbilly announcer for a dollar an hour. I quit WOLF, returning to Utica where I moved in with my parents in their new house. By this time father was station manager at WRUN. He gave me a job as a summer replacement announcer. I hoped that a permanent slot would open up at WRUN. But after a few weeks of working at the station I realized I didn't want to work for my father. Being the boss's son was a problem—even if I did a good job there would always be somebody who could say, "Well, he's here because his old man runs the place." I was working too hard to prove myself to get put down like that.

I was determined to make my own way. Not only did I quit WRUN, but I changed my name to Dick Clay. My father's name is also Dick Clark and I didn't want there to be any confusion. I'm sure this bit of egotistical radicalism offended both my parents. I also hated being Dick Clay—it didn't seem like me. But I was stubborn enough to stick with the change until I moved to Philadelphia, where I went back to being Dick Clark. (Funny thing, Dick Clark is such a simple name, yet people have always asked me what my real name is.)

My next job was with the sole TV station in Utica at the time, WKTV. The station was located on top of a mountain—

we'd freeze our asses off getting up there in the winter time. We only had two cameras but lots of energy. I went there to be a newsman. I wound up writing copy for commercials, moving scenery, and hosting a country music show as Cactus Dick and the Santa Fe Riders.

I replaced a guy named Bob Earle at WKTV. Bob was a good-looking young guy with thin blond hair who went on to MC the "GE College Bowl." At WKTV he was a newscaster. Passing the studio monitor one night as Bob was about to do the news, I stopped to watch him. I was astonished. He looked straight into the camera and talked the news, as if he had it memorized. Only occasionally did he look down at the script in his hand. I couldn't understand how he did it. For the next three nights I stayed late to watch him give this performance. Sure enough, each night he looked right at the camera and reeled off the news. Finally, I couldn't stand it anymore. After the newscast ended I walked into the studio to confront him.

"Bob, how the hell do you do that?" I wailed, sure he'd tell me he had a photographic memory or some other magic talent I'd never acquire.

He laughed. "Are you sure you're ready to find out?" he said.

"I'm ready, I'm ready! I've watched you for the last four nights straight. It's making me nuts!"

Bob made a pretense of looking around to make sure no one was watching us. He motioned me to follow him behind the set.

"Meet Elmer, my helper," he said with a wave of his hand.

There was no one there. Then I noticed a tape recorder on the floor out of view of the cameras.

"I don't get it."

Bob smiled. "I record the news on tape just before the broadcast. I run a cable to an earphone and I play the tape when I do the news. That way I repeat it as I hear it in my ear." Producing a small earplug-sized earphone, he showed me how he ran the cable from the tape recorder across the floor onto the set, under his jacket, up the back of his neck, and around behind his ear so the whole thing was invisible from a front camera angle.

"I do 15 minutes of news without batting an eyelash."

Eventually, I became a newscaster at the station. I did the news with Stu Lucas, another reporter. At six o'clock I did the sports, Stu did news; at eleven I did news, Stu did sports. I immediately got my own Elmer. I bought a tape recorder and earphone and set out to develop the system a little further than Bob had.

I got the appliance store where I bought the tape recorder to connect a stop-start foot pedal so I could walk around the studio, turning the tape on or off at will. The effect was amazing. I'd go on-camera and reel off the baseball scores or a complicated news story without once looking at the copy. The earphone was so well hidden that viewers could never tell. During the commercials I passed the earphone to Stu and he used the recorder to do the sports.

Assembling my stories on the tape each evening before airtime, I left a space at the end of the tape for Stu to add the sports. One night, I put on my news show and left the studio. Stu came in, did his sports on the tape, then ran the tape back into the middle of my news, cueing it up to a spot where I said, "Today, in Washington, President Harry S. Truman said . . . " Stu erased my story and dubbed in "Blow it out your ass, you dumb son of a bitch."

Looking into the camera that night, I repeated as it came through the earphone, "Today, in Washington, President Harry S. Truman said . . . " I stopped short at what I heard next. For a split second I thought, knowing Harry's affection for salty language, maybe he did say that. Then I saw Stu grinning at me just off-camera. I ad-libbed my way out of the story.

I've never known anything about any sport in the world. So when I did the sports I'd call my friend Al Cole at WRUN to ask "What is the Brooklyn baseball team . . . the Dodgers?" And "It's the *New York* Yankees?" Once Al gave me the authoritative scoop, I put it on tape. On-camera doing the warmup for the World Series, I ran off statistics like a baseball fanatic. After the show I often stopped by Big Bill's, the bar we all frequented, and people would come up to tell me, "You've got a phenomenal memory. I was just telling Joe here you probably remember when Joe Doakes hit a home run in the third inning of the fourth game of the 1912 World Series."

"I really don't know all that stuff," I admitted. "I have this friend named Elmer who coaches me."

Occasionally, I made it with a waitress from Big Bill's in the backseat of my 1941 Olds sedan. I had fantasies that someone would come along with a flashlight, shine it in on us, and say, "I know you, you're Dick Clay!"

I had a great time at WKTV, learning the ropes as a performer. The pay was only $52.50 a week, but I didn't need much money as I was living at home with my parents.

I'd been doing the news for a few months when Gordon Alderman, manager of WHEN-TV in Syracuse, called and offered me a job. He said, "You communicate better than anybody I've ever seen on television." I didn't know what he meant, I just knew it was a compliment. What he saw was the style I'd developed to do the news. At twenty I didn't have the authoritative look of a newscaster like John Cameron Swayze. So I conversed the news: "Say, did you hear what happened down in Mobile today?" Many early TV performers addressed the camera like they were speaking to an audience of millions. I always kept in mind the feeling Arthur Godfrey gave me when I listened to him on the radio—there's only one person listening—I talked to the camera like it was one human being.

Nothing came of Alderman's job offer because Mike Fusco, the manager of WKTV, got wind of it and called Alderman to tell him to keep his hands off me. Fusco did give me a raise, however, up to $75 a week.

After six months at WKTV I was getting what would be called extraordinary reviews. Everybody knew Dick Clay. I knew I was doing a good job. I thought, if this can happen in Utica, I ought to be able to do the same elsewhere. I decided to apply to stations in a few larger cities. My father and I talked it over. He told me he'd heard of a TV station in Schenectady that was looking for an announcer. Then he suggested that he might call a man he knew named Roger Clipp, who ran WFIL-AM-FM-TV in Philadelphia.

Dad called Clipp, told him about me, and persuaded him to arrange an audition for me. Clipp got me an appointment with Jack Steck, the program director of WFIL-TV.

Steck was a short man with a ruddy, Irish complexion. He

was friendly and had a penchant for doing benefits anywhere, anytime. He ushered me into his office with the utmost courtesy, politely asked me about my previous experience, then pulled a handful of papers out of a file on his desk and handed them to me. He said he'd give me a few minutes to go over the material and had his secretary direct me to the studio.

Steck gave me the usual jawbreaker, tongue-twisting copy every station keeps around to test potential announcers—"And here's Nikolai Rimsky-Korsakov's *Scheherazade*"—hardly anything to throw me as I'd learned to announce classical selections at college. Besides, I brought Elmer with me. I set up the tape recorder in a corner of the studio, quickly read the tongue twisters onto the tape along with copy for a commercial for RCA TV sets he gave me. When I finished I moved the tape recorder out of sight, put in my earphone, and adjusted the foot switch.

Ten minutes later, Steck poked his head in the studio door, nodded to me, then went into the control room. He looked at me through the glass partition; saying something to the engineer on duty, he bent over the intercom mike. "All right," his voice boomed out at me, "if you'd go ahead."

Taking a deep breath, I spit it all right back at him verbatim. He damn near dropped his teeth. After I finished he stood there staring at me for a couple of seconds. He leaned over the intercom again, thanked me, asking me to come back to his office with him.

He wrote a memo about the audition that he told me about years later. It said, "The kid is good, and despite his college education he seems to be smart."

Back in his office he said, "I haven't got any openings in TV at the moment, but if you'd like to come to work for us as a summer replacement announcer on WFIL radio, I think Felix Meyer who's our radio program director could use you."

I asked him if I could have a couple of days to think it over. He told me to let him know one way or the other by the following Monday.

I had to make up my mind between the TV station offer in Schenectady and the radio in Philadelphia. I chose WFIL in Philadelphia because it was closer to New York City and I always considered myself a New Yorker. Calling Steck, I accepted the job at WFIL.

I asked to see Mike Kallet, owner of WKTV, to tell him my decision, but he was too busy to see me so I met with his assistant, a Mr. McNeely who was known around the station as the "hatchet man."

"What's this we hear about you thinking of leaving, Dick?" said McNeely as I walked into his office. He was a dark, gruff man with the habit of massaging his hands together as he spoke.

"Well, Mr. McNeely, I've had these offers."

"What do you mean, *offers?*"

"I think I can get a job in another—"

"You mean to tell me you're seriously thinking of leaving? You've made a lot of progress in the short time you've been at WKTV. Don't go off half-cocked thinking that you're big time. I always thought you were a smart boy." I never felt NcNeely was a bright man or particularly clever, but he had an intimidating way of getting ahead of you in a conversation. He made me nervous with his warnings, but I knew what I had to do. I'd talked the situation over with my father, whose opinion I respected, and he agreed.

"I'm leaving, Mr. McNeely. I accepted a job with WFIL in Philadelphia."

"How could you possibly think of leaving Utica for Philadelphia?"

"Well—"

"Haven't we treated you well? Got you a raise?"

"Yes, sir."

"Are you gonna stay?"

"No, sir."

I thought he'd hit the roof. Instead he shrugged, saying, "It's a backward step, going into radio, you'll be sorry."

Standing up, I looked him in the eye. "WFIL has a TV station too," I said, then walked out of his office.

# Bob Horn's "Bandstand"

WFIL's radio studios were next to Wanamaker's department store, across the street from City Hall in downtown Philadelphia. I wanted to save as much money as possible because Bobbie and I were to get married in June, so I got a room at the "Y" for two months, only a few blocks from the station. It wasn't a room, it was a cell. It was barely large enough for the single bed with lumpy mattress, rickety nightstand, and worn wooden chair it contained. The bathroom was at the end of the hall. Down the street was Horn & Hardart, where I ate most of my meals.

On my first day I presented myself to general manager George Koehler. He was in a meeting, but he'd left instructions with his secretary that when I arrived I was to see the radio program director Felix Meyer. I found Meyer in the announcer's lounge.

"Welcome to the Monday morning pep talk," said Meyer, motioning me into the room with a swing of his long, skinny arm. He sat at one end of the room on the arm of a chair; around him were half a dozen guys, some sitting, some standing. Meyer was a tall, gawky guy with a gentle manner that appealed to me. "Gentlemen, this is Dick Clark." He introduced me to Joe Novenson, Jim Felix, Jim McCann, Allen Stone, Neil Harvey, and Jerry Grove. They were all older than I was and more experienced; but from the first they were courteous and tolerant of me. Meyer went back to reading a memo about keeping the announce booth clean, a couple of guys made rude comments, and he called the meeting to an end.

Radio announcing days at WFIL, Philadelphia, at twenty-one.

"Let me give you the Cooks' tour, then put you to work," he said, leading me out of the lounge. As we walked along the corridors he asked me about myself, how I'd gotten the job, what my experience was. I told him about my audition with Steck. He laughed. We ended up in a small, triangular-shaped room with a tiny desk surface wedged into one corner where two microphones were set.

"This is the announce booth. You work in here. See that," he said, bending his head back to look up at the ceiling. I did the same. There was a purple light bulb in a fixture. "That's an ultraviolet light, you might want to snap it on for a couple minutes before you use the booth, kills germs; otherwise one of you guys gets a cold, you all get it."

By lunchtime I was fully versed in my responsibilities which mainly consisted of doing station breaks between Mary Margaret McBride and Tennessee Ernie Ford. Between announcements I sat around with the other announcers in the lounge where we smoked, read the paper, and listened to the ABC radio network feed on a speaker that carried the station's broadcasts into the room.

For about six months, I did this old form of radio. Occasionally, I got the chance to do one of the voices in a radio drama or narrate a local origination. Most of the time I did station ID's, commercials, and newscasts.

At the beginning of June, Bobbie graduated from college. She then moved back to Salisbury, Maryland, to live with her mother until we could make plans to get married. I asked Felix Meyer for some time off. He gave me Saturday and the following Monday of the last weekend of that month. Bobbie and I set the wedding for Saturday evening at eight o'clock, June 28, 1952.

It was impossible to get away until the actual weekend of the wedding because I worked six days a week. The only assurance Bobbie had that I'd be there was my word on the phone. She had to make all the arrangements herself. She bought her own wedding ring, got the license, and rented a cottage at the beach for two days for our honeymoon.

Andy Grass drove down from Mount Vernon to be my best man. Bobbie gave him the ring to hold; in order not to lose it he put it on his little finger. We were in front of the minister, at the point where Andy was to hand me the ring, when he found he couldn't get it off his finger. For a moment it seemed the only solution was to marry Andy. My father reached over, grabbed Andy's little finger, and pulled hard. Andy yelled as father got the ring off with a twist and handed it to me. I always felt guilty about that ring; Bobbie had obviously chosen something economical because of our financial condition. When our first child, Richard, was born, I bought her a second wedding ring as a surprise when she got home from the hospital.

Our first apartment was a sublease in a Philadelphia suburb. Bobbie taught school for the first two years while I worked at WFIL from noon to 9:30 P.M.

It was a hectic life for me, and from the first we didn't keep normal "husband-works-all-day-and-is-home-for-supper" hours. My last announcement was the 9:30 station break. At first, we didn't have a telephone in the apartment, so I ended the break by giving the time, and then said, "This is WFIL, AM and FM, in Philadelphia." The *in* Philadelphia meant I'd get home on the 9:44 train. If I said, "This is WFIL, AM and FM, Phila-

June 28, 1952—with my high school sweetheart, whom I married, Bobbie Mallery.

At the Salisbury, Maryland, wedding reception, Bobbie and I posed with her uncle and her mother. On my left, my mom and dad.

delphia," leaving the *in* out, she knew I'd get the 10:17 train.

In August WFIL radio moved to join WFIL television in a new building at Forty-sixth and Market streets. We were in the new facility about three weeks when George Koehler called me into his office.

"Dick, I want you to talk to Mr. Clipp," said Koehler as he stood up and took me into the office across the hall from his. A short, trim man with a square jaw and pencil-thin mustache, Roger Clipp had built the Annenberg broadcast empire. Although most employees saw him as a demanding former accountant, he and I took an immediate liking to each other.

Clipp shook my hand, then motioned me to have a seat. He had a way of barking instructions which was amusing, as his voice was high-pitched without any authoritative rumble to it.

"Mr. Koehler and I have decided to make you part of the new WFIL radio," he told me.

I murmured that would be nice. He kept talking. "We're cutting back on the network shows and going local. We'll play records, have announcers host the programs, do the local news and weather at regular intervals. We want you to have your own show in the afternoon."

"Sounds great!" I said. The other stations in town had already switched to this format; I doubted if WFIL had any choice other than to join the trend.

"It's a good opportunity, Dick," Koehler told me as we walked back to his office. "We'll be completely local within a few months. You'll be one of our new disc jockeys. It should prove an exciting change."

The next day Felix Meyer called to tell me that within the week I'd be the host of "Dick Clark's Caravan of Music" weekdays from 1:45 to 6:00 P.M. Meyer summoned me to the record library later in the day to show me what records I could play. I knew then something was cooking—WFIL was adapting the local radio format, but Clipp and Koehler weren't planning to play "Hit Parade" songs. The station was to become instant "easy listening."

The local radio scene was dominated by two popular music stations, WIP and WPEN. Mac McGuire, the morning man on WIP, was the highest paid personality in town. He'd been in

Philadelphia radio since the stone age and it was rumored he got $900 a week. Another big personality on WIP was Bob Horn.

WPEN had the most popular program in town. Hosted by Joe Grady and Ed Hurst, it was called "The 950 Club" after WPEN's position on the AM dial. They played records and gabbed about local events for three hours every weekday afternoon and Saturdays. I disliked the show. Grady played a very formal straight man. Hurst was a nice guy who did all the gags, except he wasn't really funny. To promote the show, they invited teen-agers to stop by the studio after school. They let the kids dance while the records played. From time to time, they allowed them to introduce themselves over the mike and talk about their high schools. Grady and Hurst got top ratings with their mixture of popular music, unsophisticated patter, and kids.

WFIL had hired Bob Horn, a husky man in his late thirties with an appealing radio style, from WIP to attract attention to our station. Horn did two shows a day on WFIL. One from six to seven in the evening, the other from eleven to midnight. The second show had one sponsor for the whole program, Eslinger Beer. Besides Horn, the lineup included me in the afternoons; Phil Sheridan, the morning man; a lady named Marge Weiting who was on from midnight to one in the morning; and a couple of other announcers.

Although I knew the music I played was dated and not likely to attract a young following, I didn't worry too much about it. It was the commercials that kept me on the air. In those days announcers worked like patent medicine salesmen. Each announcer got talent fees—base pay plus a fee for every commercial he did. I concerned myself with how many commercials I could deliver during the course of the day.

Off the air I did auditions for TV commercials. The local sponsors had used all the other guys, I was a new face on the scene, so I hardly lost any of the commercials I auditioned for. "Call right now, a dollar down, a dollar a week." I was a great pitchman. I sold pots and pans, vacuum cleaners, diamond rings, Mrs. Smith's pies, the works. Eventually I landed the Schaefer Beer account. I did one hell of a beer spot.

37

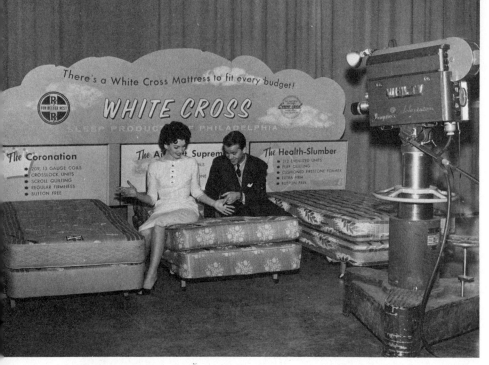

In the mid-fifties, Marge Weiting and I hustled mattresses on Philadelphia local TV.

On the left is Bob Horn listening to a record pitch from Philadelphia promoter Harry Finfer. Tony Mamarella is on the right.

I did so well for Schaefer in Philadelphia that they brought me to New York to do the beer commercials on the TV wrestling. I commuted back and forth, making what seemed like a fortune at the time—$300 a week doing beer commercials. It was great until one night Rudy Schaefer looked in on one of the New York spots, saw me, and said, "My god! Get that kid off television. He's not old enough to drink our beer!" I lost my big thing.

In those days we drank beer on camera during the spots. One week when the wrestling was broadcast from Philadelphia, I did both a beer commercial and a spot for Ritter Finance. The beer sponsor sent cases of beer to the studio for the three guys in the TV crew and me to drink. We'd sit there in the middle of the night, downing bottles of beer while we watched Gorgeous George and Killer Kowalski go at it.

One night, after consuming considerable amounts of beer, I started the commercial for Ritter Finance. There were several branch offices of Ritter Finance and this commercial opened, "You folks up there in Frankford will find a Ritter Finance office located near you."

I looked straight into the camera that night, saying, "You fucks up there in Frankford." With that the three crewmen lay down on the floor in complete hysterical collapse and that was it for the commercial. Running through my head I'm saying, "Oh, my God, what have I said. I'll be banned forever."

There wasn't one phone call. Wrestling was one of the highest-rated shows on the Dumont network, yet there wasn't a call. I can picture the viewers out there in the Delaware Valley.

"Albert, he didn't say what I thought he said, did he?"

"No, of course not, he couldn't have."

Another extra job I landed was announcer for Tasty Kakes, who sponsored the Philadelphia Phillies and Athletics ball games. I was probably the only commercial announcer they ever had who hated baseball. In between doing the sports I took a newspaper and my portable radio, climbed high up into the stands, and listened to music through an earphone while I read the paper. The baseball fans must have wondered about the lunatic who thought Connie Mack Stadium was a reading room.

# 5

## "The more I heard the music, the more I enjoyed it"

"The old English movies we're showing in the afternoon aren't making it," George Koehler told Roger Clipp over lunch one day in late September 1952.

"Dump 'em," was Clipp's reaction.

"And substitute what?"

"I don't know. Let's do a local origination of some sort. Why not use some of the Snaders and Officials?"

"Oh, God!" Koehler groaned. "Not that!"

"Why not!" Clipp said defensively. The station had been talked into buying several thousand dollars' worth of short films, each a musical performance, and he was anxious to put them to use. The better ones were in the Snader Musical Films Library—artists like George Shearing, Peggy Lee, and Nat King Cole doing their big numbers. Another part of the package was the Official Films Library. The Officials were made in Cuba by Jimmy Roosevelt before World War II and Fats Waller was the most contemporary artist in the catalog. "String them together, figure something out, they're all paid for," Clipp told Koehler.

Back in his office, Koehler called in WFIL's top DJ, Bob Horn.

"Bob, got any ideas for an afternoon TV show?" he asked. As Horn started to speak, he raised his hand. "Let me rephrase that. How'd you like to do a show with the Snaders and the Officials?"

Horn knew about the films by their reputation around the station as WFIL's folly. He also saw the door open to get on

TV, so, despite serious reservations as to how long he'd last with the Snaders and Officials, he agreed to give it a shot.

Horn called his radio show "Bob Horn's Bandstand." Keeping the name "Bandstand," he came up with a simple concept to fill the two-and-a-half-hour afternoon slot vacated by the axing of the English movies. The first "Bandstand" opened with Horn seated at a table. He said hello, then introduced Dizzy Gillespie, a longtime friend of his who happened to be in town. Gillespie came on, sat down next to Horn, and they chatted for a few minutes about Gillespie's upcoming recordings and current tour. Turning to the camera, Horn announced a film performance and they cut to a Snader of Peggy Lee singing "Mañana." The show continued on like that—jumping between Horn talking to whatever guests he coaxed to the studio and the films. It was a radio DJ music-and-interview show on TV.

Koehler and Clipp assigned a young member of the production staff, Tony Mamarella, to produce "Bandstand." Tony got to know Horn better than any other person at WFIL. He says Horn was aware of how terrible the first shows were and that Horn agonized over how he could convert the show into something that would sell.

Horn knew from the start that he was in the right ballpark—put successful elements like music and talk from radio on TV. He also knew that as the show stood it was nothing but a time killer. Then he came up with the idea that changed the course of his life and mine: make kids dancing the visual portion of the program. He took the idea of Grady and Hurst's "950 Club" radio show and put it on television.

Horn went to Koehler with his idea. After several meetings, Koehler and Clipp decided to let Horn give it a try.

"You can use the studio, bring kids in to dance, and the whole jazz, but you've got to have a partner, it has to be a team," Koehler told him.

Horn frowned, his thick black eyebrows moved together as he wrinkled his forehead. It gave his face a fearsome look. "There's no reason for that," he told Koehler bluntly.

"We've contacted Lee Stewart. You take him as your partner; at least you'll have Muntz TV from the day you go on the air," said Koehler with a take-it-or-leave-it air.

Lee Stewart was a local radio personality who had one account, Muntz TV. He was on every radio station in town for Muntz, selling TV sets for $129.95 apiece. He'd do an hour show with the commercials jammed together and bits of records in between, so there'd be more commercials than records. Stewart sold Muntz TV's by the truckload and was respected as a super radio pitchman.

Horn wasn't happy with the partnership, but he wanted to be on television so he agreed. Koehler explained that he and Stewart would be co-MC's. Stewart would be the funny man, Horn the straight guy—like Grady and Hurst on WPEN. The only amusing thing about this combination was the very idea that anyone could possibly find them funny.

The switchover to Horn's new "Bandstand" format took place the first week of October 1952. It was on Tuesday of that week that they started. All the previous week and that Monday the station promoted the new show. It was a big promotion, the brunt of it being an invitation for kids to come to the show. "Come to the 'Bandstand,'" "Teen-agers Come to Dance on 'Bandstand'" were a couple of the more inspired spots that plugged the show.

Over a thousand kids showed up that first afternoon. The cameras just shot Horn and Stewart introducing the records and the kids dancing. They could only get two hundred kids at a time into the studio, so they showed a long Snader film every half-hour, while they emptied the studio and brought in a new bunch of kids.

The show originated in Studio B, which was a large sound stage at the back of WFIL with sliding doors that opened into the parking lot behind the station. Horn and Stewart devised a set at one end of the studio—a canvas drop painted to represent the inside of a record store. A small stage was placed in front of the drop and a record counter set on it. They stood on the stage behind the counter with the canvas painting behind them.

From the beginning the show was a hit. Phone calls jammed the WFIL switchboard every afternoon—everyone liked to watch kids dancing on TV. The success of Grady and Hurst's "950 Club" was repeated a hundredfold when the audience could see it as well as hear it.

Horn and Stewart were television's first odd couple. They did the show together from 1952 to 1955. It was obvious to anyone watching that they didn't care for each other.

Horn, who was in his late thirties, was heavyset with a double chin, long, narrow nose, and greased-back black hair. He wasn't really typecast for the part. Off-camera his personality was abrasive, egotistical, and aggressive. Most people around the station found him less than charming.

Tony Mamarella says, "Horn was a great promoter. He had a very good public relations sense, and he also had a very commercial mind. He knew the kids, what made them tick, and how to exploit it. He got to trust me and taught me things about music and about different records and sounds."

Stewart on the other hand was a stumbler. Without the Muntz account he would never have gotten on TV. He was a homely man, small and dark with a pudgy face. He wore glasses which emphasized his big nose. He was a nice man, but he didn't fit into the role he found himself in. He had no sense of humor at all. He wanted to be taken seriously. He was up against Horn who was much more of a pro as a personality. It was obvious when you saw them together on the show that Stewart was out of place.

Before the show each day, Horn and Stewart met in the record library to talk about what they were going to do on the show. They planned contests and phone-ins and a million other things. For them the teen-age audience dancing to records was a springboard to bigger things. Stewart talked about how he would come up with a lot of funny gimmicks, most of which never came off. Horn, however, had a sense of what was happening that I don't think anyone else had. He knew he'd struck gold, and now he wanted to mine the vein. The first thing he did was to start playing rhythmic music for the kids to dance to. He was aware of rock 'n' roll disc jockey Alan Freed and of what the successful pop music stations were playing. He invented the record ratings. Once or twice a show he crooned, "We have company," and a guest star like Eddie Fisher or Patti Page came on to lip-sync their current record. Joni James was probably the first pop music star created by "Bandstand."

Stewart's end on the show came in 1955. Horn was scheduled

to go on vacation. Before he left he went to see Koehler, telling him he didn't want to leave the show in Stewart's hands alone. He wanted Tony Mamarella to be co-MC while he was away. Koehler agreed.

Each day while he was on vacation in Canada, Horn called in when the show was on the air. Stewart always answered the phone and said hello to Horn. The first thing out of Horn's mouth was "Let me talk to Tony." Tony got on the phone and Horn asked how things were going and talked about his vacation for a minute. Then Tony handed the phone back to Stewart. Horn said, "In a rush, got to go, people are waiting for me, call you tomorrow." You couldn't miss Horn's cold shoulder.

When Horn got back there was a meeting with Tony, Koehler, and Horn.

"Tony, you know something about the show, what do you think we should do with Bob and Lee?" asked Koehler.

"I've produced this show for three years now," Tony said. "I don't think it's a two-man show. I never have."

"Well . . ." Koehler started in defense of the idea.

"If it is a two-man show, you've got the wrong two men," Tony countered. "But it really is a one-man show. The kids could care less about two people. They only get in each other's way."

Koehler nodded. He looked at Horn. "Okay, let me handle this. I'll speak with Lee."

A week later Lee Stewart left "Bandstand." Koehler gave him a morning TV show of his own. It was called "Lee Stewart's Coffeetime." Stewart tried to make it an adult early-morning version of "Bandstand." It was a failure.

A year or so after "Bandstand" established itself locally, Felix Meyer sent me a memo that my "Caravan of Stars" radio show would henceforth be called "Bandstand." I went to Meyer to ask him where I should get the records that Horn played on TV.

"You don't," he told me. "We're changing the name of the show, not the show. Keep getting your records out of the library."

I didn't make a big thing of it. I wasn't all that conversant with Horn's "Bandstand"; I was on the air while it was broadcast and only caught bits and pieces of it on a monitor outside the announce booth.

So there was TV "Bandstand" and radio "Bandstand." The next move was a bit more outrageous. Either Meyer, Koehler, or Clipp, I've never figured out who, decided Horn should come onto my radio show for the first and last 15 minutes each day.

Horn showed up to do the introductions. "This is Bob Horn with 'Bandstand,'" he'd say. "I'll be here playing the best sounds in town." Two records played, then he came back to the mike, "Well, I've got to get the platters spinning on TV 'Bandstand.'"

At that point, I said, "Bob will be back in a while; in the meantime, I'm Dick Clark and here's one of The Four Aces' best."

Horn was shilling for the radio show. He did 15 minutes, then didn't come back for three and a half hours, at which point he did the wrap-up and invited everyone to listen in tomorrow.

This situation annoyed him. He'd worked hard to get where he was and was protective about his position as host of "Bandstand." He had misgivings about this baby-faced kid who was always winning auditions for TV commercials. He was minimally polite to me. He put up with me. He was friendly and jovial when we shared the mike at the start of my show, but when I ran into him in the hall or outside the station I seldom got more than a sour nod.

The more I worked with Horn the less I liked him. It was hard for me, in my early twenties, to appreciate that competition can be so fierce. As the years have gone by, I've mellowed in my feelings towards him. I realize that the man I cared so little about created a TV show that influenced my whole adult life. Bob Horn was a rock 'n' roll pioneer, and he should take his rightful place with Alan Freed and the other fathers of rock. He found a formula for a music show as impressive in its durability and appeal as "Grand Ole Opry" and "Your Hit Parade" before it.

There was a constant problem with radio "Bandstand" because of the easy listening music WFIL had me playing. They couldn't understand why I didn't get bigger ratings, why people didn't tune in radio "Bandstand" the way they did TV "Bandstand," where Horn played the latest rhythm and blues records. Felix Meyer, then Koehler, and finally Clipp, had meetings to discuss the problem with me. I tried to explain that I wasn't playing the same music as on TV "Bandstand." They refused to listen.

The WFIL management came up with a solution. They sent me to Pittsburgh to sit in a hotel room to listen to a DJ named Jay Michaels who had great ratings at the same time in the afternoon I was on. For three days I sat there, listening to Michaels play the hits, Top 40 music. I went back to Philadelphia. "I can imitate Jay Michaels better than he can do himself," I told Meyer. "But you won't let me play the music he's playing."

Meyer came up with another idea. He arranged for me to do remote broadcasts from the lobby of the Tower Theater. Every afternoon after school, the kids were invited to drop by the Tower to see Dick Clark broadcasting live. Very few teen-agers showed up to see me playing my antiquated hit parade.

In the fall of 1955 I got my first chance to substitute-host TV "Bandstand." Horn was on vacation. For some reason, Tony Mamarella, who normally substituted for him, couldn't make it. So I did the show. It was only one afternoon, but it whetted my appetite. I realized I could really progress if I could get out of radio and get a TV show like "Bandstand."

Since I'd done the show that once I could say I was the substitute guy. I decided to take a chance on the basis of my one appearance. I called a guy named Hanrahan who was the general manager of WEWS-TV in Cleveland.

"I'm Dick Clark, the substitute man on 'Bandstand,'" I told him—by then the industry knew about the show. "Would you like me for your station?"

"I don't want to put that crap on the air. I don't even want to talk to you," he shouted into the phone.

He was a snotty son of a bitch; I'm glad he turned me down. I've often thought, God, if I'd gone to Cleveland to do a copy version of "Bandstand," nothing would have ever happened to me in TV.

About five o'clock one afternoon in the summer of 1956,

George Koehler got a call that Bob Horn had been arrested for drunken driving and was in jail.

At the time, the Philadelphia *Inquirer*, WFIL's owner, was conducting a campaign against drunken driving. Horn was fired immediately. It's my impression that somewhere in the back of management's minds they had been looking forward to the day when they could get rid of Horn. There was always an unspoken feeling that they wanted to see someone younger and better-looking do the show. Koehler and Horn didn't really get along. Horn was often arrogant with Koehler, refusing to kow-tow to management demands. More than once Koehler or Clipp called Horn to arrange a morning meeting only to have Horn laugh at them over the phone.

Horn never returned to the show. The drunken-driving charge was followed by a statutory rape charge which involved a fourteen-year-old girl; apparently several local radio and TV personalities were making dirty movies out in the country at a place called Hound Dog Hill. To make matters worse, Horn was arrested a second time on charges of drunken driving. He was eventually acquitted on the rape charge and was still fighting the drunken-driving charges when the IRS showed up and accused him of not paying taxes on $392,500 worth of income.

Horn was exiled from radio and television. He moved to McLendon, Texas, where he did a local TV dance show for a short time. The station eventually found out about his past and yanked him off the air. He continued working for them as a radio time salesman. He died there of a heart attack several years later, a pauper, and one of his old regular dancers paid for his funeral.

For the next three months Tony Mamarella was the host of "Bandstand." Tony was a regular. The kids knew him and he was instantly available to keep the show going.

There was some in-fighting as to who would get the show. Jack Steck wanted Tony to do it. Koehler and Clipp wanted me. It was finally settled in my favor.

Koehler called me at home one morning the first week in July 1956; he wanted me to meet him in his office as soon as possible.

When I arrived Tony was already there waiting in Koehler's outer office.

"What are we here for?" I asked Tony, knowing damn well what it might be.

"They're giving you the show," Tony said. He smiled and patted me on the back as we went into the office.

"Forget the radio show and come over and do the television thing," Koehler said. "Tony's going to produce the show. He'll give you all the help you need."

I was elated. I tried to remain as serious as possible. "Okay," I said. "You want me to start today?"

"Yup," he said. He stood up and extended his hand. I got up and shook it. Koehler grinned. "Good luck."

I was twenty-five years old and not a little astonished at my good fortune. I left Koehler's office and called Bobbie to tell her the news. Then I searched out Tony.

"It's going to be rough today," Tony said. "There're kids outside picketing the station." Horn's regulars were upset over his dismissal and had somehow gotten the news that I was to be a permanent replacement, ending their hope of Horn ever returning to the show. They were marching up and down Forty-sixth Street with placards demanding he be put back on the air. The leader of the protest was a young kid named Jerry Blavat, who years later become a top DJ in Philadelphia.

I arrived on the "Bandstand" set at two that afternoon with only a foggy notion of what the kids, music, and show were really about. My only opinion was that I always thought Horn did a poor job relating to the kids. His conversation with them was stilted; he never associated with them as equals. I talked to the kids on the same intellectual level. I never became a teen idol or a father figure. I tried as hard as possible to be their friend.

From the start I was also terrified because of what had happened to Horn. I've never been sexually attracted to very young girls. It may not be the secret of my success, but it sure as hell kept out of a lot of trouble. I knew one rock idol in the early sixties who'd gather twelve- to sixteen-year-old girls in his hotel room, have them strip naked, then select his companion for the night. I get nervous thinking about such things. From the first day, I established the most platonic of friendships with the kids.

Tony met me on the set. He handed me the list of records to play and gave me a rundown on the day's commercials.

"What's happening outside with the kids?" I asked.

He shrugged. "I went out to talk to them a few minutes ago. They're pretty riled up about Bob being fired."

"Still?"

"Still. We have enough kids for the studio audience without them, so don't worry about it."

"Should I talk to them?"

"If you want."

I took a deep breath and walked out the studio door onto the sidewalk. On my right was a line of teen-agers waiting to be admitted to the show. On my left were about two dozen kids holding signs—"No Bandstand Without Bob," "Bring Back Bob Horn." I went up to the kids with the signs.

"I'm Dick Clark. I've got the job as the new host of 'Bandstand.'" I stopped. The kids didn't say anything; they just stared at me.

"I know how you felt about Bob. But there's nothing anybody can do about it. I know he was your friend. I hope you don't dislike me because I was chosen to replace him."

They still didn't say anything.

"I've got to get to work. If you want to come in, please do." I turned and went back into the studio.

Tony looked at me quizzically. "So?"

"I don't know. I tried."

A couple of minutes before airtime, Tony gave me the high sign from where he stood next to the door letting the kids in. He pointed at a group of kids who'd just come through the door. I recognized some of the crew I'd talked to. I breathed a sigh of relief.

"For the first month Dick Clark was horrible," my old friend Red Schwartz is fond of saying about my start on "Bandstand." "When he started he didn't know anything. I remember him saying, 'I don't understand this music,' and Tony Mamarella telling him, 'Don't worry about it, I'll take care of the records and the music.'"

49

Red's criticism was partially true. I really didn't understand the music Horn played on "Bandstand." When I took over, the number-one record was "Stranded in the Jungle" by the Jay Hawks. I don't think I knew more than one or two tunes on the music list that afternoon.

It didn't take me long to get into doing the show. The more I heard the music, the more I enjoyed it; the more I enjoyed it, the more I understood the kids. I began to loosen up. I listened to the kids and let them tell me what they liked. I knew that if I could tune into them and keep myself on the show I could make a great deal of money.

At first, Tony Mamarella and I didn't hit it off. He was the producer of the show and knew more about it than anyone else. I knew that any animosity between us would spoil my chance of establishing myself on the show. So I decided to confront him. I went into the office late one day after the show and found him getting ready to leave.

"Have a drink with me?" I asked.

Tony smiled. "Sure, just let me straighten this up and call Agnes to tell her I'll be a little late."

We walked down to the Brown Jug, an old Irish saloon and restaurant where we often ate lunch. We had a couple of beers, chatted about details of the show.

I finally broached the subject. "Look, Tony, I want to make the best of our association. It was a management choice that I get the show."

"I never had any illusions that I would get the show permanently," Tony said. "It's been the story of my life at Channel 6. I MC the shows when anybody gets sick. I've done everything but dress up as Happy the Clown—and that includes one show that I sat in for a couple of years ago where I had to sing!"

I laughed. "Is there anything the matter then?" I asked.

Tony took another sip of beer. He paused for a moment, lit a cigarette, and inhaled. "It comes from having worked with Bob for so long," he admitted. "You and Bob are two completely different people, except I have a feeling you both like to make money. Bob was a pro. He didn't always have a professional approach, but he was a pro. I liked him. I'm upset over what's happened to him.

"You're an amateur at this point, but you're still more professional when it comes down to it than Bob was. Just give me some time to get used to the change. I like you, Dick. I know we can work together."

We decided that our association on the show was a shotgun marriage and we should make the best of it. Tony walked with me to the stairs that led up to the elevated railroad, where I got the train home. As I climbed the stairs I caught my heel on the iron steps, tripped, and landed flat on my ass. I sat there and started to laugh. Tony offered me a hand up. I dusted myself off, he laughed, and we shook hands.

"Okay, Mr. Clark, we'll work together."

"Great, Mr. Mamarella. If I don't fall off the el and land on my head, I'll see you in the morning."

# "Roll Over Beethoven"

It took 20 minutes to drive from our apartment in Drexel Hill to the WFIL studios, so I left home every morning about 10:15 or 10:20 because for a while I co-hosted a local radio show from 11:00 to 11:30 with a woman named Nancy Lewis—it was a dreadful music quiz show called "Music Break."

On the way, I stopped at the cleaners in downtown Drexel Hill to pick up a freshly pressed suit and drop off another to be ready the next morning. Then I drove in, past the Tower Theater in Upper Darby, to West Philadelphia where the station was located.

WFIL built their TV station on Market and Forty-sixth Streets next to a four-thousand-seat sports emporium known as The Arena. The idea was they only had to go next door to cover boxing and wrestling "on location." The elevated railroad ran down the center of Market Street into and from downtown Philadelphia with a stop at the front door of WFIL, half a block from The Arena. In the late fifties The Arena was used for concerts, and it was there that for the first time I saw Elvis Presley perform.

In those days the area around the station was heavily Irish and black. There were two parochial high schools and a large public school within walking distance of the station. From these schools came the first studio audiences for "Bandstand."

Only executives at WFIL had assigned parking spaces in the lot behind the studio. I was making them a small fortune, yet they wouldn't give me my own parking space. They didn't want to alienate the other employees. It had been a touchy situation since Bob Horn's day. As "Bandstand" rose in popularity, Horn bought a Cadillac and a cabin cruiser—there'd been a great deal of jealousy about his display of wealth. For that reason I drove a Buick. When I bought a second car for Bobbie, it was a Plymouth station wagon, so I wouldn't upset anyone.

Finding a space, I pulled in. With great care I took the suit off the backseat and held it up so it didn't trail on the ground. With my free hand I grabbed the dozen records I'd listened to at home the night before, then made my way like a balancing act into the building.

The powers-that-be gave "Bandstand" one of a row of cubbyhole offices on the first floor. Only the pile of mailbags left leaning against the door each morning distinguished it from the other tiny offices along the hallway.

"Bandstand" was another show in the daily schedule. There were Howard and Mary Jones who did a talk show—Howard also broadcast as Farmer Jones with a farm report. In later years Howard, who couldn't stand children, became Happy the Clown. There was Chief Halftown, a full-blooded American Indian, who also did a children's show. There was Sally Starr, a buxom bleached blond who dressed in white cowgirl outfits and hosted the Western movies at six o'clock. And there was me, just another personality in the lineup, who happened to have a network audience of millions.

Stepping over the mailbags, I opened the office door. The office was about 30 by 20 feet, partitioned off into three areas. Near the door there was a wooden bench that record men sat on while waiting to see Tony or me. To the right was Marlene Teti, the secretary Tony and I shared, plus chairs for four other girls who opened and sorted the mail. In the left rear corner I put up two wall panels to form a room where Tony and I could have a minimal amount of privacy. It wasn't more than 10 feet long and 6 or 7 feet deep. In it we had a double desk against the back wall, a record player with its speaker hanging in the corner, a bulletin board, and the door to the closet that I used as my dressing room. The walls were covered with drawings sent in by kids, awards and citations given to the show, and copies of the top record charts torn out of *Billboard* and *Cashbox*. It was a chaotic office that gave ample proof how unpre-

53

pared WFIL was as a local TV station for the production of a network show.

Eventually, we got a slightly larger office, then promptly added two more mail sorters. By the time I left Philadelphia there were ten of us at work in one office. It always reminded me of that bit at the circus where a car drives into the center ring and clowns pour out until it seems impossible that the car could hold any more of them and yet they still keep coming out.

The office was a mess; rarely could we coax the cleaning ladies to venture inside. Every available surface was littered with piles of mail or 45 RPM records or gifts the kids mailed to the show—candy and cookies (which I was afraid to touch for fear they'd be poisoned), homemade plaques, a shrunken head, a giant ceramic pretzel, and hundreds of stuffed animals.

I came in one morning to find Marlene sitting at her desk with tears rolling down her face. I asked her what was the matter. She sobbed, blew her nose, and motioned at the mess around her.

"I'm sorry, Dick. I can't stand it. I put my notebook down last night. This morning I spent half an hour looking for it and I still can't find it. Dick, please, do something."

"Calm down, I'll think of something," I said. I rummaged through a pile of records I had brought in from the studio the afternoon before and retrieved her notebook.

That night after everyone left I borrowed a stepladder from Nat Elkitz's workshop and set to work. When Marlene came in the next morning she found all the stuffed animals gone—until she looked up at the ceiling. There they were, hanging from the crossbraces by lengths of string. She laughed nervously, looking at me like I'd escaped from a looney bin. The dangling animals became a permanent fixture.

Tony had started at the station on weekends as a part-time switchboard operator, then worked as a cameraman and stage manager until he joined the production staff in 1952. He knew the ropes. There wasn't anything that would faze him. I relied on him to make the show run smoothly.

Tony was a pleasant man to work with. He had a ready smile, curly black hair, a partiality for bow ties, and a calm manner. I had three names for him: Tony, Anthony, and Mr. Mamarella.

My secretary Marlene Teti. Two or three times a month, we sent stuffed toys and other goodies to a local Philadelphia orphanage. We were always inundated with gifts from viewers.

At the negotiations and business meetings it was always Mr. Mamarella. In the office it was Tony. And when I was in trouble and needed his help it was Anthony.

We worked on the show as partners. He shared all the off-the-air responsibilities with me. During the broadcast he made sure the kids stayed in line, the guest acts showed up, the sets were right, the crew and production staff knew what was happening, and any sponsors we had roaming around were kept happy.

The phones were already ringing when I came in the door. There was an older gentleman in a Navy uniform sitting out front where the promotion men usually sat. Marlene stood with the girls who sorted the mail, showing them how to arrange the fan mail into piles. I waved in her direction and went into the backroom. Tony was at his desk, talking on the phone. He still

As usual I'm doing two things at once, talking on the telephone and picking a high school beauty contest winner.

wore his overcoat so he couldn't have arrived more than a couple of minutes ahead of me. I let the pile of records I held slide out of my hand across the desk, opened the closet door and hung up my suit, and then sat down to work. Tony gave me a wave, and grimaced at the phone—it was the only part of the job he disliked. He said good-bye and put down the receiver with a sigh.

"Publishers!" he said deprecatingly. "They don't do anything for a record except take their piece, but they think they've got to check with me every time they go to the can." He stood up and struggled out of his overcoat.

"Who's the naval gentleman outside?" I asked. "Don't tell me he's cut a record."

"Oh, my God, I forgot he was out there! He's been here since the crack of dawn. You know that life preserver we got in the mail yesterday?"

"Yeah?"

"It was stolen off a Navy ship and he's come to collect it."

"Oh, no," I shook my head in disbelief. "Where'd we put it?"

"Nat took it to the prop shop. I called him and told him

someone'd be by to pick it up and not to paint it any bright colors in the meantime."

I went out and gave the officer a hearty good morning. Then I escorted him to Nat Elkitz, who reunited him with his life preserver.

Tony was going over the list of commercials for that day's show when I got back. I never went on the air unprepared. It shows in your presentation if you don't prepare for a broadcast, and I was determined to build the show, not coast along with it. He called Marlene in and handed her the list of spots to be typed up.

"Harry Ascola just called. Tony Bennett's single 'Firefly' is slowing down and Columbia wants to send him in to do the show. I told them next Thursday." Tony came over to my desk and showed me the list of guests for upcoming shows. We needed at least ten acts a week, so we always tried to keep the supply ahead of the demand.

"I talked to Dave Appell last night and he's planning to have a new single out called 'Rocka something' in a couple of weeks. I told him to stop by and play it for us when he gets copies. I also spoke to Red Schwartz about Vee Jay flying in Gene Allison to do 'Have Faith' while its still hot and somebody from Brunswick in New York called with a group called The Accents who've got a single called 'Wiggle Wiggle.' They'll be in New York for the next week recording so we can have them down any afternoon we want. That's it, except RCA called wanting to know when we could use The Ames Brothers."

"I'll get back to them on that one. I listened to the new Bobby Helms record last night," I said, rummaging through the singles on my desk and pulled it out. " 'The Fool and the Angel.' It's not bad. You want me to call Decca and find out where he is?"

"Yeah." Tony opened the large bound diary we kept. He wrote in the names of the guest stars on the day they were available.

Marlene came in with the commercials list and handed us each a copy. She went out, reappearing a second later with a tall pile of records. "The morning mail," she said as she carefully balanced them on the end of my desk. She got out the door before the pile slid sideways and the discs joined the others scattered across my desk.

Selecting records for the show was a time-consuming job. One day Tony made up the list, one day I did. We listened to records that came in and chose what we thought were potential hits. "Bandstand" wasn't always a big breaker of new records, although we had that reputation. Usually we didn't play a record unless it started to break somewhere else. Sometimes we heard a hit the first time we played the record—Chuck Berry's "Sweet Little Sixteen" was like that. Sometimes it was apparent that a record was breaking big in another market—we added The Crickets' "That'll Be the Day" to the play list after it took off in Cleveland. Occasionally we played the hell out of a record and another version of it became the best seller—we played somebody else's version of "Tequila" for the longest time while we watched The Champs's version climb the charts.

Every few days Tony and I checked out the local Philadelphia radio scene to see if any records were creating excitement. If two or three local stations were on a record we'd add it. We paid special attention to WDAS, the most popular black station in town. I became friends with Georgie Woods, one of WDAS's top DJ's. He was my line to the black music market. Many records played on "Bandstand" came on first as hits that were brewing on WDAS.

Tony and I must have heard four to eight hours of new records every day. Some of the records came in the mail, but most were brought in by the local promotion men. Philadelphia was a strong radio town in the late fifties; it was known as a breakout market. There were huge radio personalities, powerful stations, and the chance that if a record hit on local radio it would get on network TV. So the record companies in New York, Chicago, and Los Angeles each had one or two men working for them through their local distribution outlet whose sole job was to get their records heard and played on local radio and, if possible, on "Bandstand."

The promo men had free access to the radio stations in those days. They could walk into any station day or night and hype the DJ's directly. Whatever time the DJ was on the air, that's when the promo men went to work. Red Schwartz, one of the top local promo men, used to show up at six A.M. to bring Tom Donahue, the kingpin DJ at WIBG, coffee and doughnuts when Donahue went on the air. Donahue (who later became the father of underground FM radio in San Francisco) had a crew cut, a blue suit, white socks, and brown shoes. He always wore white socks.

The promo men were fiercely competitive. Their jobs depended on convincing a handful of DJ's that *their* records were hits. They went to WIBG where Joe Niagra, Hy Lit, and Donahue held court; to WDAS with its lineup that included Georgie Woods, Kae Williams, Leon Fisher, and Jocko Henderson; to WPEN to see Larry Brown, Bud Brees, Jack O'Reilly, and Red Benson; and to WHAT to see Reggie Lavong, Lloyd "Fatman" Smith, and Bill Curtis. And they came to see Tony and me at "Bandstand."

The promo men made every effort imaginable to curry favor. If a guy liked booze, they got him booze; if he liked broads, they got broads; if he liked money, they got him money.

Tony and I never put any pressure on these guys. We knew they had a tough job. We tried not to make it any tougher by demanding special treatment, since we knew they wouldn't forget us in the long run. We maintained a friendly, open-door policy. They could stop by whenever they wanted to and drop off their records. There was always a lineup of visitors. We listened to everybody who came in. It's amazing how many people are connected with any one record—the songwriter, the songwriter's wife and five kids, the publisher, the artist and all his relatives, the guy who sold the master, the distributor, the owner of the record label, the distributor's rep and his cousins— as many as thirty or forty people interested in the future of a single record, and all of them tried to catch an ear at the "Bandstand" office.

One of my best friends among the local promo men was Red Schwartz, a high school buddy of Tony's. Red had been a car salesman who sold practically everybody at WFIL a car. He was the only white DJ at WDAS. Finally he became a promo man.

Red went to Chicago to visit Vee Jay Records shortly after "Bandstand" joined the network. He met with Ewart Abner, then head of Vee Jay and later president of Motown. Abner played Red many of their latest master recordings. One record stuck out. Red said he loved that song. Abner said he didn't think Vee Jay would release it because it was too slow. Red convinced Abner to give him three copies of it to take back to Philadelphia—one for himself, one for Georgie Woods at WDAS, and one for Dick Clark. Dick Clark!!? Abner told Red that I would never play the record.

"Just give me three dubs. I think the song is great," said Red.

He flew back to town and the next day walked into our office. He went over to the play list for the day, crossed off the record that was scheduled to be played at 4:30, and wrote in the name of the song he'd gotten from Vee Jay.

"What the hell are you doing!" I yelled at him. "Are you crazy?"

"Dick, play this record from Chicago," he said, and handed me an acetate disc.

"You're nuts," I said as I took the record out of its sleeve and put it on the turntable. "At least you could let me listen to it."

"With your ears, what's the difference, just play the record," he said jokingly.

"Let me hear the goddamned record," I said and put it on. It sounded, well, slow. I turned to Red. "The kids will die out there with this kind of a record."

"Dick, please, do me a favor. Play it one time. Play it at 4:30, that's 3:30 Chicago time. I'm gonna call Vee Jay to tell them you're gonna play this record."

"Okay, Red," I said. "I'll do it because you're funny and you sell everything like it's a new Chevy."

Red grinned. Then he convinced me to let him use the office phone to call Chicago to tell them that at 3:30 their time Dick Clark would play the record on "Bandstand."

It turned out they didn't have a TV set at Vee Jay. They had to run across the street to Chess Records to borrow one. Chess only had a huge console TV—it took four guys to carry it across the street just to hear the record.

The song everyone but Red thought was too slow turned out to be one of the biggest hits of 1958. It has since become a classic—"For Your Precious Love" by Jerry Butler and The Impressions.

WHAT ACTORS LIKE MORE THAN MONEY—see page 20

# TV GUIDE

Local Listings • October 4-10

15¢

DICK CLARK

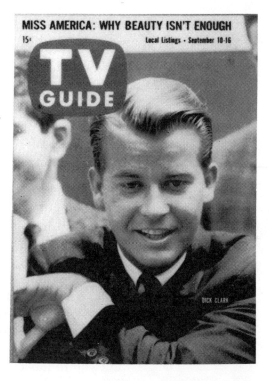

MISS AMERICA: WHY BEAUTY ISN'T ENOUGH

15¢

Local Listings • September 10-16

# TV GUIDE

DICK CLARK

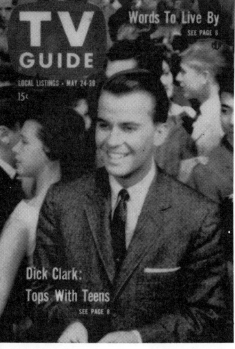

# TV GUIDE

Words To Live By
SEE PAGE 6

LOCAL LISTINGS • MAY 24-30

15¢

Dick Clark:
Tops With Teens
SEE PAGE 8

LOCAL LISTINGS
AUG. 25-SEPT. 4

# TV GUIDE

15¢

STYLE
TIPS
FROM
A TV
SCHOOL
BELLE

DICK CLARK

Another afternoon Red brought in a new single called "The Book of Love" by a group called The Monotones.

"I got a smash for ya, Dick," he said in his ebullient manner. Tony pulled his jacket up over his ears and picked up the telephone. Red pulled the single out of the sleeve and put the record on the turntable.

*"I wonder, wonder who, who wrote the book of love . . . "* rocked through the office. Tony sat up and put the phone down. He was soon nodding his head in time to the music.

"I like it," Tony said when the record ended. "What do you think, Dick?"

"I don't think it's a hit."

Red looked at Tony and shrugged. He pointed at me and then at his ears and shook his head mournfully. He walked out of the office without saying anything.

The next day about noon Red walked into the office. Behind him were five black youngsters.

"Dick, I want you to meet The Monotones," he said. He put the record on the turntable. As the record played the five kids mouthed the words and did a dance routine with hand motions and steps in unison. When they finished, Red trouped them out of the office, then came back alone.

"Well?"

"I like their act. On second listen, maybe I should play the record," I conceded.

"Yeah?" said Red.

"Yeah."

"Well, then, I gotta tell ya, Dick. Those weren't The Monotones. Those were five kids I pulled off the corner of Market Street on the way over here. I rehearsed them in the record library to mime the record."

I collapsed on the floor laughing. "Okay, you win, I'll add the record to the play list."

Records weren't the only thing we were pitched. Anybody who had anything to do with teen-agers found their way to our office.

A short, fat little man came in one day. He carried a giant plastic hoop.

"Can I help you?" I asked.

"Mr. Clark, I got a great new item I want you to see. Art Linkletter's doing it in California and making a fortune." He held out the hoop.

"What do you do with that, beat it with a stick?"

"No, no," he assured me with the utmost sincerity. "You do it like this." He pulled the hoop over his head down to his belly, gave the hoop a jerk, and with an agile wiggling motion, kept it spinning around his middle. He continued until his face turned red and sweat broke out on his forehead. I sat there in awe of the entire performance.

"What do you call that dumb thing?"

"Hula hoop," he gasped.

Somebody help me get this nut out of here, I thought. I thanked him politely and told him I didn't think we could use it on the show.

Another time, Mr. and Mrs. Handleman, who owned the Mattel toy company, came to see me.

"You're the expert on the teen world, tell me what you think of this," said Handleman. He described a new toy doll he wanted to manufacture.

"That's for little kids, you can't sell it to teen-age girls," I told him.

I was right in that regard. Fortunately, I didn't discourage him from going ahead with the Barbie doll.

I had a few winners like that.

At lunchtime Tony and I walked half a block down Market Street to the Brown Jug. There was a small room at the back of the dining room connected to the main room by a large service window with a doorway next to it. Some of the biggest record deals of the fifties were made in that back room.

In the center of the room was a large oval table that seated a dozen people. It was a down-to-earth Irish saloon—drab green walls, unmatched chairs, a faded oilcloth on the table, cafeteria-style silverware, and water tumblers half an inch thick.

Regulars at the table included Tony, Red Schwartz, and me, Harry Ascola of Columbia Records, Harry Finfer of Universal Distributing, Matty Singer of ABC Records, Teddy Kellem of Marnel Distributing and his brother Manny of Capitol Records' A & R department, Harry Rosen and Harry Fink of David

Rosen Distributors, Larry Cohen of Epic Records, and Bruce Davidson of Capitol Records.

Over lunch, artist and record deals were signed, publishing copyrights were swapped, masters were sold, and hits were predicted. Tony and I kept our ears open—a guy would come in and say he had a legitimate hype on a record that had broken in Minneapolis. Back at the office we'd call the Minneapolis distributor to find out if it had broken there and how well it was doing. If it looked like a hit, we'd drop it on the show. There were no plug sheets in those days, so our gossip over lunch was a prime method of information. Next to the Brill Building in New York, more music deals were made in that back room than anywhere else at the time.

After lunch we sat around and swapped stories. Red Schwartz got to his feet one afternoon and hit his water glass with a spoon until he got our attention.

"Gentlemen, please, a moment of your time." He raised his hands for quiet. "No, I cannot be silenced. This is about our own Dick Clark and I feel it is my duty to tell you this story. I spoke to one of the young ladies on the show about him and she told me this." Complete silence.

"It seems that Dick Clark picked up this young girl after the show one day. He took her to the movies, for a soda, and then for a ride in his car. They wound up way out in the woods. He pulled the car off the road. They get out of the car and he strips off all her clothes. Then he strips off all his clothes. He whips his tool out and says to her, 'Do you know what this is?'

"She grabs it and says, 'Yes. I'm Mary Jones. I'm sixteen and I'd like to hear 'At the Hop' by Danny and The Juniors.'"

With the Bob Horn scandal fresh in their minds, the place broke up in nervous laughter. I've since heard that story in bars, train stations, and airplanes. Thanks, Red.

At the end of the meal inevitably one of the record men picked up the tab. It was a running joke as to how many of the guys put Dick Clark and Tony Mamarella on their expense account for lunch. If the IRS ever looked into it, they'd find Tony and I must have eaten eight to twelve lunches a day.

Another half-block from the studio at the corner of Market and Farragut streets was Pop Singer's drugstore. Only the kids called him Pop. His first name was Simon and I called him Si. His drugstore was bedlam after school. There was a counter with a row of stools on the right as you went in, a row of booths on the left, and a pharmacy at the far end. Si couldn't have made a dime from the dozens of kids who used to jam into his booths, all taking their time over a five-cent Coke, but he loved the youthful atmosphere.

Across the street from Singer's was Herman's Deli. Herman's was a cut above Singer's when it came to ordering lunch out. Next to Herman's was the barber shop where I got my hair cut for $1.25 once every three weeks.

There was also an empty storefront next to Singer's on Farragut Street that I rented to record a syndicated radio show that I did. It was called "The Dick Clark Radio Show" and was an imitation of "Bandstand"—there would be sounds of crowds cheering as I introduced the acts. I actually recorded my portion of the show in a bedroom at home in Drexel Hill. We used the storefront to record stars who were appearing on "Bandstand." We'd shlep them down to the corner and they'd tape, "Hi, Dick, here's my latest record." Then I'd send all the tapes to a radio syndicator in Connecticut, who'd piece it all together.

# "I played the music, the kids danced, and America watched"

"Keep it simple," Tony Mamarella had cautioned when I took over "Bandstand." He spoke like a chef describing the recipe for a special sauce. "The secret formula is the kids, the music, and you. That's also the order of importance. We can't go wrong so long as you remember that."

I understood perfectly. Tony and I were constantly on guard against anyone complicating the show. Invariably a director got tired of the kids dancing and tried to set up artsy camera shots, someone in management wanted to know why we couldn't play just one Mantovani record, a potential sponsor wanted the set changed. We ignored all the brilliant suggestions. We knew that we knew what we were doing.

The "Bandstand" format was simple, that's why it worked. One network executive said that if anyone had come to him with the idea he'd have fired the man for being an idiot. A newspaper columnist said: "Clark is convinced that teen-agers can have a lot of fun without strong refreshments, or having to throw off their inhibitions." Tony and I saw it this way: I played records, the kids danced, and America watched.

The show went on the air every afternoon at 2:45. We chose that time because at 2:30 the nearest school, West Catholic High, let their kids out and it took them 15 minutes to get to the studio. School holidays and summer vacation was another matter. Then kids arrived as early as eight in the morning. They ate lunch, listened to portable radios, read fan magazines, taught each other dance steps, and camped out until a uniformed guard showed up at 2:30. He put a chain along the sidewalk to divide up the kids—girls on one side, boys on the other so that as we let them in we could keep the mix fifty-fifty. Usually twice as many girls as boys came to be on the show.

Tony opened the doors at 2:40 and in streamed the kids. Each of them got a "Bandstand" membership card at the door. They were also checked out by the studio doormen, Pop Higby and Bob Clarke. "*You*, chewing gum, in the basket with it," was their most famous line.

There were rules of dress and behavior that had to be adhered to for the kids to get on the show. The dress code required that boys wear a jacket and tie, or a sweater and tie. Nobody dressed that way in real life, but it made the show acceptable to adults who were frightened by the teen-age world and their music. Girls couldn't wear slacks, tight sweaters, shorts, or low-necked gowns—they had to wear the kind of dresses or sweaters and skirts they wore in school. No tight toreadors or upturned collars.

No one under fourteen or over eighteen was allowed on the show. From experience Tony and I found that thirteen-year-olds were too giddy and difficult to control. Eighteen-year-olds tended to be blasé about the show, and that limit kept the soldiers and sailors out. All we needed was: "My daughter, dancing with a sailor!"

We kept the set elements to a minimum. There were pine bleachers for the kids to sit on, the podium where I stood, the Top 10 board to list the hits, the map of the United States to promote ABC affiliates who carried the show, the autograph table to keep the stars busy after they did their lip-sync. We didn't want to distract our viewers with too many unnecessary visuals. We knew they tuned in to watch the kids dance.

At 2:30 I put on my suit and did my makeup. I didn't have a big wardrobe, so whenever I bought a suit I made sure it was dark and nondescript. That way I could wear it a couple of times a week and no one would notice.

Then I went out to the podium where I took my official position, halfway between the cameras and the kids, able to bend down to speak with them, but only mingling with them during my trips to the bleachers. Behind it was a shelf where I kept my hand mike, an assortment of stuffed animals, letters, and other junk. I also had the phone on the podium to communicate with Tony in the control room.

"Okay, if you'll all give me your attention," I yelled to the one hundred and fifty kids who filled the bleachers and dance floor. "We go on the air in five minutes. If any of you have any emergencies the bathrooms are down the hall, down the flight of stairs, boys to the left, girls to the right. Now, Tony Mamarella, our producer, would like a word with you."

Tony came out of the control room and walked toward the kids, stopping just past the cameras. "On the floor here is a broken red line. This is the camera line. On your side is the dance area. On my side is the camera area. Please, stay on your side, otherwise the cameramen can't move their cameras properly." Tony spoke with a note of defeat in his voice. He was always fighting the battle of the red line. As soon as he turned his back kids would sneak up on the line as they jockeyed for the best camera positions.

At 2:44 there was a hush. Tony returned to the control room. The kids and I watched him through the window. He looked down at his watch, raising his other hand above his head. He stood like that until 2:44:59, when he dropped his arm. Frank Kern let the turntable spin and the sound of "Bandstand Boogie" filled the studio. The kids started dancing. The cameras focused on a group of kids dancing as seen through our cutout map of the United States. The camera view pulled back, the music came down, and the red light on camera two went on, pointing right at me.

"Good afternoon, welcome to 'Bandstand.' I'm your host, Dick Clark. This afternoon that swingin' daddy himself, Buddy Knox, is our special guest. The Quin Tones will also be here to sing their latest smash 'Down the Aisle of Love.' But right now, let's get rocking with The Nu Tornados and 'Philadelphia, U.S.A.'"

The cameras cut back to the kids dancing. Camera shots of the backs of heads, shoes, elbows and rears, blank stares, mouths singing the words, a couple of morose-looking kids sitting it out. The WFIL crew caught it all.

"You housewives, roll up the ironing board and join us,"

I said with a shy smile for the camera, "as we hear a brand new one from Jackie Wilson, it's called 'Lonely Teardrops.'"

The sound of the records in the studio was deafening. I think we were the first to play music at such an ear-splitting level. Tony said if we can hear the artists singing while they're doing a lip-sync then the music's not loud enough. You couldn't hear anything else in the studio. If I wanted to talk to someone I had to go over and put my mouth up to his ear. We developed special headphones for the cameramen so they could hear the director. Nobody had ever done a television show with loud music before. We also had problems with people in the building, complaining they couldn't work with all the damned noise going on.

I started to have pains in my left ear after I'd done the show for six months. I went to see an eye, ear, and nose specialist. He didn't know who I was. He inspected my ear and pulled out a giant piece of ear wax from my ear. "Do you work in a factory near loud machinery?" he asked.

About 3:15 we would vary the pace by rating records. I selected four kids for the rating panel—three to rate the records and one to average the scores. I played three records for them. After each one they gave it a rating, from 35 to 98—on the theory that no record is completely bad or completely good.

Out of the Record Revue came the wonderful lines: "I give it a 95."

"Why?"

"I like the beat. It's easy to dance to."

Another version of that was an off-camera joke among the kids: "I'll dance to it, but I won't buy it."

The lowest-rated record we ever had on the Record Revue was put out by my friend Ross Bagdasarian (David Seville). It was the "Chipmunk Song." The kids hated it. They gave it a 35. That was the first week in December 1958. By the end of the month it had sold a million copies.

We always had a Top 10 board to emphasize the music on the show. When we went network we changed the name of the board to the "American Bandstand Teen-age Top 10." We called it that because it had no relationship to any of the other charts in the country. Tony and I made it up ourselves. We didn't even have the same songs on it that *Billboard, Variety, Cashbox,* or the other trades had on their top ten. We sat in the office and figured out our own hits. We had no formal yardstick, only what we heard through the mail, on the phone, at the Jug, from gut reaction, and from the kids. It's amazing how often we were right.

From time to time I explained the board to the kids. "One of the things that amazes people when they look at this list," I said as I went over to the board and leaned against it, "especially people who don't follow music maybe as closely as you do, they say 'What is this?' Somebody will look at this and say 'What are you talking about? Who ever heard of this thing called "Get a Job"?' Because we have it on here about six weeks before it gets on the—we won't mention any names—but before it gets on the big lists. And they say, 'You're out of your mind, who ever saw a top tunes list like that?' Only because it's about six weeks ahead of every other one and when it gets to the top with us it stays there for a while and *pfft* it's gone. This is the only reason why the 'American Bandstand' top tunes list is the authentic list, because you let us know through the mail, you write to us, we see about 400,000 people in person every year; it's a pretty accurate thermometer or pulse of the music business.

"Once again let me thank you for letting us know of the records you like, because that's the fastest way in the world to get the hit list—'American Bandstand,' P.O. Box # 6, Philadelphia 5.

"From bottom to top, this is how they shape up this date, January 9, 1958. Number 10, dropping down after a long stay at the top is Pat Boone with 'April Love'; number 9 is 'Get a Job' by The Silhouettes; number 8, 'Maybe' by The Chantels; number 7, 'Don't Let Go' by Roy Hamilton is moving up very rapidly; number 6, 'La De Dah' by Billie and Lillie; number 5 is 'The Stroll' by The Diamonds; number 4, 'Raunchy' by Bill Justis; number 3 is 'Why Don't They Understand' by George Hamilton IV; number 2 is 'Great Balls of Fire' by Jerry Lee Lewis; and number 1 is 'At the Hop' by Danny and The Juniors.

"Let's swing on down there all the way and pick up 'Maybe,'" I said, bending to point to the title on the board.

"Maybe" filled the studio and the cameras cut to the kids getting off the bleachers and starting to dance.

We also had guest stars on the show. We needed a lot of stars, two a day, five days a week. We had the biggest: James Brown, Bill Haley, Jerry Lee Lewis, Frankie Lymon, Patti Page, Lawrence Welk, Debbie Reynolds, Sal Mineo, The Everly Brothers—an endless succession of stars. Ricky Nelson and Elvis Presley were two stars who never did the show. Elvis did do phone interviews when he went in the army because his manager, Colonel Parker, was anxious to keep his reputation alive at that point. Ricky only appeared on the "Ozzie & Harriet Show." He just wasn't available for "Bandstand."

The biggest single ovation that any artist ever got on the show was a guy named Norman Brooks who did an Al Jolson impersonation while singing a song called "Hello Sunshine." Usually the artist would sing the "A" side of his record, then the "B" side. Brooks's appearance marked the first time an artist sang the "A" side twice in a row.

The day Al Hibbler was on I knew that the kids didn't know who he was. Here was one of the great jazz singers of the era, and I was afraid the kids would misinterpret him. Before he came on I explained the situation to them. He sang beautifully and while he sang it was like church, that quiet. When he finished they applauded madly. They could be wonderful kids.

Over the years there have been more than eight thousand musical performances on "Bandstand." Yet, out of that number of artists, I think I know a few dozen really well. One reason for that was that artists would rarely arrive to do the show until about 15 minutes before they were scheduled to go on. Tony met them at the door, escorted them into the cellar to use the boys' or girls' room to freshen up, then they came up to do their bit. Al Martino walked in late one day in the middle of a snowstorm and performed in his overcoat with the snowflakes melting on his shoulders.

Tony talked to the stars, asking them if there was anything special—an upcoming show or record—they wanted me to mention. Tony made a point of keeping them out of the studio until they were ready to go on because he didn't want the kids to be distracted by them. He hid Fabian and Frankie Avalon in our office until just before their spot; otherwise the kids would have gone crazy. The only time I got to know the artists was at record hops or later when we did the "Caravan of Stars" tours.

We came under fire constantly because the artists lip-synced to the records instead of actually singing. Critics said it was a cheat. We never made any bones about it. We used to compliment the stars, "You do a great lip-sync." It didn't make any difference to the kids. Every musical motion picture ever made has used the lip-sync technique. I explained the process to the kids and they learned to distinguish between a good lip-syncer and a bad one. We used lip-sync primarily because it was cheaper, but also because it was impossible to duplicate the sound of the record—and it was the record that kids wanted to hear. That was what they bought.

Once Paul Anka came to do "Diana" and in the middle of the chorus the record stuck. Paul repeated the line a couple of times, a look of panic on his face, then broke up laughing. But things like that rarely happened.

Phil and Leonard Chess sent Chuck Berry to Philadelphia to do the show. Chuck was a giant star, and he'd even written Philadelphia and Bandstand into the lyrics of a song, "Sweet Little Sixteen." Chuck, a very mercurial performer, got to the studio about 20 minutes before he went on the air. I greeted him at the door and took him into the office. We exchanged pleasantries, then he said, "Ain't going do any dancing."

I didn't know what he meant. I thought he wasn't going to dance with the studio audience. "You don't have to dance, just do your record," I told him.

"No dancing," he said.

I told him to stay right there. I went across the hall to the control room and got Tony. "Go talk to him, will you. I don't know what the hell he's mumbling about."

Tony went over, talked to him, and came back with the news that Chuck wasn't going to lip-sync the song and he wasn't going to do his little duck-walk steps for the cameras.

I stormed out of the control room and back into the office. Chuck sat in a chair, relaxed and nonchalant.

"Chuck, I don't know what to say to you, man. We've talked about it, we've announced it, and you're here."

"No," he said, looking past me. "I'm just not going to do that."

I started to fume. I went into my office, grabbed the phone, and told Marlene to get me Leonard Chess in Chicago. When Leonard came on the line I said, "Hold on a minute, Chuck wants to talk to you." I went into the outer office, telling Chuck Leonard Chess was on the phone.

I heard none of the other side of the conversation, but I can imagine what they must have said to him, "Get your ass out there and do that thing, motherfucker."

Chuck did the show. He's done it a thousand times since. He's never gotten any easier to get along with; he's still an ornery son of a bitch, but I love him dearly. He is indeed one of the great fathers of rock 'n' roll.

An on-the-air embarrassment arose the day Connie Francis came on the show to sing her new record, "Plenty Good Loving." I've always been aware of women's hair styles because of my father's background in the cosmetic business. I can see a woman maybe a year after I've last seen her and know she's got a new hairdo. Connie came on the show, and instead of her hair being its normal black, it was red.

"Oh, my God, kill it!" I said on-camera in a very ungentlemanly outburst. "What have you done to your hair?"

Connie's face turned as red as her hair. I was just as embarrassed myself. I got out of it as best I could and Connie sang her song.

The next day she got over one thousand letters at her fan club, agreeing with me that she was much cuter with black hair. Connie gave in.

Fats Domino came on the show regularly. Once before he sang his latest hit, I asked him how it had come about.

"Well, Dick," he said in his soft-spoken way, "I've been very successful, thank God. I've got seven or eight cars, a big house, all those things. One day I went for a walk in the neighborhood and a fella came up to me. He says to me, 'You've got all those cars, what you doing walking?' I said, 'I just felt like a little exercise.' He looked at me, shook his head, and muttered to himself, 'Ain't that a shame.'"

There were a number of kids who considered "Bandstand" like a club, like their corner candy store. They were the "regulars." Around the studio Tony and I called them The Committee.

The Committee came about because we needed continuity. We couldn't have completely different kids every day—we felt the viewers wanted some identification with the kids, that they wanted to be able to recognize at least a few of the kids if they tuned in regularly. So we picked some kids who could externalize, who could dance. They became the nucleus of The Committee, and we gave them special membership cards. Every so often they'd come to Tony or me and say they wanted to make a friend of theirs a Committee member, so we'd let them. We gave them the guidelines and rules for the show, and they kept the other kids in line by telling them how to behave. They were very willing to follow the rules themselves because as members of The Committee they became top dogs in Philadelphia and they were on the show every day.

By the time we hit the network The Committee consisted of over thirty kids. So we knew that even if there was a blizzard thirty kids were going to show up. We kept a daily mail count of how many letters came in for each kid. If somebody got a hell of a lot of mail, he or she was immediately made a Committee member. We had a roll call every day and introduced twenty or thirty kids. We knew the viewers could relate to these people, figure out who they were. We still do it: "Your name and your age."

The single most popular kid on the show was while it was still a local show. His name was Tommy DeNoble. Tommy had a greater impact locally than any of the kids had when the show went network.

At one point Tommy was asked by a priest in Mahonoy City —which is in the coal region of Pennsylvania, about 90 miles from Philadelphia—if he'd go up there to attend a parish dance. Tommy agreed. It was front-page news there—"Tommy DeNoble to Visit Mahonoy City, St. Mary's Dance, Come See Him, Talk to Him, Shake His Hand." Normally, they got 150 kids at a parish dance. Fifteen hundred kids showed up to meet Tommy. There weren't 1,500 kids in the whole town. They came from miles around.

74

Sometimes the girls on the show got dirty mail. Since we had permission to open their mail, we'd throw the pornographic stuff out. There were always people who sent pictures of themselves in odd poses in various states of undress. Occasionally, somebody sent money with promises of more for a visit.

Everyone who watched the show had their opinion of who the most popular regulars were. I'd say the two most prominent couple were Bob Clayton and Justine Carrelli in the late fifties and Ken Rossi and Arlene Sullivan in the early sixties.

Bob Clayton was a handsome boy with a head of greasy blond hair. He lived in Wilmington, Delaware, and after he saw Justine on the show he came to Philly to meet her. He made the hour train ride every day to be on the show and dance with Justine. They wound up going steady. And they won the first "American Bandstand" National Jitterbug Contest with close to a million write-in votes. For that they each won a jukebox with two hundred records. They eventually made the mistake of considering their dancing fame as show business. They made a record together called "Drive-in Movie." The record flopped and they split up.

Kenny and Arlene weren't quite as stylized as Bob and Justine. Their torrid togetherness at fourteen and fifteen was compared in *16* magazine to Rossellini & Bergman and Hargitay & Mansfield. Arlene used less makeup and her hair wasn't quite as done as Justine's. Kenny's was more teen idol than Bob's greasy-haired rock 'n' roller. Kenny had fairly close-cut, curly hair and an easy smile; he was Bobby Rydell compared to Bob's Duane Eddy.

People sat at home and fantasized about these kids. They wrote their own scenarios about Bob and Justine or Kenny and Arlene's love affairs. We gave the viewers just enough information without really saying anything, so they could do their own little mind trips. Each of these kids got several hundred pieces of mail a week. The big status symbol on the show was to dance with big wads of envelopes sticking out of your pockets or to be seen off in a corner reading your mail.

The viewers could tune in every day for the latest regular in-gossip: Eddie Kelly had a romance with Bunny Gibson; Joyce Shafer and Norman Kerr invented some new dance steps;

Bobby Darin at the "Bandstand" autograph table. Behind him is our giant Platter Puss.

The kids played the old "pass-the-matchbox-with-your-nose" game at our Halloween party in 1959.

Sitting it out at our skating party at the Drexelbrook Country Club.

Neither rain nor sleet kept the "Bandstand" kids from their daily visit. This 1960 snowball fight took place at the back door where they were admitted.

*Left:* Whenever snow fell while we were on the air, we opened the back door to the studio. The reaction we got from places like Phoenix, Arizona, and California was amazing.

*Right:* In a world filled with rock 'n' rollers, Johnny Mathis became a superstar. He made his television debut on "American Bandstand" in 1956. Here, he returns to sing "It's Not for Me to Say" in April 1957.

The kids line up outside the studio in front of the Market Street elevated train waiting to be admitted.

Barbara Levick left the regulars to work after school; Mary Burns got rid of her long braid for a shorter hair style.

Some of the mail was heart-rending: "Please, Dick, as a special favor to an old farm woman I would like to see Tex in another spotlight dance. Please do this as Tex reminds me of someone I loved long, long ago and lost by death."

The regulars had their own fan clubs and got cookies, cakes, and presents in the mail.

I'm always asked whatever happened to this regular or that. The truth is, nothing extraordinary ever happened to any of them. Bob Clayton owns and operates several ladies' boutiques in Wilmington, Delaware; Justine Carrelli is married to Paul Dino and they live in Las Vegas, where they're in the real estate business; Arlene Sullivan has been married and divorced, and works in a local Philadelphia hotel; Arlene's former boyfriend, Kenny Rossi, is a Philadelphia talent agent; Carole Scaldafieri is in advertising, is widowed, and raising her young daughter; Jimmy Petrose is a hairdresser; Carmen Jiminez teaches retarded children; her sister, Yvette, lives in New York City and is in retailing; Pat Molitierri has been divorced and is now remarried; Angel Kelly is a Keno girl in Las Vegas; Gary Levine is a disc jockey; Charlie "Rubber Legs" Hibib is a tailor; Billy Cook is married and working for the city of Philadelphia; Peggy Thompson is a housewife with two children; Doris Olson is married and a model in Philadelphia; Michele Leibowitz is a mother of two and lives in Philadelphia with her husband.

It's hard to keep track of all the "Bandstand" graduates. But one thing that's kind of interesting is that none of them ever became stars. And like every other group approaching middle age, they don't think too highly of the young people today. They make the same criticisms that their elders made of them.

Backstage we dealt with the kids pretty much as we did on-camera. We had the thing they wanted most, the visibility. The worst thing that could happen to them would be if Tony or I banned them from the show for a week. We never had any real problems, no fights, no stabbings—contrary to the image rock 'n' roll fans had gotten during the riots in New York and Boston at Alan Freed's rock shows. I'm not sure why, except that we used about 80 percent of the same people over and over and we had a fair amount of supervision: Tony and I, a lady attendant in the girls' bathroom, the doormen, and Si Singer, who hung out backstage during the show as an unofficial chaperone.

Many churchgoers in the fifties were upset about the dancing on the show, which they considered lascivious. Certain priests and other religious spokesmen had their own particular opinions of the show. The Catholic girls wore their school uniforms on the show. The nuns at West Catholic High said no more of that, cover it up. So the kids wore a sweater over the uniform and their little white dicky collars would stick out of the top. Girls all over the country tried to buy what they called "the Philadelphia collar."

Fanatics in the Bible Belt screamed bloody murder about the show. I could never say "going steady" on the air. We had a teen-age language code. I'd never ask the kids, "Are you going steady?" I always said, "Are you going with anyone?"

There was no sex in the fifties. "Nobody got nothing" in those days. Children were conceived immaculately. How Pat Boone ever had as many daughters as he did is still a mystery! We just didn't deal with sex.

One of the small embarrassing moments of my young life happened on the show. I was about to go into a commercial and had a couple of minutes to fill with gab.

Turning to two girls standing near me, I asked one of them, "What's that hanging around your neck?"

"A tiki god, I bought it in a mail-order catalog."

I turned to the other girl, who had a little pin on her bosom. "What's that pin?"

She said a mumble pin.

"A what?"

She leaned into the mike and said loudly, "It's a virgin pin!"

I thought to myself, oh, God, my world has come to an end. I turned to the camera. "That's nice, we'll be back in just a moment."

Around Christmas time of 1958, one of the cameramen wrote a mash letter to one of the girls on the show, Carole Scaldafieri. He was a quiet, young, introverted man who, as I remember, was going bald. He watched this girl dance and he'd fallen desperately in love with her. But someone found out about the note and the station heartlessly fired him on Christmas Eve.

Most of my contact with the kids off the show was in the nature of first aid. Tony and I mended broken heels, supplied nail polish to stop runs in nylon stockings, loaned carfare home, and always kept a supply of pins in our pockets. There seemed to be no more basic need among the girls than for a pin. They came to Tony and me with that desperate look, like we were the ultimate, last resort, and asked without any real hope, did either of us have a pin? We did, which saved innumerable hours of hysteria.

"Bandstand" was a segregated show for years. It became integrated in 1957 because I elected to make it so. In the early days of TV, if a black performer and a white performer appeared on a show, and the white MC gave the black girl singer a friendly kiss on the cheek, there'd be an agency conference and a network blackout; at the very least, station affiliates would drop off the line.

For a moment in time Alan Freed had a local TV dance show in New York. On one show the cameras caught Frankie Lymon dancing with a white teen-age girl. The show was canceled.

I was aware of all this. I was also aware that rock 'n' roll and "Bandstand" owed their existences to black music and the black artists who sang it. By the time I had the show a year I knew it had to be integrated. Tony and I made sure we had black representation which increased as the years went by.

I was terrified the first day I put a black teen-ager on the Record Revue. What would the reaction be in the South? After the show I rushed into the control room. There hadn't been one phone call. It was like so many of the things we feared in the fifties, once we confronted it we found there was nothing to be afraid of.

Sponsors were another important part of the show, at least to my industrious mind. The first sponsor "American Bandstand" had on a national scale was General Mills with Cheerios and its other products. The second sponsor was Ivan Combe, who ran a small business making an acne remedy and was a neighbor of the president of ABC, Ollie Treyz. Ollie told him to advertise his remedy on the show. So Clearasil became our second sponsor. I supported Clearasil because of the skin problems I had had growing up. As you get older you forget how awful it is to go around with a face covered with pimples.

The commercials on the show occasionally ran two or three minutes. There was a different yardstick in those days—the FDA, FTC, and other government agencies weren't quite as hard on the claims made.

Around 4:30 I did a Rice-A-Roni spot. We'd brew up a pot full of Rice-A-Roni and I'd eat it out of the pan. At 4:30 in the afternoon when I hadn't eaten since lunch it tasted great. The cameras would cut back after the commercial while a record was on and get a shot of me and three or four kids standing around the pot gobbling the stuff up. It was the greatest ad in the world.

Betty Crocker sent a cookie lady from the agency when we did spots for their cookie mix. She handed out cookies and cakes and the kids helped themselves, probably ruining their dinners, but munching away until it was all gone.

Bosco was another sponsor. I sold hundreds of thousands of "Dick Clark All-Time Hits" records as a special premium for them. Other sponsors were Popsicles, Mounds, Almond Joy, 7-Up, Dr Pepper, and the Purple Cow (somebody convinced the Welch's people that if they mixed grape juice and milk together they could make a fortune selling it as the Purple Cow—and I have to say that much as I love Welch's grape juice, adding milk to it makes a pretty awful concoction).

The first time I did a Dr Pepper spot I took a swig of it and said, "Gee, this stuff is good!" They freaked. They wouldn't let me call it "stuff." It had to be this *drink* is good. I said, well, whatever, I didn't fight it, but sometimes it was difficult for me to be myself and be credible with a product.

To get sponsors for the show I traveled the advertising agency circuit on Madison Avenue. I still do. I talked to them about the kids and they listened. Eventually I started an advertising consultation agency and spent a great deal of time explaining young people, their likes, dislikes, and buying habits to the pros on Madison Avenue.

One time I couldn't convince an executive to buy "Bandstand." I knew it would sell his product. As a last-ditch measure I begged him to send someone to Philadelphia to watch the show for a couple of days.

Tony picked up a very glum account executive at the Thirtieth Street Station. The guy figured he'd been assigned to Siberia. We took him up to the sponsors' booth and made him as comfortable as possible.

The first afternoon he noticed a cute girl with a ponytail.

The second day he was into the dance steps.

The third day he was humming along to some of the tunes.

At the end of the week he returned to his office on Madison Avenue. I got a copy of a memo a few days later that he'd sent to his boss as his report. It was three short lines:

> It's a great show.
> We ought to buy it.
> Don't ask me why.

An effective method of attracting the attention of our viewers, the network, and sponsors was to have contests on the show. The crazier the contest, the more mail we'd get. We had one to name Frankie Avalon's new house in South Jersey. Another, to name the first American satellite (the prize was a week in Philadelphia—W. C. Fields would have loved that!). We had dance contests of all sorts and weird prizes. We gave away three-wheeled automobiles one year, another time it was sets of *American Peoples Encyclopedias* "in full leather bindings together with unique coffeetable bookcases."

The last really big contest we had was the strangest. It was in 1964, when Ira Sidelle, one of the fellows who'd worked on concert tours with me, became the road manager of the first Beatles tour of the United States. I called him, asking him to gather up pillowcases, sheets, cigarette butts, and pop bottles, any Beatles debris, and send it all to me properly identified. We had a giant drawing for all the stuff. We got over a million pieces of mail in a week—for George Harrison's cigarette butt and Ringo's pillowcase.

Another promotion for the show was to go on location. I used the Drexelbrook Country Club down the street from our apartment for many of these location shows—the swimming party, skiing party, and ice-skating party were held there. We went to Willow Grove amusement park for the fun house party. We rented a big barn on a farm outside Philadelphia for a barn dance party, got the kids, crew, and equipment out there, only to find someone had forgotten to bring along video-tape. We had a Frontierland party at an amusement park in New Jersey. It rained 5 minutes before the show so we opened with the kids dancing ankle-deep in mud.

By the time the show went off the air at five o'clock I played upwards of thirty-five records, had as many special events, guest artists, and other activities as Tony and I could manage to round up before airtime, and had been on my feet for two and one-half hours.

Immediately after the show Tony and I went back to the office to take phone calls from local stations who carried the show and kids who watched. For an hour or so we talked to program directors and viewers about the show, the music, and how particular songs and artists went over. It was this feed-back that kept us on top of the music scene.

We also got numerous calls from the phone company. Kids would call us on the family phone, run up a tremendous bill talking to us about what was happening in Hartford, Miami, or Chicago, then deny they knew anything about it when the phone bill came in. The phone company would call once or twice a day to verify a number.

# "American Bandstand"

"We better get our asses in gear on this and do something," I told Tony Mamarella in May 1957 when "Bandstand" was still a local show. I stubbed out my cigarette, sipped my vodka and 7-Up, then lit another cigarette.

"Don't I know it," he said. He motioned for the waitress to bring us another round. It was six o'clock and we were at the Brown Jug, relaxing after a tough day at the office. For the fifth time in the last few months, a program director from a local TV station in the Midwest had appeared in the office, asking to see Tony. The story was always the same; they wanted to do a local version of "Bandstand" and could they have a few minutes of Tony's time.

"I don't think we have too much to worry about," said Tony. "I sit down and tell them exactly how the show is done, but I know most of them don't believe me. Number one, they think I'm holding out on them. Number two, they all have MC's who are egotistical enough to think I'm lying and that the MC has to play a much more important role."

"I know that, but there's another complication. I heard from Jack Steck today that ABC is dropping their old English movies and have approached all their affiliates to carry a new program."

"Well it took them long enough."

"Steck didn't know what the replacement would be, or if it would affect the show. He said it was Clipp and Koehler's decision."

"Dick, they won't cancel "Bandstand." If ABC came to them

and said 'Cut that show, we've got a replacement,' they'd tell 'em what they can do with it. FIL makes too much money out of 'Bandstand' to give it up."

"You think?"

"It's a money machine for them."

"I'm not so sure. I think we've got to do something."

On the way home that night I thought over our conversation. "Bandstand" did okay locally, but it had come to a standstill. It was the top-rated daytime show in Philadelphia, but where did I take it from there? Or was it a question of moving on from the show?

Six months before, NBC had sent down a guy from their daytime programming division. He'd stayed two days, watching the show, asking questions. Tony and I had had delusions of network grandeur. A week after he went back to New York, Tony had called him. He told Tony that NBC wasn't interested.

By the time I got home to Drexel Hill, I had an idea. I called Tony.

"Hasn't ABC ever expressed any interest in the show?" I asked him.

"Not that I know of."

"We should get a kinescope of the show and get it to New York to the powers-that-be at ABC."

"You know, Dick, I seem to remember that Koehler said something about a kinescope a month or so ago. Do you suppose he or Clipp are already pitching them?"

"Interesting, I didn't know that," I told Tony.

The next morning I called Ted Fetter, director of programs at ABC, and got an appointment to see him. Then I went to George Koehler's office.

"George, Ted Fetter's interested in 'Bandstand' as a possible network replacement for the afternoon movie."

Koehler ran his hand over his crew cut, smiling at me. "Really?" he said, as if he knew damn well Fetter hadn't called me, I'd called him. Koehler didn't say anything for a minute, it seemed like he was making a decision what to say to me. Finally he spoke. "Some of the network people have already seen the kinescope."

In the end Koehler and Clipp's efforts coupled with my

youthful enthusiasm created enough curiosity about the show so that they viewed the kinescope several times. They told us they'd let us know.


I had a week's vacation coming and I arranged to take it in the middle of June. I went to Utica to visit my parents. I called Marlene every day to see how things were going. The morning of June 19, 1957, she told me I'd gotten a letter from Ted Fetter. I asked her to read it to me.

"Regarding your teen-age dance show," wrote Fetter, "we have viewed it with interest and pleasure. I personally want to take this opportunity of congratulating you on the excellent job you do. If you are ever in New York why don't you drop in and say hello. Sincerely yours, Ted Fetter."

I canceled the rest of my vacation and flew to New York. I was naive enough to misread Fetter's "Don't call us, we'll call you" missive for an open invitation. I rushed into Fetter's office and pleaded with him, "Give me a chance, put the show on for a couple of weeks." I didn't know anything about thirteen-week cycles or how complex network decisions were. Fetter was a bit taken aback, but between the show and my own excitement he agreed to see what he could do.

In the middle of July he called me. He, James Aubrey, who was the head of ABC-TV, and Aubrey's assistant, Daniel Melnick, would come to Philadelphia to see the show. I danced around the office after the phone call. We just might pull it off.

Tony was on vacation that week, relaxing at home. I called him. "Anthony, come back," I yelled. "How would you like to be the producer of a network television show!" Tony took it with a grain of salt, but agreed to be in the office the next day to prepare for the network visit.

Two days later Jim Aubrey, Army Grant, Daniel Melnick, Ted Fetter, and a couple of others came to see the show. Tony ushered them to the sponsors' viewing room. He sat with them as the show went on the air.

Almost immediately everyone in the room had suggestions to make or criticisms about the show.

"How come the kids don't stop and applaud at the end of

every record? They would if this were a regular dance."

"Why don't we put a picture of the artist on camera every time Clark announces a record, then we could put all the pictures in a book and sell it?"

"The lighting is terrible."

"I think Dick Clark is a little sloe-eyed, don't you?"

"How come the kids aren't wearing any makeup?"

Tony started to do a slow burn. After all, the show was the most successful show in Philadelphia, drawing 60 percent of the local audience for its time period.

Aubrey must have sensed that Tony was angry. He turned to Tony, "Tony, would you walk down to the studio with me? I want to ask you some questions about the studio."

He and Tony left the room. He stopped Tony in the hall. "Tony, I don't want to ask you any questions about the studio," he said. "You tell me, why does the show work, why is it successful?"

"It has three ingredients, Mr. Aubrey. It has kids, and kids like to watch kids and adults like to watch kids; we play the music of the day that the kids dig; and it has an MC. You couldn't do the show without kids, it wouldn't be interesting. It also wouldn't be interesting without the music. And somebody has to MC."

Aubrey nodded his head when Tony finished, then said, "Why would kids in Texas or California or Cleveland like the show?"

"The show goes all over Pennsylvania already," said Tony. "Our range is over a hundred miles, and we have all sorts of kids watching, in Philadelphia, in the coal regions, all over, and they all like the show. One of the kids on the show attended a dance in Mahonoy City, two hours from here, and there were headlines in the paper."

"You know, we always have a concept that a local personality has to be changed somewhat in order to be acceptable networkwise," Aubrey told Tony.

"If you make any change, it will have to be gradual, because if you change Clark or the show you'll send it down the tubes. Dick Clark has just established himself being Dick Clark the way he is right now. If you're gonna impose phony changes on him you might as well take a phony guy from New York and put him in front of the show."

Aubrey was silent.

Finally, Tony asked him, "Well, what do you think?"

Aubrey smiled. "I'd never tell you what I think, but I will tell you this: you will hear from us in three days with a 'go' or a 'no go.' Certainly there's no argument that you've got the hottest local thing. I wouldn't worry too much about it."

Later that afternoon in the office Tony and I tried to figure out what Aubrey was thinking. We figured he meant that even if he wasn't interested we still had a hot local show—so either way we'd come out all right. I made Tony go over the entire conversation twice, to try to get some clue to what was going to happen.

We were both on pins and needles for the next three days. The morning of the third day the phone rang; it was Ted Fetter.

"We liked it," Fetter told me. "There're problems, but we're giving you a shot. We're putting you down for a four-week trial run beginning August 5. I'm sending down some of our people to build you a new set and change the lighting."

Once we went network we had two openings for the show. The first was at 2:45 when we went on the air locally. The second was 3:00 when we joined the network.

A few months after the success of the show on the network, I learned my first lesson about network wisdom. ABC had a game show called "Do You Trust Your Wife?" that they wanted to promote. They figured that if "Bandstand" was doing well, why not stick this other show in the middle of it to boost its ratings.

So it was that at 3:30 every afternoon "Bandstand" left the network for half hour to be replaced by "Do You Trust Your Wife?" It annoyed me no end. At 3:29 I looked at the camera and said, "Many of you have written to know why we go off the air at this time. Actually, we don't; we keep on going. The ABC television network brings you another program and I hope sincerely you'll be able to join us again, in half an hour from now."

The host of the games show was a young comic named

90

Johnny Carson. I beat on his show's intrusion mercilessly. I never named the show, just said it would interrupt "Bandstand" for half an hour, hoping there would be enough mail to get it out of there. Apparently Johnny has never forgiven me—I've never done the "Tonight" show when he's been the host.

The announcer on "Do You Trust Your Wife?" was a guy named Bill Nimo. Bill was Bill the Bartender for Pabst Blue Ribbon Beer on the Wednesday night fights. He had one too many jobs at one point and couldn't hold all the announcing chores together, so he gave up the quiz show.

My associate in those days, Chuck Reeves, had an occasional drink with Carson's manager. One day Johnny's manager said to Chuck, "Doesn't your friend, Dick Clark, have a neighbor that's an announcer? We need one."

I lived next door to Ed McMahon at that time in Drexel Hill; the wall to our living room was his kitchen wall on the other side. Ed had started out making a lot of money doing the Sealtest Circus show as a clown. He'd been one of the highest-paid radio and TV guys in Philadelphia. Then he was in Korea in the service and it almost destroyed his career. He came back to Philadelphia and was doing a five-minute insert on the midnight movie; that was about it. Times were rough for him.

Chuck called me to tell me to have Ed call about the job on "Do You Trust Your Wife?" I called Ed, and he wasn't home. I finally got his daughter Claudia on the phone; she tracked him down at military reserve summer camp, and he went to New York to audition. He got the job, spent five or six years doing it, and then went on to the "Tonight" show with Carson, which he's been doing ever since.

"Bandstand" did well in the afternoon, despite the interruption. The show went to 5:30 for a while, but then ABC introduced "The Mickey Mouse Club" to take over at 5:00.

At WKTV I'd watched John Cameron Swayze sign off the network news with "Glad we could get together." I'd said to myself at the time that whenever I got in a position to do a sign-off on TV I'd develop something that wasn't just an ordinary "good-bye." So I started saying at WKTV, "For tonight, Dick Clark, good night" and I'd give a little salute. I

91

Somebody had the bright idea of dumping a week's worth of mail on the studio floor for a publicity photo. Fifteen thousand postcards and letters are not easy to pick up.

kept it at that when I signed off on "Bandstand" before "The Mickey Mouse Club." I looked at the camera, said, "The mouse is coming, and for now, Dick Clark, so long"; with that I gave the camera a salute and Mickey was on his way.

In those days the mail was the sure indication of how the show was doing—it was the computer survey of the fifties. From the very first day "Bandstand" went network I worked to generate as much mail was possible. By the time we'd been on ABC for a few weeks, the mail was pouring in at the rate of 15,000 letters a week. I took a picture sitting in the midst of a vast sea of letters that got wide newspaper circulation. Eventually the show got more mail than the most popular show on TV at the time, "Wyatt Earp."

A small percentage of the mail came from people who didn't like the show. Every now and again I did something that I think Garry Moore was the first to do. I would take one of the screwball letters and write a note to the person if he had been brave enough to sign his name and address. I'd say, "Dear Mr. Jones, We received a letter today which purports to be signed by you. Obviously some demented, sick person is using your name, and we thought you'd like to look at it."

Occasionally we got a bomb in the mail. The first time it happened it was a cardboard box with postage due. The postal authorities and the bomb squad told me they weren't impressed with its manufacture. We got many phone calls about bombs. But in those days bomb threats weren't as credible as they are today. Nobody really believed a bomb scare in the fifties. We would go on, live, in the studio with 150 young people and me rockin' 'n' rollin' while firemen and policemen walked around the studio, looked behind drapes, under the stands. Every time there was a bomb scare the Philadelphia *Bulletin* ran a story on it and we'd immediately get three or four more calls. I finally prevailed on them to ignore us.

Another time a box came in the mail that looked strange— we got so we could recognize the real crazies by their handwriting. This box had a label on it that had that look. Besides, when I held it up to my ear I could hear it ticking inside.

I told Marlene to call the bomb squad and then calmly evacuated the office. The guys in the armored suits came in with their tongs and shields and took the box in a van the size of a tank. They drove to a remote field, took out the box, and tore it open by remote control. Inside there was a wind-up hound dog.

One piece of mail I'll always remember was a medium-sized rectangular box wrapped in brown paper and tied securely with a brown cord. It had a Los Angeles postmark.

The moment it arrived in the office, Marlene brought it to me. "You better look at this, it smells godawful," she said as she placed it on my desk.

Tony, Marlene, and I gathered around the desk. Carefully I opened the package; the more brown paper that came off, the worse the smell got. By the time I had all the wrapping off the odor had filled the office.

Lifting the lid of the box, I found a very dead fish. There

was also a note: "To our good friend, Dick Clark. A souvenir caught in the beautiful blue waters of Southern California. From your friends, The Four Preps."

It took us hours to air out the office. I vowed I'd nail those four jokers the next time I saw them.

The mail was filled with thousands of ticket requests, which came in from kids who were going to have the chance to pass through Philadelphia. School groups that made their school trip to New York or Washington would often convince the teachers or chaperones to detour to Forty-sixth and Market. Tony once got a call for one hundred tickets—a convention was in town and most of the conventioneers had been persuaded to bring their kids since daddy was going to the home of "Bandstand."

It got so bad that at one point the Philadelphia post office called asking us to go easy on contests for a while. During a contest we usually had practically every mail sack in Philadelphia at the WFIL studios.

Viewer reaction to the show varied. For some kids in the fifties the big fantasy was to drive to Philadelphia. I always thought that was weird. In Oshkosh, Minneapolis, or St. Louis, a mother and father would turn on "Bandstand," look at the kids dancing, and say, "Why there's my Charlie!" I'd look up in the middle of the show and see a policeman or plainclothesman standing near the door. They'd gotten a call from Richmond or Atlanta to come pick up little Johnny Jones who was blissfully dancing with Angel Kelly.

Two housewives wrote to say they danced in front of the TV with pillows for partners because they loved to dance and their husbands didn't. The wife of a member of the 3558th Fighter Bomber Squadron at Perrin Air Force Base in Texas wrote that "the volume of 'American Bandstand' has compared favorably with the warming up of jets" as it played on the TV set where the crew waited to take off. Reports came in that infants loved to wiggle in front of the screen, that pet dogs, mothers, and grandmothers loved "Bandstand." "It makes a wonderful baby-sitter," some wrote.

Television station KTEN in Ada, Oklahoma, decided not to carry the show and got more letters of protest over its cancellation than there were people in town. In Iowa, high school girls started rolling their socks the way the girls did in Philadelphia. In Miami, despite the heat, kids got in on the fad of wearing sweaters. In St. Louis, an enterprising record store owner had a TV set installed in his "45" department so the kids could watch "Bandstand" when they came in to buy records.

The police chief of Carbondale, Pennsylvania, came into our office one day after the show. He told me how he and his force had suddenly realized that all the teen-agers had vanished from the roads and sidewalks after school, and they couldn't figure what the kids were up to. When the chief authorized a house-to-house search, they discovered that the kids were at home watching "Bandstand."

# "Land of a Thousand Dances"

"So furious is the rate of the dancing, which is mostly rock 'n' roll, that it is inconceivable that any dancer would have an ounce of energy left over to invest in any kind of hanky-panky whatsoever," wrote Anne Warren Griffith in the New York *Herald Tribune.*

"My sister and I pick up new steps watching the show," said Sal Mineo.

On "Bandstand," dancing went under many names, and, like the music, everybody had something to say about it. Dancing was the result of putting together the kids and the music. Sometimes it was the currently popular dance step. Other times I announced the Spotlight Dance—a slow dance where the cameras got in close to concentrate on one couple dancing. Or it could be a dance contest—we'd need to goose the mail count, and asking viewers to pick the best dancers on the show got us an avalanche of cards and letters. The kids danced and America watched what kids in other cities called dancing "Philly style."

America loves to dance. And ever since this country was founded, there have been dance fads. The magic of rock 'n' roll was that it was easy to dance to because it had a straightforward beat. Rock 'n' roll was less inhibited than anything that came before it.

"Bandstand" had only two kinds of dances—fast and slow. The fast dance elicited comments from adults because it was an electric dance where the partners rarely touched. In the early sixties the fast dance came in for more heat as it turned into the Twist, in which the pelvic thrusts were such that if the dancers *had* touched we all would have been arrested.

An unwritten rule on the show was that every other record was slow. In the fifties, when the kids slow-danced, they could "cop a feel." Really sensual girls threw the lower part of their bodies into the guy's groin; the girls would sort of backbend and chuck it right out. Slow-dancing was the beautiful art of getting sexually aroused with no payoff.

For years "Bandstand" determined the dance steps of teen-age America. There was the Duck, Pony, Fly, Dog, Madison, Popeye, Mashed Potato, Watusi, Loco-Motion, Twist, Hitch-hike, Harlem Shuffle, Limbo, Swim, Wiggle Wobble, Bristol Stomp, Cool Jerk, Frug, Boston Monkey, and the Hully Gully.

Of all the dances, only one was hatched by adults. Ray Anthony did a big band record for Capitol of the "Bunny Hop" and Bob Horn introduced it to the kids on the show. A Conga line was formed with each kid standing behind the next, putting his or her hands on the hips of the person in front of him. It was the simplest thing: put your left foot out, put your right foot out, hop forward, hop backward, hop forward three times.

Kids brought the new dances to the show. Except for the Bunny Hop, I don't think there was ever a dance created by Philadelphia record men or Madison Avenue ad men. Sometimes, however, a new dance step evolved without a specific record to do the new dance to. When that happened, I immediately called to tell my friends in the record business.

When I took over the show the kids did the Jitterbug and Lindy to fast records and the Fox Trot to slow records. In the summer of 1957, just before we went network, the Bop was introduced on the show and became our first big dance.

Tony and I heard about the dance during the course of phone conversations with music people in Southern California where kids started doing it to "Be-Bop-a-Lula," a record by Gene Vincent and The Bluecaps. By chance, a couple of California kids on a visit to relatives in Philadelphia came down to be on the show.

I was at the podium, getting ready for a commercial, when I noticed two kids at the far end of the bleachers whose gyrations differed from those of the rest of the dancers. I picked up

The "Bandstand" sweethearts, Justine Carrelli and Bob Clayton.

my phone and told Tony to find out what they were doing.

Five minutes later my phone lit up. "It's the Bop," said Tony. "They're here for a couple of weeks from Los Angeles. I asked them to hang around after the show to teach some of our kids how to do it. They said sure."

As soon as we went off the air I rounded up Pat Molitierri, Billy Cook, Bob Clayton, Justine Carrelli, and a few others and sent them into Studio A with the Californians to learn the Bop.

Pat Molitierri stuck her head through the office doorway half an hour later.

"How's it going?" I asked, motioning for her to come in.

Pat walked in and slumped into a chair. "I'm exhausted, but we've got it. It's like jumping up and down on a pogo stick, except every time you land, you grind your heels left and right."

Within a week all the kids on the show were doing the Bop. It was the first fast dance done on the show when we went network. In the fall, Gene Vincent released another Bop record, "Dance to the Bop," which was a Top 50 hit for him.

In 1957, the Stroll was the other important dance. Chuck Willis, who was known as The King of the Stroll, introduced the dance on the show. It was popular in the black community, danced to Willis' hit, "C. C. Rider." The Stroll was a cool, modern-day version of the Virginia Reel—two lines were formed, boys on one side, girls on the other, then the end couple would stroll in a wiggle-wobble fashion down the corridor between the two lines, separate, and become the end boy and girl at the other end of the line.

In November 1957 one of the guests on the show was a Canadian group called The Diamonds, who were managed by a friend of mine named Nat Goodman. Nat brought the boys to Philadelphia to do their current single, "Silhouettes," which was a turkey (not the Rays's version). He saw the kids doing the Stroll and remarked on the dance. I told him that the dance was popular, but that there was no specific Stroll song. On the way back to New York Nat and the group decided to record something by that name with that tempo. They commissioned three different songwriters to write a song called "The Stroll" on the theory that one of the three would come up with something. By Christmas 1957, "The Stroll" by The Diamonds was the number-one record in the country.

Between 1957 and late 1959, there were many minor dance fads. In 1958 there were the Shake and the Walk, the latter popularized by Jimmy McCracklin's wonderfully syncopated record of the same name. In 1959 there were the Shag and Sam Cooke's "Everybody Like to Cha Cha Cha." Dave Appell and The Appelljacks hit on Cameo with a redone "Bunny Hop," which made a short comeback for the occasion. There were also two dances—the Alligator and the Dog—that were banned from the show as too sexy. Those were the only dances we ever nixed.

There were other, more short-lived dances as well. There was the Circle Dance, a sort of square dance in the round; Bix Reichner and I wrote a song named after my son called "Do the Dicky Doo" but nobody did it; Tony and I saw the kids doing a combination of the Cha Cha and the Calypso which we named the Cha-lypso, had some music written for it, and sold a few copies here and there.

In 1959 Hank Ballard released a record called "Teardrops on Your Letter" that got enough airplay to make the charts for a couple of weeks, then disappeared. Ballard and his band, The Midnighters, were stars from a series of humorous, raunchy

99

records about a lady of considerable talents named Annie. After "Teardrops on Your Letter" flopped, Ballard came back with two hits, "Kansas City" and "Finger Poppin' Time." Then people began to request a song Ballard had written which was the flip of "Teardrops on Your Letter." It was called "The Twist."

Ballard's record company, King, re-released the record and it started to climb the rhythm and blues charts. Its popularity was accompanied by a new dance in the black community, also called the Twist.

I was in the middle of a show in the summer of 1960, about to do the Record Revue, when I saw a black couple doing a dance that consisted of revolving their hips in quick, half-circle jerks, so their pelvic regions were heaving in time to the music. The white kids around them watched, fascinated. Some started to imitate the dance.

"Tony! For God's sake, keep the cameras off that couple near the Top 10 Board!" I yelled into the phone. I was terrified. It looked like something a bellydancer did to climax her performance.

"Go into the Record Revue, then announce a Spotlight Dance," said Tony, not sounding any too calm himself.

I followed his instructions, and once the kids were quietly fox trotting to the Drifters' "This Magic Moment," I walked over to the couple. "Pardon me, what do you call that dance you were just doing?" I asked.

"The Twist," they said, with a tone that suggested I should be a little more up to date on such matters.

The next afternoon I noticed that the Twist was spreading. Already there were half a dozen couples who'd gotten the hang of it. Tony and I discussed it and decided to let it go and see what happened. In the meantime I called Bernie Lowe at Cameo Records. I asked him if he remembered the record Hank Ballard had done a year or so ago called "The Twist." Bernie said he did.

"Well, the kids are doing a dance to it, except they're doing it to other music," I told Bernie as specifically as possible. "It looks like it'll catch on. Why don't you turn the song upside down or sideways or whatever and do it again."

Bernie took my advice. He recorded the song with a relatively unknown singer he'd recently signed named Ernest Evans.

"I cut the record," Bernie called to tell me. "The interesting thing is, there's no sense turning it upside down, it's too simple. We just did the same song."

The Christmas before all this happened I'd had the idea of sending out a record instead of a Christmas card. I wanted the record to be an imitation of stars wishing our friends a "Merry Christmas" and "Happy New Year." Bernie had agreed to make the record for Bobbie and me and I had gone to the Cameo studios one evening to be at the session. In the studio that night was a handsome young black singer, Ernest Evans, doing imitations of Elvis, Fats Domino, Jerry Lee Jewis, and others for our record. Bobbie looked at him, turned to Bernie, and said, "He's cute. He looks like a little Fats Domino. Like a chubby checker." Ernest has lived with that name ever since. He laughingly calls Bobbie his godmother.

Chubby had been looking for his big break for some time. He'd gone to South Philly High with Fabian and Frankie Avalon. Frankie was on to him before anyone else. He brought record people to see him sing, but hadn't been able to help him because Chubby had no original material.

Chubby worked as a chicken plucker in a market owned by Henry Coltapiano. Chubby sang to entertain the customers and carried on about how he wanted a career as a singer. Henry Coltapiano agreed to see what he could do, and eventually Chubby connected with Bernie Lowe and Kal Mann at Cameo. Chubby's first break was doing our Christmas record. Then Bernie decided to release a commercial version of the record. It was called "The Class" and Chubby debuted it on the show, imitating famous stars right down to pretending to strum an invisible guitar.

Then came the Twist. Part of the promotion of Chubby was purely visual. He was young, good looking, and a born ham whose hip-wiggling version of the dance often looked more like a tricky exercise. Chubby sold the dance as he sold the song. It was an incredible event for all of us. The Twist was the big-

*"It's What's in THE CASH BOX That Counts—INTERNATIONALLY"*

Early "Bandstand" favorites Arlene Sullivan and Kenny Rossi received several hundred pieces of fan mail each week.

"American Bandstand" goes on location to a barn dance in the early sixties.

A Christmas party shot of "American Bandstand." Look at those faces! No wonder people used to say, "Why don't they smile?"

The first publicity photograph taken of me on the "Bandstand," in July 1956. I had just taken over a television program whose format would last over twenty-five years.

gest dance in the history of popular music. Hank Ballard went on the charts with his original version in 1960. Chubby went to number one with his version in 1960 and again in 1961. Others got on the bandwagon as the Twist sensation spread: The Isley Brothers' "Twist & Shout"; Sam Cooke's "Twistin' the Night Away"; Fabian's "Kissin' and Twistin'"; Santo & Johnny's "Twistin' Bells" (a Christmas song); Gary "U.S." Bonds's "Dear Lady Twist." Chubby himself had a second hit, "Let's Twist Again," in between the times his "Twist" went to the top.

I got a call from the motion picture outfit that was promoting Jerry Lewis' latest movie. They wanted him to come on the show to promote the film. I called Joanne Campbell and asked her if she could come down from New York to "teach" Jerry Lewis how to do the Twist. It was one of the funniest afternoons we've ever had on the show. Jerry leaping around the studio as Joanne patiently tried to show him how to Twist.

The Twist broke as headline news. *Time* and *Newsweek* made it a feature story. Most of the country first saw it done on "American Bandstand." All anyone had to do was tune in between 3:30 and 5:00 to see it, live from Philadelphia. The Twist was the rage and we had the patent on it.

I was in New York one night in the fall of 1961 when Joanne Campbell took me, Tony Orlando, Glen Campbell, and a group of other friends to a joint on Forty-fifth Street called The Peppermint Lounge. It was a hangout for street people, hookers, dancers, and after-hours musicians. There was a house band called Joey Dee and The Starlighters, who were a very hip band at the time. Joey, with his producer, Henry Glover, wrote a song called "The Peppermint Twist." Then Joey, who'd never sung lead in his life, sang lead at the session where the song was recorded after the original lead singer couldn't get the feeling right. The record became a hit and Joey and The Peppermint Lounge were in the spotlight.

Ahmet Ertegun, head of Atlantic Records, began to bring his diplomatic friends and the jet set crowd to The Peppermint Lounge. The result was a wild mixture of people including Jackie Kennedy, Judy Garland, Jayne Mansfield, and Pearl Mesta, most of whom would get on the dance floor to try out

Limbo time in the early sixties. Charlie O'Donnell and I hold the limbo pole while the kids dance to Chubby Checker's "Limbo Rock."

the Twist—although most of the dancing by then was done by professionals hired to give the place atmosphere. Before long the newspapers got wind of the story with the help of a young press agent named Steve Paul—the jet set was twisting the night away at The Peppermint Lounge! And that story made the Twist a hit all over again. Anyone who might have missed it the first time, didn't the second.

From the Twist until the Beatles, "American Bandstand" continued to feed the dance craze with one new step after another. There was the Pony, Watusi, Fly, Continental Walk, and Madison as contenders to replace the Twist. When the kids saw adults trying to Twist and heard it was the rage of the forty-year-olds, they shuddered and turned to other dances.

Many of these dances came out of Philadelphia and were associated with songs done by artists on Cameo Records. There was Bobby Rydell with "The Fish," The Dovells with "Bristol Stomp," Dee Dee Sharp with "Mashed Potato Time," and Chubby Checker with one dance record after another, including "Pony Time," "Limbo Rock," "Popeye," "The Hitchhiker," and "Slow Twistin'."

This continued into 1963 with Major Lance's "Monkey Time" and even into 1964, when The Larks introduced the Jerk. From then until the seventies the dances ceased to have names. It wasn't until the return of discothèques as discos and the introduction of the Hustle and the Bump that dances again had names.

As for me, well, I dance very poorly. Most of the time I'm too embarrassed. It's been an inhibition since I started on "Bandstand." Mr. and Mrs. Arthur Murray lived next door to me and my parents in Mount Vernon, and when I was about thirteen they gave me a set of dance lessons at their famous studio. I can still cut a mean Fox Trot. The last dance I learned was the Twist. But usually I sit it out. People think I ought to be able to dance very well, therefore I don't even attempt to learn because I know I'll never fulfill their expectations.

# "At the Hop"

It was after six on a Friday evening near the end of June 1958. Tony and Marlene were gone and I was alone in the office making a halfhearted attempt to straighten out my desk in the hour before I left for my record hop. From outside in the hall I could hear the janitors shouting to each other over the steady drone of their floor-waxing machines. I stood up and stretched.

I was sorting through the records on my desk, putting those I'd take with me that evening in a large cardboard box, when the office door swung open and in walked Ed McAdam. Ed was a burly ex-marine, a gruff fellow who was actually the kindest and gentlest of men. I'd hired him the year before as a bouncer for record hops and he stayed with me for many years, eventually becoming road manager of my "Caravan of Stars" tours.

"Hi, the car's out back. Where're we off to tonight?" Ed sat down at Tony's desk, opened the paper sack he carried, and extracted a container of coffee and a ham sandwich.

"Berwyn Roller Rink tonight, the Starlight Ballroom in Allentown tomorrow. Did you get the quarters from the bank?"

"Mmm," he said, chomping on his sandwich.

"Good. We'll leave in a half hour or so. The act is meeting us here."

Ed sipped his coffee, then asked, "Who's on tonight?"

"Bobby Darin. He can come only tonight, so Duane Eddy will go with us to the Starlight. Which reminds me, I guess it's too late to call them. Hell! I hope they remember to bring the dubs of their new records."

While Ed worked on his sandwich, I finished loading the cardboard box with the records I wanted to play. Besides the current hits, I took half a dozen new singles that'd come into the office during the week. Tony and I had set them aside as possible hits. Record hops were the natural place to test them before a teen-age audience. If the kids liked a record they applauded or came up in droves to ask me about it; if they didn't like a record they ignored it. One night I'd taken a record by an unknown named Dale Hawkins to a hop. The record was called "Suzi Q." I had to play it for 21 minutes straight before the kids had enough of it. Needless to say, it went on the "Bandstand" play list the next day.

At seven the night watchman knocked on the office door. "There's a gentleman here to see you, Mr. Clark, a Mr. Darin."

"Send him in." I turned to Ed. "All set? Oh, I almost forgot. Get a box and take twenty-five or thirty of the records in that pile in the corner for prizes." While Ed gathered the records, I pulled on my jacket and straightened my tie.

"Richard, how are ya!" Bobby Darin said as he came in the door, grabbed my upper arms, and hugged me.

"Not bad, Robert. And you?"

Bobby turned to Ed to say hello, then held up his hand. "One second, before we go, I have a little something I want you both to hear. It is, in fact, my next record."

I glanced at my wristwatch.

"Where we going tonight?" asked Bobby.

"West Philadelphia, to the Berwyn Rink."

"Even on roller skates it won't take more than a half hour to get there, sit down and shut up."

I sat down and lit a cigarette. Ed stood in the corner grinning. Bobby went over to the record player and put on the dub he'd been carrying. "*Splish splash I was takin' a bath long about a Saturday night . . .*" the sound boomed through the room as Bobby cranked up the volume. He shifted his shoulders back and forth in time to the music, snapping his fingers occasionally to accent the beat. When it ended he turned to me. "So?"

"Robert, I think you've finally done it!"

"You know what? I think so, too!" Bobby took the dub off the turntable and handed it to me. He went over to Ed and

110

feinted an uppercut. "Hey, Ed, after it hits you come to work for me; you can be in charge of keeping the thousands of screaming girls at bay. The surplus'll be all yours and I can assure you it'll be more exciting than fighting off the occasional grandmother that this one attracts."

In the parking lot we loaded the records into my station wagon. Ed had already put in the turntables, amplifier, and speakers we carried with us to the hops. We got in the car and Ed started up and pulled out of the lot. I turned to Bobby, who was stretched out on the backseat.

"So, when does it come out?"

"Week after next. But Atlantic will have copies for me on Monday. They also think I've finally got a big one. *Splish splash.*"

"How in hell did you come up with that?" I asked laughing.

"You won't believe it. It was at Murray "the K" Kaufman's house about a month ago. We were sitting around shooting the shit one night and we got to talking about writing songs. I open my big mouth and say I can write a song off any idea; give me an idea and you got a song. So Murray says 'Okay, wise guy. Write me a song that has "splish splash I was takin' a bath" as one of the lines.' I went right to his piano and did it."

We pulled into the lot next to the Berwyn Roller Rink at about a quarter to eight. It was an old movie house where somebody had torn out the seats and installed a roller rink. There seemed to be a blight in the roller rink business in the late fifties; we were invariably booked to do hops in them. Ballrooms were another place we did hops—they couldn't support themselves any longer booking big bands. And, of course, we did hops in high school gyms. Often the coach wouldn't let the kids dance on his varnished hardwood gym floor unless they took off their shoes—and so the sock hop was born.

We got out of the car and Ed went into the building to scout out the crew for the evening. We hired six guys at $1.50 an hour to act as bouncers. I tried not to have any uniformed police at the hop unless the hall insisted; it ruined the atmosphere.

Bobby and I stood by the station wagon until Ed returned. In about five minutes Ed came out with six fullbacks. He had

111

one watch the car while the others helped him carry the records, amplifiers, speakers, and other paraphernalia into the rink. As Bobby and I started for the back door of the building, a car pulled into the lot and honked at us.

It was Si Singer wih Bob Clayton, Justine Carrelli, Pat Molitierri, and Billy Cook. Si often drove some of the regulars out to the hops. They'd sign autographs and add a little color to the evening in return for getting in for free; also they loved the "star treatment" they got. Bobby and I said hello to them and told them we'd meet them inside.

The doors opened at eight o'clock. Before that Ed set up the two turntables, a mike, and the PA system on a raised platform at one end of the floor. They put it all on a couple of card tables. Compared to the kind of equipment carried by today's rock groups, it would seem pitifully small, but in those days it made more than enough noise. I took my position on the platform.

Ed was at the front door. The kids paid seventy-five cents to get into the hop. Inevitably they'd have a dollar bill. So I sent Ed to the bank on Fridays to get rolls and rolls of quarters. Ed would sit at the door and the kids would pass by him on the way in. Lightning-quick, he'd take in a dollar and hand back a quarter, throwing the dollar bills into empty "45" record boxes. Ed was a sweater. He sweated through his hands, his forehead, his chin; as he worked, the perspiration would run off the end of his tie into the box of bills, making a mess. At the end of the night we had five or six boxes full of crumpled, wet dollar bills. The boxes of bills wound up in the extra bedroom of our apartment. Once or twice a month Bobbie and I sat for hours, counting them into bundles before we took them to the bank. It was a good business—I made about $50,000 a year from the hops. I was meticulous about reporting all that cash, although I was smart enough to form a corporation to channel it through—that was the first corporation I ever formed, the Click Corporation (a contraction of Dick and Clark).

The kids didn't really come to the hops to see Dick Clark. Once the hop was set up and running it wasn't much more than a mating game. I understood this and didn't make any big to-do about the records. I announced them and played them, much as if it were a "Bandstand" show. From time to time during the evening I'd announce a Ladies' Choice or a Spot Dance. The Spot Dance meant that I'd pick up the turntable arm in the middle of the record and tell everybody to freeze. Ed would be walking around the dance floor with the box of prize records. Wherever he was when I said "Freeze" he'd give the couples around him a few records.

To make sure trouble was kept to a minimum, Ed and I developed a security system using the six guys we hired. Ed positioned the six guys on the floor, four of them worked the corners of the room and a couple plus Ed drifted through the dance floor. We assigned numbers to the corners of the hall— the far left was 1, far right, 2, and so on, with the center of the dance floor designated as 5. From my position on the platform I could see the whole room. If there looked like trouble, I'd just say, "Number 5" through the PA and the guys closest would descend on the middle of the floor.

I checked my watch. It was nearly 9:30. I picked up the mike after the record on the turntable ended. "We have a special guest star this evening. He's got a new record that's very exciting. Let's give him a big hand, and welcome Bobby Darin!" Bobby stepped up on the platform and acknowledged a scattered burst of applause. I handed him a dead mike we used for the occasion and put on the acetate dub of "Splish Splash."

There, in front of several hundred sweaty kids, working on a creaky plywood platform, Bobby danced and moved like it was opening night at the Copa. He was a terrific performer and always knocked kids out with his stage moves, even in the days before he had his first hit record. As "Splish Splash" ended the kids roared their approval. Bobby gave them a big grin, took a deep bow, and jumped off the stage. I played "Splish Splash" twice more that night. It was obvious the record had it.

"Ricky Nelson sings it, and it's the number-one record this week," I announced, and let "Poor Little Fool" spin on the turntable. I jumped off the platform and went to find Bobby. He was drying his face and hair with a towel in the boys' room.

"Great, they loved it," I told him. "Can you do it on the show the week after next?"

"Oh, I think I may be able to fit it in; I'll have to consult my social secretary." Bobby gave me a big grin. "Did they really like it?"

"It's gonna be a smash," I told him in low, confidential tones.

Bobby and I soon became close friends. He was always on hand to do hops for me and though we saw each other rarely between his trips to Philadelphia, it was a strong friendship.

He demonstrated his potential as a performer at the hops. I got so I could tell how well an artist would do from the reaction he or she got doing a record hop lip-sync. Fabian got screams though he couldn't sing a note. Bobby Rydell was another instant success, though what caught my attention was the way he had his hair whipped into a pompadour that looked like it'd been sprayed with gunite. Sam Cooke had the little girls swooning over the romantic atmosphere he created. Duane Eddy refused to smile at the first few shows he did because he had a chipped front tooth. We had it capped and he became a new man, outgoing as could be. Chubby Checker was far from being the world's best dancer when he started doing hops. Then there was Brian Hyland, who always looked like he'd rather die than go onstage (I've never met a more introverted performer), but the kids seemed to love him because he was genuinely shy. Freddy Cannon had modest musical talents but a tremendous ability to build audience participation until they did his act for him.

The hop ended at midnight. I closed every hop with Jessie Belvin's wonderfully romantic "Goodnight My Love." The couples snuggled together and shuffled across the floor. Then the lights came on and Ed and his crew cleared the hall as quickly as possible. Within a half-hour he had our gear back in the station wagon and we were on our way home.

# 11

## "We want to put the show on Saturday night"

Christmas week of 1957 I should have been counting my blessings. It had been a momentous year for me: "Bandstand" and I had been swept into the national spotlight and in a few short months been proclaimed a roaring success. At twenty-eight I'd made it. But instead of enjoying my good fortune, I was depressed. My career had gotten out of control.

My mood resulted from what anyone else would have seen as a vote of confidence. ABC had shown their interest in my potential as a personality by presenting an evening version of "American Bandstand" on Monday nights. When they approached me to do it I agreed without thinking. The result was a show over which I had no control—an ill-conceived, poorly executed program put together by people who had obviously never bothered to watch the afternoon show.

"Here he is, boys and girls, Mr. Gloom," intoned Tony Mamarella as I walked into the office. He'd been trying unsuccessfully to cheer me up all week. I sat down at my desk and busied myself with the morning mail.

Tony spoke again, continuing to address an invisible audience rather than speak to me directly. "Fortunately, there are no windows in our office, so he can't jump, and if there were it wouldn't help as we are located on the first floor. I will, however, increase his moroseness by handing him this sheet of paper." Tony leaned back in his chair and flipped the paper onto my desk. It was the network rating report for Monday night "Bandstand," which was abysmal and only confirmed my opinion of the show.

"That does it, Tony, we've got to do something," I said.

"Maybe they need a teen dance show in Rio?"

"Please be serious, I need your help."

"Ah, well, I'm perfectly willing to help, but you've got to stop acting like Clark Kent the day they took away all the phone booths. You've been positively impossible."

"I know. I'm sorry. Let's go down to the Jug and figure this one out, what'd you say?"

"Nothing to figure out," said Tony, getting up. He came over to my desk, picked up the receiver of my phone, and handed it to me. "Call Ted Fetter and tell him."

"You think?"

"I know. 'Bandstand' is a hot property and you're their boy wonder. Tell 'em the Monday night show stinks."

I grinned at Tony and took the phone. Why the hell not. There must have been a trouble-making glint in my eye, for Tony laughed. I smiled at him and told Marlene to get me Ted Fetter at ABC in New York. He came on the line.

"Ted, Dick Clark. Listen, the Monday night show is a disaster. It hasn't gone right from the first show. Let's call it quits, please. It's not doing any of us any good."

Ted tried to soothe me. I kept at him. "Can't you speak to Melnick or Aubrey and ask them what's going on? They must know what the ratings are." Tony made a twisting motion with his arm. "I really can't take too much more of this; it's making me nuts and I'm sure it's going to start affecting my performance on 'Bandstand.' "

I got off the phone with Fetter and looked at Tony, "Thick enough?"

He smiled. "They know it's a dog. This'll be the straw that'll make 'em dump the whole thing."

Tony was right. Two days later Danny Melnick called. He broke the news that the Monday night show was being canceled immediately. "Don't be discouraged," he said, "I'm sure something will turn up that'll work out better."

In the middle of January Jack Steck dropped by our office.

"Just between us," he said, "I got a call today from the network people in New York. I don't quite know what they're planning, but they've got something in the works; I'd bet it's a new show for you, Dick."

116

"Thanks, Jack, let me know if you hear anything more." I raised my eyebrows at Tony. He gave me a who-can-tell shrug.

A few days later Danny Melnick called.

"Dick, we want you to be part of our new 1958 lineup," he said. "It's quite an impressive group—Frank Sinatra, Pat Boone, Guy Mitchell, Patrice Munsel, Maverick, Zorro—and we've got an idea for a show that I'm sure you'll like."

I tried to sound interested but not too enthusiastic.

"I'd like to come to Philadelphia sometime next week with Louis Heyward. Do you know him? He wrote and produced shows for Garry Moore, Ernie Kovacs, Faye Emerson, and Bell Telephone. I think he'll be the perfect producer for your new show."

"Okay, come down when you can," I said.

"Right. One more thing, we want to put the show on Saturday nights."

That took my breath away. I got off the phone with Melnick and told Tony. He calmed me down with the observation that if it wasn't the right show it wouldn't matter when it was on.

Danny Melnick showed up with Louis Heyward on Tuesday afternoon of the following week. They watched "Bandstand" from the clients' room, then came down to meet with me. I took an immediate liking to Louis Heyward—he was called Deke by everyone—although I wasn't so sure about him as producer for a show for me.

"We're supposed to build a show around you. What do you do?" asked Deke as soon as we met.

"Nothing," I told him. "I know the music. I know the stars. But I don't do anything myself. We can get you the stars, like the Everly Brothers."

"Bob and Ray Eberly?" asked Deke.

I turned to Melnick. "Listen, if we do this show, Tony and I have to have total control of the artists who appear on the show."

We eventually hammered it all out. Melnick assured us that they wouldn't make a step without checking with us, that we would book the acts for the show from Philadelphia, and that they'd gotten us the Little Theater in New York. Tony had the idea to do the show in the round, but ABC insisted on the Little Theater—it was an old radio theater they'd con-

In 1959, during the shooting of my first feature film *Because They're Young*, we originated "The Dick Clark Saturday Night Show" from Los Angeles. I'm talking here with Paul Peterson of "The Donna Reed Show." The young lady next to him is his co-star, Shelley Fabares.

A close friend and favorite performer, Bobby Darin.

Tony Mamarella and I shared these extraordinarily cramped quarters at WFIL.

Jerry Lee Lewis makes his network debut on the Saturday night show, complete with leopard lapels. It's a wonder they let us stay on the air.

That's a pretty interesting conglomeration. February 1958, backstage after the premiere of "The Dick Clark Saturday Night Show." From left to right, Johnnie Ray, Dick Clark, Pat Boone, Jerry Lee Lewis.

My thirtieth birthday, November 1959. Around to celebrate were (left to right) Bobby Darin, Sal Mineo, Frankie Avalon, Pat Boone, and Dave White of Danny and The Juniors.

verted for television. "Mr. Firstnighter" and other radio dramas had come from there. And it was really little; it had only 498 seats.

The show was named "The Dick Clark Saturday Night Show." It was a rock 'n' roll stage show. Our idea was to present a fast-paced lineup of stars. For half an hour we had the tops in pops and rock zing across the screen with as few interruptions as possible. The show wasn't at all like "Bandstand"— there was no dancing—the kids instead were the screaming shouting studio audience. The format was one star after another coming out to lip-sync his or her latest hit, usually in some kind of low-budget production number dreamed up by Deke Heyward and the set designer Don Eaton. I announced the acts and at the end of the show came out to run down the Top 10 for the week.

The first show was on Saturday night, February 15, 1958. When I boarded the 10:30 train at the Thirtieth Street Station that morning it was snowing. By the time the train pulled into Penn Station it was a blizzard. Abandoning any hope of getting a cab, I trudged through the storm to Forty-fourth Street. I made that trip from Philadelphia to New York every Saturday for two and a half years. At first I took the train, later I took the bus, and finally I had Ed McAdam drive me in the station wagon—I'd put down the backseat and sleep on the way in and back.

When I got to West Forty-fourth Street there were barriers at the end of the street and a policeman was diverting what little traffic there was. There were three sellout shows in theaters on that block at the time—*Bells Are Ringing, Auntie Mame,* and *The Music Man*—but as I walked down the street I knew that the groups of kids milling around hadn't come to see a Broadway show. I went into the Little Theater looking like Frosty the Snowman and greeted Deke Heyward, who was standing by the door talking to a policeman.

Deke nodded at me and motioned me toward the control room. Garth Deitrich, the show's director, was preparing the rundown when I walked in. He pointed to the coffee machine.

"Why me, I ask you, why me?" muttered Deke as he came into the room. "How are you, Dick? The cops, as you probably noticed, have closed off the street. They're not too happy; they've done this out of sheer desperation."

"Why?"

"Well, it seems that out there in that blurry white stuff are approximately 1,500 kids who want to get in to see the show."

"God! How're we going to manage that?" I asked.

"Let 498 in for the rehearsal, 498 in for the show tonight, and tell the rest of them to come back another time. There's not much else we can do. The cops say they'll keep the street closed until seven, so it won't really be a problem, although I'm sure we'll be finding bodies in the snowdrifts when it begins to thaw."

Deke sat down next to Garth. "Call lunch, then have everyone back in an hour for the run-through." Garth nodded and made the announcement through the house PA system.

"Everything set?" I asked Deke.

"Yeah. Don Eaton got the sets in place and the floors painted late last night. I got here at six and we had the lighting done by eight. We started to do run-throughs at ten and everything seems to be well organized. Have you got a copy of the script?"

Deke handed me my cue sheet and left me to go over it. The

control room had emptied out for the lunch break. About 1:30 the crew reappeared. Through the control room window I saw Deke onstage with The Royal Teens, explaining to them how they would come out onstage.

The rehearsals started again, with The Royal Teens moving around the stage as "Short Shorts" played and they did their best to lip-sync and follow the choreography. Deke stood in the middle of the theater, watching their performance. I walked over to him.

"It's gonna be louder than that when the kids come in, isn't it?" I asked.

"What!" he screamed back over the music.

"It's gonna be louder than that when the kids come in?"

"What are you talking about, I can't hear you!"

"It's got to be louder," I yelled into his ear. He looked at me like I was a madman.

Just then one of the studio pages came down the aisle looking for me. He handed me a package wrapped in tissue paper with a ribbon tied around it. There was a note attached to it that said: "Good luck on your new show, I'll be watching." It was signed Bobby Darin.

Undoing the ribbon, I tore off the tissue paper to find a cigar box. I opened the box. It was filled with horseshit sprayed with gold paint.

Deke walked away shaking his head.

(Two weeks later Bobby Darin did the show. After the rehearsal he was in the shower in his dressing room. I sneaked into the room and took all his clothes, leaving him stranded there nude until 10 minutes before he went on.)

At three o'clock I went to the stage door for a look outside. It was still snowing and the kids in line were turning blue. I went to find Deke.

"The kids are freezing out there," I said.

"What can I do, I can't let them all into the theater," he said.

"Buy them hot cocoa."

"What!"

"Buy them hot cocoa." Seeing that he didn't believe me, I took twenty-five bucks out of my pocket and handed it to him. Deke took the money and sent one of the crew out to buy the kids hot drinks. He told me later I was the first performer he'd ever met who actually cared about his audience. What he didn't realize, I'm afraid, was that behind that bland twenty-nine-year-old face lay the heart of a cunning capitalist. I knew that if the kids got cold enough they'd probably go home, and since the show depended as much on audience reaction as it did on the stars, the last thing I wanted was for the kids to go home. It's something I've realized through the years—the audience is the most important part of my shows.

"From Broadway, the street of celebrities, street of bright stars and smash hits, the American Broadcasting Company takes pleasure in inviting you to the television premiere of 'The Dick Clark Show'!" The announcer's voice rose to a crescendo as the cameras panned up and down Broadway, catching a blurred picture of the lights and traffic through the snowstorm.

The cameras cut to me. I was out in front of the Little Theater, standing under the marquee, half-frozen to death.

"Man alive! Have you ever seen anything like this! Welcome to Lower Slobovia! I never thought Forty-fourth and Broadway would be quite like this," I said, hoping the metal casing of my hand-held mike wouldn't freeze to my hand. Turning to the kids crowded behind a barricade, I said, "It's real nice of you to come. I wish everybody could get in. But we gotta scoot 'cause things are going." I gave them a wave and moved into the lobby, where the first act was ready to go on.

The Royal Teens did their number in the lobby. The cameras cut to four guys in black shortsleeve shirts, tan Bermuda shorts, and socks up to their knees, sitting on the stairs that led to the balcony. "*Who likes short shorts, we like short shorts . . .*" they chanted. A pretty girl wearing very short shorts came up the stairs. Still singing, they followed her while she pretended to make a call in the phone booth in the lobby, and then walked down the center aisle and onto the stage where they finished the song.

The cameras panned across the audience, zooming in on me where I was sitting in a seat on the aisle.

"This is Elaine Berman on my immediate right, left, right?"

I turned to the young girl seated next to me. "Elaine, how does a working girl get to be the president of the Johnny—I was going to say Johnnie Ray, I'm all shook up, you'll hate me forever—Jerry Lee Lewis fan club? A lot of people know about fan clubs and their presidents and so forth, but what does a fan club president really do?" I stopped, sure no one had understood a word I'd said.

"Well, Dick, in the last eight months I've sent out five thousand photos of Jerry Lee Lewis," she said.

"All by yourself?"

"No, I have my co-president here with me."

"You write the letters too and all?"

"Oh, yes, fifty letters a day."

"What keeps you the busiest, Elaine?"

"Oh, hopping around town visiting disc jockeys."

"What's the furthest away you ever had to travel?"

"To Little Falls, New York."

"It cost money."

"Oh, yeah, seventy-five dollars."

"Who pays?"

"Me."

"Out of your own pocket?"

"Yeah."

"I'm awful glad that isn't a regular sort of affair. Elaine, I think you've really truly earned the honor of introducing the man you've been so devoted to." I pulled a slip of paper out of my pocket and handed it to her. "It's written out if you want to read it, you can say it any way you want to."

Elaine took the slip of paper. "Okay, here's the man whose records have sold over two million copies, who plays to standing-room-only all over the country, he just flew in from Nashville, Tennessee, to be with us tonight, his name is Jerry Lee Lewis!"

The kids screamed and yelled as the curtains parted to reveal Jerry Lee seated at a white piano with a drummer and bass player behind him. Jerry Lee was the only act who refused to lip-sync, so he'd brought his band with him. He ripped into "Great Balls of Fire" and the theater resounded with the sound of the kids squealing and clapping along. He was dressed in a

125

On the opening night of the Saturday night show, Pat Boone, a student at Columbia University at the time, was gracious enough to stop by.

black tuxedo with leopard spot print lapels and leopard edging on the pockets and sleeves. Flashes of fire went off behind him as he shouted the lyrics and banged the keyboard.

As he finished the number the cameras cut to me sitting at the edge of the stage. "There he goes, Great Balls of Fire, Jerry Lee Lewis! He will be back with us again, don't panic." I waited for the applause to die down. Then I introduced Connie Francis.

Opening with a shadowy outline of her profile, the lights came up on Connie in a floor-length gold lamé dress standing in front of an artsy Parisian street scene drop. She did an intense lip-sync to her hit "Who's Sorry Now?"

I gave Connie a kiss, squeezed her hand, and turned to the cameras.

"Here's a man who's reached the number-one spot a good many times in his life, let's greet Mr. Pat Boone!"

The kids broke into a screaming uproar as Pat did "Everybody's Gonna Have a Wonderful Time up There," snapping his fingers in time to the beat as the kids clapped along. Towards the end of the song he walked forward out the short runway that was located at the front of the stage. He sat down on the edge of the runway and the little girls went crazy.

I went over to him when the song ended.

"I see you've made yourself at home."

"Yeah, sit down, Dick."

I sat down, looking at the kids in the front row. "I think this gal's gonna faint if you get any closer." I turned to Pat. "How's school going?" I asked him. He was in his freshman year at Columbia University. We chatted a few more minutes and then I brought back Jerry Lee Lewis to close the show.

When the show was over, Deke Heyward called his mother. She was a nice Jewish lady then in her sixties. Deke had had a classical music education and had gone through law school. His mother was proud of the fact that he produced "The Bell Telephone Hour" because, as Deke explained, "It had mostly dancers with Russian names."

Deke gets her on the phone and says, "Mama, did you see the show?"

There was a very long pause.

"Mama, are you there?"

"I'm here."

"Mama, did you see the show?"

"I seen the show."

"Mama, what did you think?"

Another long pause, then she said, "My boy, you're not friendly with any of these people, are you?"

That night after the show was the first time I was scared by a crowd. Bobbie had come to New York in the afternoon and we were leaving the theater to go to dinner and celebrate. We were walking from the alley behind the theater across the street to our hotel, the Manhattan. Suddenly a group of 200 to 250 little girls, harmless little preteen and teen-age girls, backed us up against the stage door which was locked from the inside. There was no way out. Finally one of the studio guards heard the commotion outside the door and rescued us.

The first week there were no commercials on the show because we didn't have a sponsor. But we did have an audience. We doubled the ratings ABC had for that time slot. A Trendex survey showed 51 percent of the viewers were adults.

One viewer was Bud Kloss who had the Beechnut Gum account at the Young & Rubicam advertising agency. Kloss told the agency he thought the show was ideal for Beechnut Gum to sponsor. They didn't think so.

Kloss got a kinescope of the first show and made an appointment to see the owner of Beechnut, Ed Noble, an old man who was known for shooting from the hip. He watched about 10 minutes of the kinescope, then told Kloss to turn the damn thing off. Kloss thought, uh-oh, I've had it.

Noble glared at him, then said, "That's terrible. That's the worst thing I've ever seen. But it'll sell a lot of my gum. Buy the show."

Beechnut Spearmint Gum was our fulltime sponsor from the third show on. The story of what we did for the Beechnut people is unbelievable. I would lay sincere, genuine pitches into the camera about "Wrapped in green and made for a teen, Beechnut flavor*ific* gum." The cameras would pan across the kids in the audience, all of them chewing gum and wearing "Ific" buttons. The kids sent me clothes made from the wrappers. It was phenomenal; I had rooms full of hats, jackets, even slippers made out of Beechnut wrappers. On my thirtieth birthday I was presented with a life-size portrait of myself made from 357 Beechnut wrappers. *Advertising Age* ran a full-page story that said in reference to the way I was selling Beechnut with my commercials: "He may replace Arthur Godfrey as the number-one personal salesman." That was the greatest commercial credit I ever got.

We booked an amazing variety of acts for the show: Paul Anka dueting with Annette Funicello, Bob Hope, Teresa Brewer, Sal Mineo, Tab Hunter, Neil Sedaka, Eddie Cochran, Sam Cooke, Johnny Carson doing a drum solo to promote "Do You Trust Your Wife?", Fats Domino, and Chuck Berry. Gordon MacRae did the show after he called to ask me if he could go on it because his daughter, Meredith, watched and thought the show was the greatest.

I finally got the chance to pay back The Four Preps for their dead fish. All afternoon they rehearsed their current single, "Down by the Station." At one point in the song they crossed downstage to the "T" mark on the floor where they were supposed to stand to finish the song. That evening when the show

A 1959 Saturday night show audience, with buttons, courtesy of the sponsor.

The reaction to the Beechnut sponsorship of "The Dick Clark Saturday Night Show" was unbelievable. Kids made everything from Beechnut wrappers—a giant birthday cake, hats, pennants, clothing, and displays.

was on live, they crossed the stage to find the "T" mark had been replaced by a large puddle of plastic vomit from a joke store. It looked tremendously realistic. Deke and I roared with laugher as they jumped back away from it, trying not to lose their places in the lip-sync. Ah, revenge is sweet.

Frankie Avalon was on, although he almost didn't survive the rehearsal. He was rehearsing in the afternoon and got the little girls so steamed up they rushed him. It was as if the seating area was a dump truck, and all of a sudden all the kids just fell onto the stage knocking Frankie flat. I ran out, waded into the mass of bodies, and pulled Frankie out. His jacket and shirt were torn to shreds, but he took it in stride.

Don Gibson was on the show. Deke thought we'd make him feel at home by building a stable and having a real horse on the set so this country fella would be comfortable with us rock 'n' rollers. Damned if the horse didn't step on Don's thousand-dollar guitar. He took it very graciously.

The Crests were on to do their hit, "16 Candles." We had a set for them where they sat in a rowboat in the middle of an artificial sea. The afternoon dress rehearsal before an audience went well. The evening show came, I was in the balcony doing the announce, I can see it now: "Ladies and gentlemen, here they are, the fabulous group who have such a big hit with '16 Candles,' The Crests." The curtains parted, the cameras zoomed in on the rowboat, but there was nobody in the boat.

The group had gone home. They thought the dress rehearsal was the show.

Antoine "Fats" Domino did the show a few times. Fats was terrified of appearing on TV. When he came to the Little Theater I always had a case of Teachers scotch waiting for him and his band.

One Saturday morning he was late for the rehearsal, so I went to his hotel to get him. It was about eleven in the morning. When I got to his room, he'd just gotten up. He stood there in his underwear, brushing his teeth and drinking a can of beer.

"Antoine, come on, let's go downstairs. We'll have a little breakfast and then go to the show."

He looked at me. "No, no, Dick," he said, sipping his beer, "I can't eat on an empty stomach."

The show was going well, everything was fine, when Ed Sullivan tried to throw a monkey wrench into the works. He was a miserable bastard in those days. He tried to do us in, to kill the show. He tried to put clauses in his contracts that if an artist did his show the artist couldn't appear on any other show a week before and eight days after their appearance on his show. He couldn't understand how artists like Tony Bennett did my show for $155, then hit him for $5,000 to $7,000 for an appearance on his show. He was convinced I put a pistol to Tony's head. Sullivan didn't understand that "Bandstand" and the Saturday night show with their huge teen-age audiences sold records. Tony would call me to tell me his contract was coming up for renewal and that he needed a booking to boost his record sales.

Sullivan went to AFTRA, trying to establish that I was pressuring the acts into appearing on the show. I had a huge argument with the union over that one. Sullivan didn't understand the music, he was too busy booking trained seals, ventriloquists, and Russian dancing bears.

At one point he offered Fabian $10,000 to do his show, if Fabian agreed not to appear on the Saturday night show. Bob Marcucci told Sullivan he was sorry but they'd have to skip his show. Eventually, Sullivan came back to book Fabian even though he'd done my show the night before.

I wrote Sullivan pleading letters. I wanted his acceptance and his blessing. He saw me as a young upstart. He treated me much the way Bob Horn had—as a young guy who couldn't be anything but a threat. It was almost ten years before we met and became friends.

I'm not sure exactly who decided to send the Saturday night show out on location. Maybe the network wanted to add a little glamour to the show, I don't know. In June 1958, we started a series of location shows that took us around the country with stops in Miami, Atlanta, Los Angeles, and Binghamton, New York (where a new station was joining ABC).

The first remote was on June 21, 1958, from Atlantic City. Deke Heyward didn't get any extra money to produce the show as a remote, so he followed a common practice of those days; he got whatever he could "clout," which meant we'd trade goods for a plug on the show. He went to Atlantic City a few days early to see what he could round up.

He called me on the Wednesday before the show. "I worked out a deal with the Shelbourne Hotel," he told me. "We mention them at the beginning of the show and in return we can use their boardwalk and they put you up in a suite."

"That sounds good," I told him.

"Yeah, well, they weren't interested in putting up anything more than that. So to put up the rest of the cast and the crew I made a deal wih Max Malamud's Empress Motel, which is only about ten miles from the boardwalk," said Deke, his voice filled with irony.

"Yeah?"

"Yeah, and in return you have to work it into your opening remarks on the show that Max Malamud's Empress Motel has a new swimming pool."

"*What!*"

"This connection must be bad, I can't hear anything but static, I'll see you on Saturday morning," and he was gone.

Then Deke called Leon MacNamara who worked for Young & Rubicam and was in charge of the Beechnut account. Poor Leon, he was a long-suffering individual whom Deke turned to whenever he had an idea for the show and couldn't find anyone else to pay for it.

"Leon, Deke. I'm in Atlantic City and I've got the greatest opening for the show!"

"Yes?"

"You want a big opening for the show don't you, Leon?"

"Oh, yes. I'm with you."

"I need two airplanes."

"What do you need two airplanes for?"

"One will carry a banner that says Beechnut Gum, the other will have a banner behind it that says Dick Clark. Now won't that be one hell of an opening, those planes flying into view over the shore and soaring over the boardwalk?"

"Deke, I'll see what I can do, can you call me back?"

Deke waited a half-hour, then called Leon back. Leon, kind soul, agreed to the expenditure.

Bobbie and I flew to Atlanta, Georgia, the site of the first integrated rock 'n' roll concert in the history of the music business. While this picture was being taken, we both knew that the concert might turn out to be a violent disaster.

Just before showtime Deke got a call from the airplane people. It turned out that the banners were too long for the planes to pull. Deke told them to skip the Beechnut part, have the first plane pulling the banner that said *Dick,* the second pulling the banner that said *Clark.*

The opening credits rolled that evening and out of the sky flew two planes. But unfortunately they got their cues wrong so the banners read *Clark Dick.*

Then I drove a golf cart up the boardwalk to where the cameras were situated. I got about fifty feet from the mark when the batteries ran down and the cart stopped cold. This was followed by an interview I was supposed to do with twenty girls in the Miss Atlantic City beauty pageant. I did the introduction, then turned to ask them each a question. There were only nineteen of them; 15 minutes before the show one of them had announced she was pregnant.

I got used to the remotes as we did more of them. In October Deke called to say we were going to Atlanta for a show at the Lakewood Park Fairgrounds as part of the forty-fourth Annual Southeastern Fair. Tony and I booked Paul Peek, Sam Cooke, Dave Appell and The Appelljacks, Conway Twitty, Danny and The Juniors, and Joni James for the show.

Tension was high as we televised Sam Cooke's appearance in the first integrated rock 'n' roll show held in Atlanta. The National Guard and Klu Klux Klan members attended a rock 'n' roll show together! Despite threats of violence, we didn't cancel the show.

Deke and the crew arrived five days ahead of time to set up the show. He hadn't been there for more than a half hour when he was on the phone to me.

"Dick, I don't know if you knew it, but this is the first integrated show ever held at the Atlanta Fairgrounds. There's been a lot of publicity that the blacks are going to be seated with the whites. There may be trouble."

"Do you think it can be avoided?" I asked him.

"Yes, I think so."

"Okay, keep me informed how it goes."

Two days later Deke called me again.

"Everyone in the crew has been getting threatening letters and phone calls," he said.

"Jesus! Are you all all right?"

"We're fine. I was a little shaky yesterday. I got a phone call from a guy who said the KKK was gonna fix our asses. I called the local police and the National Guard. I also went out and bought a gun."

"Deke, you sure everything is okay?"

"Yeah. It'll be all right."

"Good. I want the show to go on if possible."

On Thursday I flew into Atlanta and went directly to the motel where Deke and the crew were staying. I found Deke and Sam Cooke together in Deke's room. Sam had arrived a couple hours before me. There'd been some trouble about him checking into the motel; they didn't want any blacks, but Deke had prevailed on them.

Sam gave me a smile and we shook hands. Deke had been talking with him, and he continued as I stood on one side and listened.

"Sam, here is exactly what we have. We've gotten letters, we've gotten phone calls. I can't guarantee anything."

"I'm going on," said Sam.

"I talked to the National Guard. One of the junior officers came to me, told me there's a good sprinkling of KKK members in the Guard, and that if there's trouble we shouldn't depend on them. Then another of the Guard officers, an older guy, said we could depend on them. Your guess is as good as mine."

"I gotta go on," Sam told us. "That's all there is to it."

"That's it, Deke, Sam is with us so we do the show," I said.

"You got it," Deke said.

The night of the show we were all on edge. The stadium told us if we wanted to set up our equipment we could use the colored men's room. Half an hour before airtime there was a bomb threat to our control truck. We moved the control truck two blocks from the stadium and demanded the National Guard throw a ring of men around it.

Deke was making last-minute checks of the stage area as the audience was coming in when he looked down to see a group of black nuns come in and take seats in the front row. He walked down to where they were seated.

"Sisters, excuse me, but you know there may be some trouble tonight?"

One of the nuns looked up at him, giving him what he later described as an angelic smile. "If we don't sit here now," she told him in a soft voice, "we may never sit here. We'll be all right, don't you worry."

Despite all our worries the show went smoothly. Deke had conned Leon MacNamara again and he had two expensive special productions for the show. First, all the acts came in on floats, which probably wasn't the safest idea considering the atmosphere. Then, at the end of the show there was to be a huge display of fireworks that would light up the sky to spell out B-E-E-C-H-N-U-T G-U-M. When the time came, the fireworks went off but all they spelled was N-U-T. Poor Leon.

The Atlanta show was one of the few ballsy things I ever did. We went up against the authorities and told them they either took us as we were or the hell with them.

We were back in New York rehearsing one of the shows when Deke Heyward got a phone call that Bobby Darin's mother had died. Deke had also become friends with Bobby. He came down to the stage to tell me. I hadn't spoken to Bobby in a couple of weeks and the news came as a surprise. I asked Deke when the funeral was. He told me it was that afternoon.

"I'll be back in time for the show," I said. Before he could protest I was out of the theater. I got a cab and had him drive me to the funeral services. It's not my nature to do such things, but I did. Bobby never forgot that. He thought it was a very thoughtful thing to do. I'm afraid sometimes I'm not a thoughtful person; I want to be thoughtful but I'm often off the mark. But I made that one gesture, and Bobby always remembered it.

# 12

## "Person to Person"

As I got out of the car I felt the chill in the air. It was the middle of April 1958, the day had been sunny and warm, but the ground had just started to thaw and spring was a few weeks off. Doublechecking that the car doors were locked, I buttoned my jacket and walked briskly along the cement path that led to the door of the garden apartment Bobbie and I had moved into the year before.

Through the living room window to the left of the door I saw Bobbie sitting at the end of the couch. I tapped on the window pane with my door key, she looked up, and returned my grin.

As she opened the door I kissed her.

"I thought you went to Allentown for a hop," she said, helping me off with my jacket. Sinking into the easy chair facing the couch, I loosened my tie and slipped off my loafers. Louie, our deaf miniature dachshund, waddled out of the kitchen to snuggle at my feet.

"Put me down for a long day. No, the hop was moved to next Friday."

Bobbie made a face. "Why don't I make dinner, then we'll look in the paper to see what's playing at the Waverly. If it's anything good, I'll get Mrs. Quirk to sit with Dickie. We could go to the early show."

I agreed. On the way to the kitchen, she bent to give me a quick hug.

Gathering up my shoes and jacket, I climbed the stairs to the second floor where the apartment's three bedrooms and

It's hard to believe that I was already a millionaire, living in a three-bedroom garden apartment in Pennsylvania, when the Edward R. Murrow crew came to visit. That's my record collection behind me and an RCA color television set, one of the first in existence.

only bathroom were situated directly above the ground floor layout of living room, dining room, and kitchen. This was the third apartment we'd had in the area. Drexelbrook was an old golf course that had been converted just after World War II into a housing development. It was a pretty neighborhood, hilly with plenty of trees, and quiet winding streets along which were spaced two-storey red brick apartments with black trim casement windows. Our first apartment had been a one-bedroom for $67 a month, the second, a two-bedroom at $87, and the present three-bedroom was $110 a month.

Our son, Dickie, was almost two years old, and Bobbie had quit teaching to take care of him fulltime. The door to his room was open a crack, I looked in. He was asleep. I watched him for a couple of minutes. Finally I pulled his door closed and went back downstairs.

Bobbie was still in the kitchen, so I put on a coat and took Louie out the front door. I had 20 feet of clothesline that I used as Louie's leash. Attaching the line to his collar, I walked him around the back of the building where the backdoor from the kitchen opened on to a playground area and beyond that a steep hill down into ten acres of woods.

Moving back to the front, I had a look at the little flower patch by the side of the front steps under the living room window. The tulips I'd planted the year before looked as if they might break through the hard ground any day. Measuring off the patch with my feet, I considered what I'd plant when spring arrived. From inside the house the telephone rang.

Bobbie came to the door, a spatula in her hand. "It's Tony. Keep it short, dinner'll be ready in five minutes."

It took less time than that to hear what Tony had to say. Replacing the receiver, I went into the kitchen.

"Bobbie, you won't believe this. After I left the office today Edward R. Murrow's office called from New York. They want us to be on 'Person to Person'! I told Tony maybe we'd see him later at the RDA for a drink."

"Dick, that's great." Bobbie beamed at me, then suddenly her face clouded. "Oh! Does that mean they'll come here?"

"Not only will they come here; it means you and Dickie will be on the show with me. They said it was an *at home* with Dick Clark."

At three o'clock that morning the phone rang. Bobbie got to it first, then came and shook me awake. I went to the phone with every intention of giving whoever it was a piece of my mind and going back to bed.

"Dick, you know who this is, but don't say anything. I just want to tell you to watch out. Jerry Lee Lewis married his thirteen-year-old cousin and all hell's gonna break loose. You're promoting the daylights out of him, you'd better be careful." Then the connection was broken.

Sitting at the dining room table the next morning, sipping a cup of black coffee Bobbie had put in front of me, I stared out at the woods in the back yard, trying to sort out what I should do about Jerry Lee Lewis. "I've got to be crazy to put him on the show," I thought to myself. "On the other hand, he certainly has done me enough favors. I should go ahead and use him. Why not? If we use him it could be all over for us; the sponsors will get nuts, the network will be all over my back. I've got enough troubles." I must have sat there for a half-hour thinking the situation over. Finally, in frustration, I decided to talk to Tony and some of my friends in the business. But I knew

From left to right, my mom, dad, Bobbie, Dickie, and me, on one of our yearly "American Bandstand" Christmas parties.

We allowed the fan magazine photographers to follow us to the Acme Food Store. Dickie and I check out the lettuce with Bobbie in the background.

Father and son: Richard A. Clark II at home in Pennsylvania.

that whatever was decided it would be my decision and I'd have to stand by it.

In a very cowardly act I decided to hold off further bookings for Jerry Lee on the show, for which I've been sorry ever since. I've apologized a million times, but he's never really forgiven me. We still see one another and do things together. I tried to make amends in the sixties by trying to "bring him back" at a period when his career was sliding. I hope someday he'll forgive me for not standing by when he could have used support.

The following Wednesday the production crew for "Person to Person" came to Philadelphia. I took them out to the house so they could have a look around. They decided to use the downstairs and the back yard. They painted the fence around the playground in the back yard. The show was to open with me seated on the backsteps of the apartment, but there were sunken trash receptacles beside the kitchen door, so they planted three honeysuckle trees to hide them.

They wanted part of the show to be me talking about my records. When they asked about my record collection, I said, sure, no problem.

The truth was, I didn't have much of a record collection. In

141

a panic I called all the promo men I knew and asked them to give me all the empty record jackets they could spare, anything they had around. There I was, supposedly the number one disc jockey in the country, with barely a record in the house. I had shelves put in under the stairs, and filled them with hundreds of record jackets. Once we did the show my record collection became famous. If they'd ever looked in any of the album covers they'd have found my collection was nothing but the jackets.

We went over the entire show point by point. There was nothing spontaneous about "Person to Person," though the show was done live and gave the impression of being unrehearsed. When Murrow came on the screen to introduce us, I knew exactly what he was going to say and how I'd answer.

The evening of the broadcast, Bobbie was scared. I tried to joke with her while we strapped on the wireless mikes under our clothes. (Hers was hidden in her bra.) The whole thing was silly and fun, but she was too tense to enjoy it.

I never met Edward R. Murrow. The show was planned out by his staff; on the actual day of broadcast they set up speakers so we could hear him asking us questions; there wasn't even a visual monitor to see him on.

The show began with a shot of Morrow seated in an armchair on a set that was supposed to resemble a living room. He wore a suit, had a cigarette clenched in his left hand, a floor-standing ashtray at his right side. He was on the left side of the screen, and he looked at a curtained-off area that was supposed to resemble a picture window.

He appeared on the screen, and said in his throaty voice, "A personable twenty-eight-year-old disc jockey by the name of Dick Clark has become just within the last year something little less than an idol to rock 'n' roll teen-agers and to some of their elders too." He went on to give a brief resume of my career, then turned to look at his "picture window"; there, superimposed on it, was me, sitting on the backsteps in the early evening. Floodlights illuminated me and the back yard. I wore my best baggy suit.

"Good evening, Dick," said Murrow.

"Good evening, Mr. Murrow," I chirped back.

142

Bobbie and I talk with Edward R. Murrow on "Person to Person." Check out those socks!

"You look as if you might be deep in thought. Were you?"

"I'm sitting here and thinking about how to get on a bus and get into New York City in time for a ten o'clock rehearsal in the morning."

"Get on a bus," he said like I'd just said something extraordinary. "You mean you have your own bus and driver? That's real luxury!"

I shook my head and gave the camera a smile. "No, not quite. We use the public service bus; it's very reliable and always seems to get me there on time."

"So you're still riding the bus. But other things have probably changed for you in the past year or two, haven't they?"

"Oh, not a great deal, Mr. Murrow. We still live here in Drexel Hill. We've lived here for about a year now, we've lived in the apartment development for about five and a half years. We have the same automobile we've had for a while. Things haven't changed too much."

"Do you still like living in Drexel Hill?"

"Oh, very much," I replied. I stood up and walked away from the kitchen steps, the cameras backed up in front of me. "We have practically everything we could ask for, one of the world's

143

smallest back yards. There's a lot of room over here in the back with a playground so my son can get out and chute the chute and up and down on the swings and all. It's very, very comfortable." The cameras cut to the newly painted fence and the playground it encircled. Then cut back to me. "Actually we have practically everything you'd want in a house."

The cameras followed me as I walked into the house and sat down in the living room. Murrow had another question. "In the course of your shows you've undoubtedly talked to hundreds of teen-agers. Do you find them as much of a mystery as some of their elders seem to do?"

"Mr. Murrow, during the course of a year I get to talk to about 300,000 teen-agers and it bothers me a little bit when older people look at young people and say what a mystery. I don't think there's anything really very mysterious about the younger generation."

"Well, Dick, what about the parents. You must get some rather interesting comments from them on the, ah, social contributions of your shows, don't you?"

"A lot of people have asked, Mr. Murrow, if we make any educational contribution in our programs. I think there's one very important social contribution that we make and many, many parents have written about it—the fact that for the very first time in their lives they've been able to look in on their children having fun doing what *they* like to do. They've finally got a common ground of understanding, so they can talk to one another for a change."

"No complaints that rock 'n' roll sort of shatters adult ears and nerves?"

"Well, we get a few, that's only natural." Again I gave my best twenty-eight-year-old grin to the camera, then said, "But I think the conception of the fact that popular music bothers adults is not right, otherwise 53 percent of the people watching us wouldn't be over twenty-one."

This man-to-man talk ended momentarily as Bobbie appeared on the screen.

"Is Dick as adept around the house as he is at spinning records?" asked Murrow.

"Yes, he's really very good." Barbara turned in the chair to point at the wall. "He made this clock on the wall behind us here from an old lampshade, an eight-day alarm clock, some pieces of model airplanes, and old pieces of cork."

I walked over to the wall to look at the clock as the camera followed me. It was a hideous construction, but I admired it as if it were a Picasso.

"Very good too," said Murrow. "It's a little fast, isn't it?"

I smiled, turned, and tapped my wristwatch. "Mr. Murrow, that's standard operating procedure in our household. The watch on my arm and the one on the wall is always about four minutes fast so that we can hope to be on time."

"Ah, Dick, getting back to rock 'n' roll, those lyrics are a little hard to understand, wouldn't you agree?"

I picked up a set of typed-out lyrics that I'd prepared for the show. I sat down on the arm of the easy chair again. "Well, kinda," I said, trying to look shy and flustered at the same time, "as a matter of fact I have a set of many different song lyrics here, one of which, the lyrics to a song which has sold one million, two hundred thousand copies as of yesterday. It's a thing called 'The Witch Doctor' and it says, 'I told the witch doctor I was in love with you, / I told the witch doctor I was in love with you, / And then the witch doctor he told me what to do, / He said, "ooh-eee-ooh-ah-ah, ting-tang, wallah-wallah, bing-bang, / Ooh-ee-ooh-ah-ah, ting-tang, wallah-wallah, bing-bang"' and so forth.'

"It's all perfectly clear now that you've explained it," said Murrow deadpan. "Very simple, isn't it. Barbara, *you* understand, don't you?"

"Oh, absolutely," said Bobbie.

"I don't either," said Murrow, then he laughed.

"Mr. Murrow, in popular music these days though, very often it's the sound and the beat of the record and that's what this record has, it has a mysterious charm that people seem to like."

"Dick, do you think the influence of rock 'n' roll music on teen-agers has been somewhat overstated?"

"Yes sir, I do. I think that rock 'n' roll is something that adults are more preoccupied with than children are. Kids seem to like rock 'n' roll, but it's only a portion of their existence, it's not quite as important to them as adults would make it."

"And they still read and don't spend all their time listening to rock 'n' roll, right?"

"Very much so."

"Well, Dick, I gather talking with you that you're reasonably convinced that teen-agers as a group aren't quite as much of a problem as they're often pictured, is that right?"

"Mr. Murrow, for thousands and thousands of years adults have worried about the young generation and what they were coming to. There would be one thing though I would say to older people regarding younger people, and that would be, rather than say, 'What is that you've got on tonight!' or 'What is that racket you're listening to?' why don't you take about 15 minutes a day and find out why they like the music they like or why they dress the way they do. They're not much different than we are. They like the same things. Perhaps they dress a little differently, but they have the same sort of problems, very understandable and likable people."

"And you think that even as little a time as 15 minutes a day might serve to improve the understanding between these teen-agers and their parents, is that right?"

"Mr. Murrow, I read a survey not too long ago that showed that the average parent spent about 4 minutes *a week* in intimate conversation with their children. And 15 minutes a day would be a million percent better."

"What a terrible indictment of the parents!"

"Well, it's not. Let us not say it's the parents' whole fault. But young people, for my money, I think they've had one problem. And that's the name teen-ager. The newspapers, the radio, and the television all say 'Teen-ager Holds up Store,' 'Teen-ager Gets in Trouble.' You never see 'Middle-ager in Trouble,' maybe there's something there."

"Dick, thank you very much for letting us come. Thank you, Barbara. And say goodnight to your son, please."

"Thank you, Mr. Murrow."

"Goodnight," said Murrow and it was over.


By the time I was thirty, I was a millionaire. I had made a million dollars and we still lived in the $110 a month garden

Eight Benton Circle, Wallingford, Pennsylvania, the house we moved into after apartment-living in Philadelphia.

apartment. To be truthful, I didn't give it much thought. I've always spent money in moderation.

But eventually Bobbie and I decided to look for a house. Dickie was ready to start kindergarten, so we wanted to be near a school. We found a house in Wallingford, Pennsylvania, about 45 minutes from the station, and just down the road from the Summit Elementary School. The house cost us $38,000. It was on the corner of Dogwood Lane, a comfortable white house on three-quarters of an acre with a brook running through the back yard and lots of cedar trees for shade.

My next-door neighbor was Joe Anderer. Joe built a small wooden bridge across the brook that ran through our back yards. When I moved to California I sold the house to the man whose daughter married the late Jim Croce. Jim told me that he and his wife Ingrid were married on that bridge in the back yard years later.

# 13

"I've got this kid named Fabian"

Rock 'n' roll hit big in the mid-fifties. Before that it was an
oddity, an amalgam of two peripheral musics—rhythm and
blues and hillbilly—promoted by Alan Freed, Bob Horn, and
other vaguely disreputable, if visionary, entrepreneurs, and
epitomized by the early success of phenomenons like Elvis
Presley. When they bothered with rock at all, RCA Victor, Columbia, British Decca, and the other old, established record
companies joined music publishers, network radio, and right-
thinking adults in condemning it.

Despite this attitude, the demand for rock 'n' roll increased.
Teen-agers liked the music; it was their music, created by their
peers. They were pleased by its discordant sound; they de-
lighted in its irreverent, sexy beat and its destructive effect on
old folks' eardrums.

With the big record companies rejecting the music and deny-
ing there was a market for it, independent record producers
stepped in. From the first generation of young postwar business-
men came producers who were hip to rock 'n' roll, rhythm and
blues, and hillbilly music. They realized that the demand was
such that a minimal investment in recording a good song could
make them extraordinary amounts of money. It was like the
early days of the movie business—there was nothing mysterious
about making records, the trick was to give the teen-age record
buyers what they wanted to hear.

As an adjunct to their South Side Chicago nightclub, Phil and
Leonard Chess started Artistocrat Records, eventually recording Muddy Waters, Howlin' Wolf, Bo Diddley, and Chuck

Berry. When he was fired as Arthur Godfrey's orchestra leader, Archie Bleyer started Cadence Records to record the Everly Brothers and Andy Williams. Two sons of a Turkish diplomat, Ahmet and Neshui Ertegun, and a young journalist named Jerry Wexler started Atlantic Records to record Ruth Brown, LaVern Baker, and Joe Turner. A Memphis businessman named Sam Phillips started Sun Records, producing the earliest records by Elvis, Johnny Cash, Carl Perkins, and Jerry Lee Lewis.

It was a pioneering era. Young, swinging capitalists went into the record business to satisfy the demand for rock 'n' roll. I wonder if any of them ever conceived that the rock record industry would grow by the late sixties to gross $2.5 billion a year!

One of the centers of this independent record activity was Philadelphia. It had a strong radio market, "Bandstand" as an important national outlet, and South Philadelphia.

People always ask me why so many stars came from Philadelphia. My answer is South Philadelphia. Originally the Irish section of town, South Philly became predominantly Italian in the late forties, with smaller Polish, Irish, Jewish, and Black communities. It was like Brooklyn—you were from South Philly first, then you were Italian, Irish, or Jewish. Lower and lower-middle class, South Philly with its endless streets of brick, two-storey row houses, was the tough part of town; the part of town where young people looked for a way out. The way out then, as it has always been for ethnic groups, was to be an athlete or an entertainer. Mario Lanza, Eddie Fisher, Al Martino, and Buddy Greco came out of South Philly in the forties and early fifties. In the mid-fifties, Fabian, Bobby Rydell, James Darren, and Frankie Avalon all grew up within three blocks of each other. When we were short a guest on the show, all I had to do was pick up the phone, call Bobby or Chubby or Frankie and they'd hop in their cars and be at the studio within 15 minutes.

The first contact I had with the local Philadelphia music business was through a young guy named Bernie Lowe. Bernie had played piano in a speakeasy when he was thirteen and in his early years cut records under the name Dizzy Brown. I first met Bernie when I was doing the Tootsie Roll commercials for the "Paul Whiteman TV Teen-Club" in the early fifties. Bernie

149

was the piano player in the orchestra that also included Arnold Maxim on violin—Arnold was later the president of MGM Records; Artie Singer on bass—Artie started Singular Records; and Dave Appell on guitar—Dave became one of Bernie's right-hand men eventually.

In 1957 Bernie started Cameo Records. He joined talents with Kal Mann, a songwriter with whom he wrote "Teddy Bear" for Elvis, and Dave Appell. Their first artist was a singer named Charlie Gracie. They recorded Gracie doing an inside-out version of Guy Mitchell's "Singing the Blues" which they called "Butterfly." Bernie didn't have enough money to pay for the recording session, so he made a deal with a local sound man, Emil Corson, to record the record in return for a piece of the profits. Emil set himself up in business from his piece of "Butterfly."

Bernie would always come to visit me when he had a record he was involved in, even when I was still on the radio. In November 1956 he came into the office with the first pressings of "Butterfly."

"Dick, listen to this," he said with real excitement in his voice. I took the record from him and put it on the turntable. It sounded like a hit to me.

"Well, after all these years of bringing around duds, I think you've got a live one."

"Listen, Dick, you've always taken an interest in my records. I want you to share with me in this one if it hits. I heard you're in the process of setting up a publishing firm. I'd like you to have 25 percent of the publisher's royalties on the song."

"Really, thank you anyway, Bernie. I don't want it."

"Please, do me a favor, Dick. Let me give you a percentage."

"Forget it. Congratulations on your first big shot," I said, going to take a phone call.

A couple of weeks later Bernie stopped by the office again. "Butterfly" had been added to the play list of several local radio stations and I'd added it to the "Bandstand" play list on the basis of the action it was getting.

"It's phenomenal!" said Bernie. "Not only is it doing great here, it looks like it might go national."

"Great. The kids are always asking for it on the show. I want to arrange for Gracie to be on in the next few weeks."

150

"You got it," he said. Then he frowned. "Dick, I think there may be a problem. I'm afraid one of the majors will cover it."

It was common in those days for the big companies, though they hated rock 'n' roll, to have one of their established artists record a "cover" version of a record by a small independent company if that record looked like a hit.

I sympathized with Bernie. Then I had an idea.

"Listen, Bernie, I've got the meeting in New York on Friday that Murray the K. is organizing. Disc jockeys from around the country are flying in to attend. Give me a dozen copies of 'Butterfly.' I'll hand them around, tell them it's a hit here, that I'm playing it on the show, and that they should listen to it."

Bernie was ecstatic. Half an hour later two dozen copies of the record were delivered to the office. I made good on my promise, spreading the word that "Butterfly" was a hit and the version on Cameo was the one to play. "Bandstand" was still a local show, but I was known as having an ear for hits.

The record became one of the biggest sellers of the year. It sold all over the world. By February 1957 it was in the Top 10.

Near the end of 1957, Bernie called me.

"Dick, I want to thank you and let you know that your share of the royalties for 'Butterfly' is $7,000."

"Bernie, forget it."

"Dick, I made a promise. I intend to pay you for your help."

"Oh, all right," I said, not realizing I'd live to regret my decision to take the money.

Besides Bernie, Kal Mann and Dave Appell kept Cameo running.

Kal was the songwriter for the company. He'd sit at his desk, dreaming up wonderfully simple lyrics. I don't mean to put him down, but they were very basic lyrics.

Dave Appell rounded out the team. Dave had a band, Dave Appell and The Appelljacks, who backed many local stars. Dave and his musicians did the bandtracks on most Cameo records. Dave came up with a number of dance novelties for "Bandstand" including "Rocka Conga," "Bunny Hop," and "Mexican Hat Rock."

Cameo and Parkway, its subsidiary label, introduced many hit artists: Chubby Checker, Dee Dee Sharp, The Dovells, Bobby Rydell, The Orlons, among them. Many of the big dance hits were on Cameo or Parkway, including the biggest of them all, "The Twist."

Bernie was in his late thirties. He was a family man with a couple of kids, and he claimed his daughter was the key to his success. "I never do anything, never put out a record, without letting her hear it first," he said. In later years when Cameo and Bernie stopped turning out a constant stream of hits everybody kidded Bernie that his daughter had lost her touch.

In 1957 a large catalog of Hollywood horror movies was released to television. For the first time the teen-ager generation enjoyed *Frankenstein, Dracula,* and other classics. Local TV stations programmed these features as late-evening fare, often accompanying the films with a local host made up as a "monster."

A sweet, homespun guy named John Zacherle was Roland, Philadelphia's reigning monster. One evening Bernie came home from the Cameo offices to have his daughter tell him about this guy on TV, Roland, whom he should make a record with.

That night Bernie tuned in the monster movie. Before the film began, he saw a white-faced, skinny rail of a man, dressed as a weirdo undertaker, come down a spiral staircase with a basket under one arm that had a head in it and chocolate syrup dripping out of the bottom. Roland gave a hideous laugh, then said, "Dinner was served for three at Dracula's house by the sea. The hors d'oeuvres were fine, but I choked on my wine, when I found that the main course was me! Ha ha! Fine, fine!"

The next day Bernie called Zacherle. Zach had a meeting with Bernie at the Cameo offices in center city, Philadelphia. They agreed to record a single with Zach.

I stopped by the Cameo studio the day Zach cut his first single, "Dinner with Drac." The studio was located in the office building with the Cameo offices. If they wanted echo they had to wait until everyone in the building went home, then they'd run a set of speakers down the hall and stick them in the john with a microphone. The studio itself was about twenty-five feet square. In one corner was a partitioned-off control room made of plywood with a little window cut in it so they could see out into the rest of the studio. In one corner of the control room was an Ampex quarter-inch tape recorder on rollers.

*Left:* Crazy and lovable John Zacherle, in his role of Roland, always visited us on Halloween.
*Right:* John Zacherle and I—complete with cobwebs—at a "Bandstand" Halloween party.

Zach stood in the middle of the studio, looking at a music stand in front of him on which he'd put a sheet of paper with the lyrics written out. Around him were The Appelljacks. There was no mixing or any other sophisticated recording.

The band started to play. Bernie listened, adjusting a dial. He went to the door of the control room and yelled, "The drums are too loud."

Dave Appell picked up an old horse blanket from a corner and spread it over the bass drum. "Try it now," he said.

The band started up. Again Bernie stuck his head out of the control room door, "That's fine, let's check Zach's mike," he yelled.

Zach was a little disgruntled because they wouldn't let him sing, though he had a fine voice. Instead, he had to sort of half-sing, half-talk the words. He started in on "Dinner with Drac."

"Too loud," yelled Bernie.

Dave Appell went over and pulled back Zach's mike about six inches.

"Got it," yelled Bernie, "We're ready for a take."

The band went into the tune, Zach recited the lines. Suddenly Bernie cried, "Hold it, stop. Dave, Zach's a little off on the rhythm, help him out, will you."

The band played it from the top. Dave Appell went over to Zach and beat time on the music stand with a pencil. The take went well.

"Okay, let's try it once more," said Bernie.

They did it again. Then Bernie rewound the tape and played it back for them.

"What'd you think, Dick?" he asked.

"I like it, but the lyrics seem a little gory in some places."

"You think?"

"Yeah, a little too bloody."

"You might be right," said Bernie. He stuck his head out the control room door and said, "Dave, come in here a minute, please."

Bernie told Dave what I'd said, they had a quick conference, deciding to rerecord one side of the record with a slight alteration in the lyrics. The record was part one and part two, so they redid part two to tone it down a little.

In March 1958 "Dinner with Drac" went into the Top 10. It became a custom on "Bandstand" to have Zach come on the show every Halloween to do his monster bits.

Other early record men in town included Kae Williams, a former disc jockey who wrote and produced "Get a Job" for The Silhouettes, originally released on his Junior Records label; Artie Singer who once ran a music school with Bernie Lowe, besides being in the Whiteman orchestra with him. Artie produced Danny and The Juniors, then started Singular Records; and Dave Miller who had Essex Records and who discovered Bill Haley and The Comets. After having hits with The Four Aces, Al Martino, and Bill Haley, Miller came up with the idea for "101 Strings." The "101 Strings" was a guy Dave had in Philadelphia who did arrangements and the Hamburg Symphony Orchestra. Miller had the music arranged, recorded it inexpensively in Germany, pressed the records in a pressing plant he had in an old plush mill outside of Philadelphia, and became a multimillionaire.

In the late fifties the Philadelphia record business produced some of the biggest teen idols rock 'n' roll had ever known.

When I took over "Bandstand" the archetypal rock star was a white guitar player who could sing. Then the nonguitar player, stand-up singer in the Sinatra/Fisher mold took the record beat from the guitar man, making it more romantic.

By the late fifties the impact of the music as revolution was softened—kids rock 'n' rolled on Saturday night, but Sunday morning they got their hair combed neat and their suit on and went to church with mom and dad. I was like that, we were all like that. Considering the times, I doubt we could have been otherwise.

Eventually the teen idols became the stars who specialized in being nice young men underneath it all instead of rock 'n' roll stars. The early spontaneity of rock 'n' roll was lost. Bobby Rydell, for example, readily admitted he took dancing, singing, drumming, and talking lessons so he could be a teen idol.

White teen idols didn't smoke, drink, or swear. Jimmy Clanton once told me what a press agent told him to tell reporters.

"If you're asked," said the press agent, "you went to a movie, went for malts or a soda, and had her in by ten."

Although he was a rock 'n' roller, Elvis was also the first teen idol. His appeal was strictly to his own age group; with them he could rock 'n' roll. When he met his elders he was always polite and respectful, even if his music wasn't. It was as if the escape from the fifties reality that rock 'n' roll provided was put in contrast by Elvis' inborn Southern politeness when in adult company. Adults met Elvis and said, "What a nice young man, too bad about his black shirt and greasy sideburns. I can't understand why he makes that racket when he sings, but he is a nice young man."

Nick and Mary Avallone and Adrio and Jennie Ridarelli wanted their kids to be stars. They used to bring their kids to the CR Club, a private club and offshoot of Palumbo's Restaurant, where the booking agent, a former boxer and dancer named Eddie Suez, would let the kids perform. Nick and Mary brought their kid to play his trumpet. Adrio and Jennie brought their eight-year-old to do his Frank Fontaine impersonations.

From that beginning, Robert Louis Ridarelli and Francis Thomas Avallone became the first of the Philadelphia teen idols: Robert as Bobby Rydell, a name Paul Whiteman gave

155

him when he appeared on Whiteman's program; Francis as Frankie Avalon, who appeared in all the local talent contests, winning a refrigerator and console radio-record player on one local TV talent show.

In 1951 Frankie sneaked into a party for Al Martino, walked into the middle of the party, and started playing his trumpet. An agent saw him, took him to New York, and he repeated the performance for Jackie Gleason. Frankie did a number of national TV shows as a child, then it all petered out. He joined a local Philadelphia rock 'n' roll band, Rocco and The Saints. He got his friend, fifteen-year-old Bobby Rydell, a job as drummer in the band and for a couple of years they played local clubs.

Two songwriters, Pete DeAngelis and Bob Marcucci, who had written a local hit called "You Are Mine," formed Chancellor Records with $10,000 Marcucci's father lent to him. Pete DeAngelis was a serious, intent-looking guy who was the more musically educated of the two. (Incidentally, his aunt used to baby-sit for Frankie Avalon.) He and Frankie would have jam sessions at Pete's house, Pete on sax and Frankie on trumpet. Bob Marcucci was a bit on the chubby side with curly hair and an easy smile. He'd also known Frankie as a kid. Pete supplied the musical direction, Bob was the promoter, manager, and dreamer.

In 1958 when they started Chancellor, Frankie came to see them, asking for an audition. They signed him and released two records, "Cupid" and "Teacher's Pet." Both were flops. Frankie, Bob, and Pete were in the studio trying to come up with a third record for Frankie. They had a song called "De De Dinah," but Frankie didn't seem to have the feel for it. Frankie made a joke about the song and pinching his nose closed with his fingers started to sing it. Bob told him it sounded great that way. Released in early 1958, that joke became Frankie and Chancellor's first hit.

At the same time, Bobby Rydell was discovered by the bass player for Dave Appell and The Appelljacks, Frankie Day. Bobby was still in Rocco and The Saints. They and The Appelljacks were working a summer resort in Somers Point, New Jersey. Usually Frankie went out for a walk when the other band went on, but it was raining so he caught the band, and Bobby.

Frankie and Bobby formed Veko Records. Bobby's first record was a flop. They signed with Cameo and came up with two more flops. In the summer of 1959 they finally found Bobby the right song, "Kissin' Time," and he had his first hit. His next record was a cover version of "Volare." His mother liked the song and suggested he record it. It sold a million copies.

Bobby was on the show once before he had a hit. It was the day Paul Evans was a guest on the show. Paul had a hit called "7 Little Girls Sitting in the Backseat." Nat Elkitz had come up with a special production for the number—he drove my car in through the rear doors of the studio, and then Paul sat in the backseat and did his lip-sync. Tony Mamarella put some kids in the front seat while Paul sat in the back. Bobby Rydell's grandmother was Tony's godmother, and Tony knew that Bobby had always wanted to be in show business. Tony called him and said, "Why don't you come out to 'Bandstand' and be a kid on the show, I'll get you seen and it'll do you good." So Tony put Bobby and Bobby's cousin in the front seat for the Paul Evans' number. Tony told me later that Bobby decided that his appearance wasn't instantaneous stardom and he didn't want to come around anymore because he didn't want to be just one of the kids on the show. Bobby didn't come back until he had his first hit record.

I got along well with Frankie Avalon and Bobby Rydell, although Bob Marcucci and I didn't hit it right off. When my son, Dickie, was born, Bob sent him a diamond ring, which I sent back. I know Bob meant it as a gesture of goodwill, not as payola, but I returned it. The next time I ran into Bob he had a record out called "Calypso Parakeet" and was giving away parakeets as promotion. I wasn't alone in thinking he was half nuts.

When "De De Dinah" hit, I scheduled Frankie Avalon for the show. The afternoon he was to be on, Tony Mamarella walked out of the office to bring Frank Kern the play list. He came back from the control room laughing.

"Dick, you're not going to believe this," Tony stopped.

"What?"

"Your buddy Bob Marcucci is outside in the hall with Frankie

Avalon," was all Tony managed to say before he was overcome with laughter.

"Now what?" I shouted out, getting out of my chair. "I can't believe that guy." I went out into the hall. There was Bob with Frankie. Behind them was a giant cardboard box set on a rolling table and a young lady who held a giant scroll rolled up in her hands.

"Hi, Dick, today's Frankie's birthday, so we brought a cake," said Bob. He opened the top of the box and sure enough, it was a giant birthday cake with "Happy Birthday Frankie" in bold strokes of blue icing. "And I also asked Frankie's fan club president to come along, she's made this drawing of Frankie especially for the show." Bob took the scroll from the girl and unrolled it down the floor of the hall.

Bob was so genuinely excited I hated to hurt his feelings.

"We usually like to plan our own special events, Bob," I said.

"Oh." He looked crestfallen. "I only thought it'd be nice. The beautiful cake, the beautiful picture of Frankie."

"We haven't had a birthday cake in a while," said Tony, who'd come into the hall, and seemed to have regained his composure. "What d'you say, Dick, why don't we use it?"

Bob and Frankie looked at me like a couple of eager kids. I began to feel like I'd suggested they cancel Christmas.

"Sure," I said, breaking into a smile. "Sure, wheel it in."

After that Bob and I became friends. He told me he'd decided when he was twelve to live his life like a Twentieth Century-Fox movie. Whenever he got in a situation that demanded a quick decision, he'd say to himself, "Now what would John Payne do in a spot like this?"

After Bob hit with Frankie Avalon, he started to look for his next teen idol. Frankie had a friend named Fabiano Forte whom he introduced to Bob. Bob named him Fabian and proceeded to tell people he'd discovered this kid sitting on a doorstep. The kid, Bob said, had *it*.

Fabian was a shy, nice kid who'd flunked choral class at South Philly High. He had good looks and a pleasant manner.

Bob called me to tell me about Fabian. He was excited.

"Dick, you know Elvis and Ricky Nelson are really hot."

158

I agreed.

"Well, neither of them are doing anything. They're not getting out there where the kids can see them, they won't let the kids touch them. I figured this out and said to myself I've got to find someone and take him and let him be touched by everybody. I've got this kid named Fabian. He looks like Ricky Nelson. I want to make him into a giant star, then put him out on the road where the kids can get close to him."

"I'm doing a hop on Friday night, why don't you bring him around," I told Bob.

That Friday Bob showed up with Fabian. He had Fabian dressed in a blue sweater, tight-fitting pants, and white bucks. Fabian gave me a smile as I introduced him, pushed back a few strands of his pompadour, and crooned into the mike, lip-syncing to an acetate Bob had brought of his first record, "I'm a Man."

The little girls at the hop went wild. They started screaming and yelling for this guy who didn't do a thing but stand there. I've never seen anything like it.

After Fabian did his number I escorted him backstage. I turned to Bob and said, "Bob, you got a hit, he's a star. Now all you have to do is teach him to sing."

It was rumored that I owned half of Chancellor Records. I didn't. My deal with Bob and Pete was a simple gentleman's agreement. I said to them, "If you find a star, allow me the pleasure of introducing him and then, on occasion, have him come back to visit 'Bandstand' after he's big." I knew that if I could help build Frankie Avalon then along the way it would be helpful to me. The same with Fabian.

Frankie Avalon had run up a string of hits and was scheduled to be on "Bandstand" to debut his new release, "Just Ask Your Heart" when he, Bob, and Fabian, who also had a couple of hits chalked up, walked into my office.

Frankie and Fabian carried large shopping bags.

"Hi, Dick. Frankie's doing the show today, so we all decided to stop by to say hello," said Bob.

"Hi, Dick," said Fabian.

"Hi, Dick," echoed Frankie. "Oh, listen, Dick. We know that you like to dress the way you do"—he stopped and he and

*Left:* Frankie Avalon shows me a part of his wardrobe during a "Bandstand" show.

*Right:* I guess I don't have a face that is easy to caricature. This is one that was done in Disneyland a few years back.

In July 1958, Fabian, Frankie Avalon, and their dates came to visit us. It turned out to be a very hectic day when their fans mobbed them at the back door.

On another occasion Frankie Avalon came to "Bandstand" and there was pandemonium. He was a true teen idol. On display here are pictures of his early days in show business as a preteen trumpet player.

Whenever we had a special occasion, we would call on Fabian and Frankie Avalon. This is an "American Bandstand" anniversary get-together at the network. We even dragged out the old "Bandstand" back-drop for the occasion.

Bobby Rydell and Frankie Avalon played in the same rock 'n' roll group before they became individual teen-age idols. Here they come back to visit on the Saturday night show.

The " 'American Bandstand' at-Home Visits," like this one with Frankie Avalon, inevitably ended up in a room where the gold records were displayed.

From left to right, Charlie O'Donnell, Dick Clark, Fabian, Neil Sedaka, Freddy Cannon, Bobby Rydell, Chubby Checker, on a "Bandstand" anniversary show.

Neil Sedaka makes his network debut on "The Dick Clark Saturday Night Show." He opened by playing Chopin and closed with "I Go Ape."

*Left:* When I visited Connie Francis in her New Jersey home, she told me of her early career as an accordionist.

*Right:* Connie's mother, Mrs. Francanero, Connie, and I posed in front of her new home shortly after it was completed. By this time, Connie had become the number one female vocalist in the world. She made her television debut on "American Bandstand" in late 1957, singing "Who's Sorry Now?"

Paul Anka was the first superstar I ever met who wrote and performed his own songs. An astute businessman and performer, he first sang "Diana" before a network audience on "American Bandstand."

From left to right, Johnny Mathis, Jackie DeShannon and, behind me, Kenny Miller came to visit at Bob Marcucci's home in Hollywood.

*Left:* It's hard to believe now that anyone was interested in the subject material listed here.
*Right:* Editor Gloria Stavers published the article in *16* magazine when the network decided to cut back on "American Bandstand" and we went to one hour once a week.

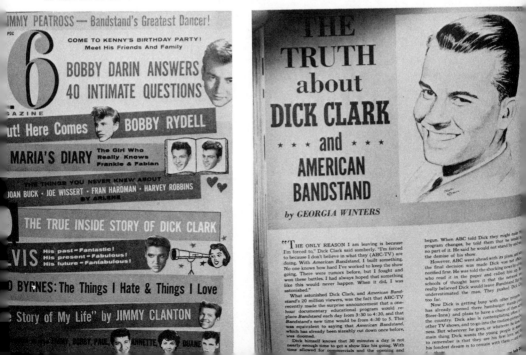

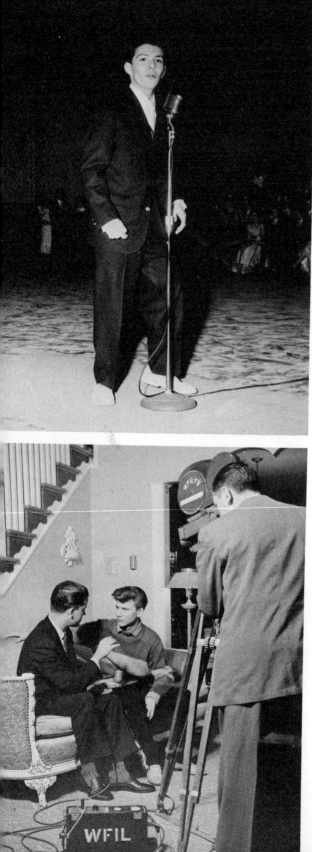

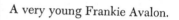

A very young Frankie Avalon.

Like so many of the stars of the late fifties and early sixties, Bobby Rydell lived in a row house in South Philadelphia where we visited him.

Fabian made smirking noises—"but we thought maybe you could use a little help."

"Yeah," interjected Fabian. "I mean we don't mind that you dress square, but at least it could be nice square."

"What the boys fail to communicate," said Bob, "is that we come fresh from Irving's Clothes Shop. And here are some presents for you."

With that they set down the shopping bags in front of me. I looked in them. They were full of clothes of the style that Frankie and Fabian wore. I pulled them out—a Fabian sweater with a wide roll collar, a pair of gray shoes like Frankie wore, a pair of white bucks like Fabian's, a pair of sneakers, several shirts in bright colors with puffy sleeves. As I looked at each item, the three of them broke up laughing. It wasn't so funny months later when Federal investigators accused Bob of giving me clothes as payola.

Later that afternoon Bob Clarke, who let the kids in, came in and found me just as the show was about to start.

"There may be trouble, Dick," he said anxiously. "The kids have found out that both Frankie Avalon and Fabian are in the building and they're acting a little crazy."

"Okay, we'll handle it, thanks." I called Tony on the intercom and told him to have Bob Marcucci keep both Frankie and Fabian out of sight.

Frankie did the show, the kids screamed and loved it, then Tony hustled him back out of the studio to the music library where we'd stashed Bob and Fabian. The show ended, the kids left, and everything seemed fine, until I got a report that there were almost a thousand kids milling around Forty-sixth Street waiting for Frankie and Fabe to come out. Tony told me the police had called; they were sending over mounted troopers to keep order.

None of us had any real experience with this kind of thing, so we foolishly agreed to help Bob, Frankie, and Fabe make a dash for their limousine which was parked in the lot behind the station.

Bob and Frankie went out, the kids made a beeline for them, but the cops moved in with their horses, Frankie ran fast, and he got into the limo.

167

Then it was Fabian's turn. As he left the studio someone in the crowd yelled, "Here comes Fabe!" As Fabian ran towards the limo one of the horses reared up, his front legs hovering in the air over Fabian's head. Tony and I watched with astonishment, sure Fabe would be killed by the horse. He managed to get into the limo.

The limousine sat there for 45 minutes. The kids climbed all over it, banging on the doors and windows. For a while I couldn't even see the limo, it was covered with a mound of kids.

An hour later Bob called.

"You must be crazy to bring those two around together," I told him.

"I know, I know," he said. "Fabe and Frankie already told me. I'll never have the two of them in the same room, house, or building together."

There were two non-Philadelphians who joined the ranks of Frankie Avalon, Fabian, and Bobby Rydell as teen idols and members of the "Bandstand" gang: Connie Francis and Bobby Darin.

Connie was born Concetta Franconero in Newark, New Jersey. Her father, George, was a roofing contractor with a love for music. He bought her an accordion as a child. Connie wound up a winner on Arthur Godfrey's "Talent Scouts," and it was Godfrey who suggested she change her name.

Connie's first five records were failures. She was eighteen by this time and had a chance for a scholarship at New York University but she decided to give singing one last try.

"Why not record that old song I used to love to hear you play on the accordion?" suggested her father.

Connie followed the suggestion and recorded "Who's Sorry Now?" The record was released, but again nothing happened.

It had been out for about four months when I first noticed it on a pile of records in my office. For some reason I took it and played it. I liked the melody and the fresh vocal approach. I played the record for Tony and he agreed it was a possible hit.

I added it to the "Bandstand" play list. We played it a lot. From there other stations picked up on it. By the middle of February 1958 it was the top record in the country.

For the next five years Connie was the top female vocalist.

Neil Sedaka wrote "Stupid Cupid" for her, she had a romance with Bobby Darin, and her song "Frankie," a hit in 1959, had us all wondering whom she was singing about.

I first got to know Bobby Darin at a record hop at Clemonton Lake Park in New Jersey after a "Bandstand" appearance. He lip-synced his record, signed autographs. and got a good deal of attention from the kids. His first couple of records didn't make it, but he was always an outstanding live performer.

Born Walden Robert Cassotto, he selected the name Bobby Darin at random from the Bronx phone book. He was an impulsive, ballsy guy, often bordering on the point of being obnoxious. He came on strong with a finger-poppin', Frank Sinatra style.

After his success, people asked me, "When did he turn into such an egotistical son of a bitch?"

I'd laugh and say, "He was always that way."

In the late fifties Bobby had great rock 'n' roll hits—from "Splish Splash" to "Queen of the Hop" and "Dream Lover."

In August 1958 he was scheduled to be on the Saturday night show. That particular installment of the show was done from Hollywood, where I was working on my first film, *Because They're Young.*

Bobby called me before he came out.

"Richard, I think I've done it again," he said, in a matter-of-fact way.

"Married, divorced, or punched out somebody important?"

"Wise guy. No, I've got my next hit."

"Glad to hear it."

"You're not going to believe it, I'm going to do 'Mack the Knife' from the *Threepenny Opera*. I'm going to debut it on your show."

I told him he was crazy.

He laughed. "I'll call you when I get to Los Angeles, bye."

I called Deke Heyward.

"Do you know what Darin is going to do?"

"I know, I know," said Deke. "He called me to tell me you were going to call me to tell me he was doing *Threepenny Opera* on the Hollywood show. I told him if he wanted to turn his career into chopped liver so be it."

Emerging from a dark stage into a misty pool of light, Bobby

169

sang "Mack the Knife" on the Saturday night show. It was a total departure from the rollicking, bouncy hits he'd come to be associated with. But he was right and I was wrong. The song became his biggest seller, hitting the number-one spot on all the charts.

Bobby had a great way of living. He was entangled with Connie Francis, then Joanne Campbell, a singer and dancer who taught both Bobby and Connie all of their stage moves. When Bobby married Sandra Dee, in the living room of a New Jersey magistrate, December 1, 1960, it was one of the highlights of his life. Bobby Darin, married to a blond movie queen. The fan magazines and gossip sheets ate it up.

The teen idol era was remarkable. My favorite memories of that era are the headlines Gloria Stavers used in *16* magazine: "What would happen if Freddie Cannon didn't go WHOO! . . . if Bobby Rydell got a crew cut? . . . if Elvis got married? . . . if Paul Anka retired? . . . if Dick Clark danced the Pony?"

Gloria was the first to discover the teen idol magazine market. I worked with her as much as the stars did. I also ran up to New York to do as many interviews as my press agents at ABC, Mari Yanofski and Connie De Nave, could set up. I was on the cover of *16, Dig, Teen,* and the rest of them. I let them photograph Dickie, Bobbie, and me in the living room—me getting out of bed answering the phone, me shopping at the supermarket, Bobbie waiting at the front steps to welcome me home, me out in the yard playing with Dickie, and the rest—things I would never let anyone do now in my "old age."

It paid off in the long run because the familiarity, the wide recognition of who Dick Clark really is is still there.

My 1959 press handout said:

"For those with a special interest in such details, we offer the following Dick Clark particulars:

| | |
|---|---|
| Size jacket: | 39 regular |
| Shirt: | 14½ |
| Sleeve: | 33 |
| Waist: | 32 |
| Height: | 5′9″ |
| Shoes: | 8D |
| Birthday: | November 30, 1929 |

If you ask Dick his favorite foods he'll probably respond to either steak and onions or hot dogs and chili."

It was during this time that I decided to go into the record business. The basic reason was that I couldn't make enough money doing "Bandstand." By the time I paid everybody out of the $2,000 a week budget there was nothing left, often not even enough for new sets or to pay all the stars who appeared on the show. So I wrote a memo to Roger Clipp. I said I want to be in the record business.

All right, he said, just don't let it interfere with "Bandstand." Famous last words.

I proceeded to get into talent management, music publishing, record pressing, label making, distribution, domestic and foreign rights, motion pictures, show promotions, and teen-age merchandising. That was how I made my money. Everything was based on TV, I realized that, but the show was only a part of my activity.

One of my first ventures was to put together the first "oldies-but-goodies" album. It was a collection of past hits called "Dick Clark's All-Time Hits." I did the first one for Cheerios. The kids sent in a quarter and a Cheerios boxtop and got a record. A year later I did a similar promotion for Bosco—for fifty cents the kids got six hits on an extended-play "45." Beechnut then wanted to do it for the Saturday night show. I did two or three such promotions for them eventually. In one week I made $200,000 on a record premium. What I did was press the record at my pressing plant, package it, make a favored-nations deal with the artists, record companies, and publishers, and deliver the records for mailing. I made ten to twelve cents a copy.

The major record companies were terribly anxious to get in on the rock 'n' roll action. RCA sent George Marek, one of their top executives, to Philadelphia to meet with me. He was a distinguished, gray-haired gentleman who spoke with an accent. He told me RCA had decided they would repackage their Ames Brothers and Perry Como sides as "Dick Clark Presents." I told him I didn't think he or RCA had any idea of what was going on out there with the kids. "The kids don't give a shit about that music you want to put out," I told him. "They don't want to hear it."

The first record company deal I got into was Jamie Records.

171

Harry Finfer, Harold Lipsius, Samuel Hodge, and I each owned 25 percent of Jamie. Harry was a record promotion man, Harold was a lawyer, and Sam Hodge was the owner of a record pressing plant. A young West Coast producer named Lee Hazlewood approached us with a guitar player named Duane Eddy. Duane got a raunchy sound on his guitar and favored instrumentals with titles like "Rebel Rouser." He was also one of the first rockers to feature electric bass on his records. A talent manager named Al Wilde and I eventually formed SRO Artists to become his managers.

There was always talk that I played more Duane Eddy records on "Bandstand" than Elvis Presley records—the intimation being that Duane recorded for a record company I had an interest in and was managed by a company I owned half of. None of my critics knew enough about "Bandstand" to know that at the end of every half-hour we played an instrumental. There were very few instrumentals to choose from. We played Jimmy Dorsey's "So Rare" an extraordinary number of times. And we played Duane because he really was the only constant hit-making rock instrumentalist around.

Al Wilde and I expanded SRO Artists to manage LaVern Baker as well as Duane. At one point Bobby Darin didn't have a manager. Al and I flew to Bridgeport, Connecticut, where Bobby was appearing at the P. T. Barnum Festival. We talked to Bobby about managing him. He thought about it and said no. In a way I'm happier I never became his manager. Our friendship remained purely personal and, for that reason, was especially significant to me.

In July 1957 I formed my first two music publishing companies, Sea Lark (for C. lark) and January Music, which was the month Dickie was born. I hired a woman named Vera Hodes to run the companies out of an office in New York and we began to keep our ears open for songs we might publish.

In December 1957 I went into the record distributing business with Harry Chipetz and Bernie Lowe. We each owned a third of Chips Distributing.

Later that month Bernie Binnick, Tony Mamarella, and I formed Swan Records. Swan was my first really complete step into the record business. At the time there was a Los Angeles company called Specialty Records. We ripped off their label, after a fashion—they had a black and yellow label with a special signature logo; we copied the label in maroon on white because we couldn't afford more than one color.

Bernie Binnick found our first hit, a group called Dicky Doo who'd written a song called "Click Clack" while riding the train from New York to Philadelphia.

I was sitting in the "Bandstand" office talking to Bernie on the phone about the group.

"I know, Bernie," I said. "Dicky Doo is the lead singer. So what do you think we should call the group?"

"I don't know, you decide," said Bernie.

"I don't know either, Bernie!"

"For Christ's sake!" Tony yelled. "Call them The Don'ts!"

So Dicky Doo and The Don'ts they became.

Tony and Bernie each owned 25 percent of Swan and I owned the other half. But we had meetings where everyone had their say about the records we were releasing. When we first decided to buy the Dicky Doo record we listened to both sides of the acetate, and the three of us agreed we should buy the master on the basis of one side. As it turned out the other side was the hit!

At the time, the Chalypso was a popular dance on the show. I noticed there wasn't a record to go with the dance, so I told two independent songwriters and producers I knew, Bob Crewe and Frank Slay, they could fill a need for a record by coming up with something to which the kids could dance the Chalypso. They came up with "Lucky Ladybug" done by Billie and Lilly. It became another hit for Swan—helped, no doubt, by the fact that we had a Chalypso dance contest and each time the kids competed we played the song.

Crewe and Slay had offices in New York and Bernie would visit them to hear tapes. One evening after Bernie got back from New York we all met at his house to listen to a master they wanted us to hear.

Tony, Bernie, and I listened to the record.

"I think it might be a hit, but I don't think it's commercial the way it is now," I told Tony and Bernie.

"There's something missing," agreed Tony.

173

"I think it needs the beat accented in some places," I said.

"Yeah, and the opening's too long," said Bernie.

I went into Bernie's kitchen and called Crewe and Slay.

"Listen," I said, "The opening is too long, and the whole song needs more of a beat, a pounding beat like this. . . . " With that I lowered the receiver down to within an inch of the kitchen floor and pounded the floor with my foot, thump, thump, thump.

"Okay," said Bob Crewe, "we'll make those changes, as soon as I recover my hearing."

The result was another big hit for Swan, "Tallahassee Lassie," sung by Freddy Cannon, a former truck driver from Boston whose mother had written the song for him.

All through 1958 I continued to expand by business interests. In March I acquired another record company and a new publishing firm; in May I bought Mallard, a record pressing plant; in July I formed Drexel Television Productions; and in November I bought another music publishing firm.

As my interests grew I got the reputation within the record industry as someone who was on the scene, who knew what was going on with rock and with the kids. In the summer of 1957 Artie Singer and Larry Brown came to me with a song called "Doing the Bop." They played it for me, then Artie asked me what I thought.

"I like the feel of the song and the beat," I told them, "but the lyrics are terrible. The Bop is almost over as a fad dance; by the time you record and release it, it'll be out of date."

They looked dejected. I'd just taken what they thought was a potential hit and turned it into a sure flop.

"I've got an idea though. Why don't you rebuild it to tell the story of what goes on at a record hop. You could call it 'At the Hop.' "

Artie and Larry brightened. I told them some of the typical scenes I saw at record hops, what the current dances were like, and the slang kids used. From this background they fashioned a new set of lyrics and recorded the song with Danny and The Juniors. It became a national hit.

"The song wouldn't have been a hit if you hadn't suggested redoing it," said Artie when they came to tell me how well it

174

was doing. "We'd like you to have half the copyright for your publishing company."

I took it. I figured, since I was already playing the song on "Bandstand" and it was already a hit there was nothing wrong in accepting a return on my creative energies. "At the Hop" sold several million copies and is considered one of the classics of the rock 'n' roll era. I'm proud to have been instrumental in it happening, even though I was raked over the coals for accepting half of the copyright.

I got into other areas besides records. I promoted a Dick Clark record carrying case on the show made by Rave Products, which Tony, a local distributor, and I owned. We got permission from the station to give the cases away on the show—in those days "plugola" was perfectly legal. We showed it at the end of every Record Revue, gave the kids on the Revue one each, and sold a few record cases as a result. I also had Startime Industries with Tony and two other guys. We made Platter Puss and Cuddle Pups stuffed animals, and Autograph Hounds, great big autograph dogs that I had guest stars sign when they visited the show. We also made little autograph hounds. I had Post-Grad Products with Tony and a few others, and we made a cream hair conditioner (an unadulterated failure, I might add).

It was much the same in 1959. I was busy forming new music publishing companies, another pressing plant, and another record company when the payola thing came down on my head.

# 14

## "They said rock was nothing but trash"

In the fifties many people feared and hated rock 'n' roll. *Look* said rock 'n' roll dragged music to "new lows in taste" and Elvis was "vulgar." A New York *World Telegram* columnist said rock 'n' roll was "contrived by corrupt men." In an interview that ran in newspapers across the country, Pearl Bailey said, "Those groups with the weird names just aren't in time. The kids are listening to bad music . . ." *Variety* said rock 'n' roll lyrics were nothing more than dirty postcards translated into songs.

These attitudes were focused on "American Bandstand" because the show was there to take a shot at every afternoon on the network. And from the moment I first announced a rock record on the show, I came under fire as a champion of rock 'n' roll.

"In general, the music is rude, restless and untamed. The best is monotonous and insistent. The orchestra—if that's the word I want—seems to consist of a hillbilly gee-tar and a hundred drums, all manned by savages. If there's a piano, it is thumped rather than played. The right hand never listens to what the left is doing. The lyrics are gibberish, repeated three times," wrote Harriet Van Horne.

One newspaper ran articles by Sam Levenson and me about our differing attitudes toward rock 'n' roll. Sam was the humorist who didn't find rock funny. I was Dick Clark, the guy who understood the kids.

Sam said rock 'n' roll was "depriving kids of good music. A kid strums three chords on a guitar and the weirder he sounds the greater his potential for success. Most teen-agers are willing to pay, not play. They buy records, they won't take lessons."

"There's more music available than ever before in the history of music," I answered. "Young people have more varied taste than Sam or I ever did. Kids enjoy all music. It's only the adults who think the kids only enjoy one kind of music.

"And as for talented musicians, Paul Anka, who's only sixteen, has written three or four big hits. He not only reads music but writes both the music and the lyrics. He will probably become one of our top songwriters. Bobby Darin, who has just turned twenty, plays six instruments. Neil Sedaka, who's still a teen-ager, has written three hits."

Sam and I bantered back and forth. Finally, Sam lit into radio stations that played only rock 'n' roll.

"Disc jockeys should sandwich in a little Chopin or a Shubert melody," he suggested. "Mention Chopin to a teen-ager and he'll look at you and ask, 'Has he got a gold record?' "

"Would Sam consider slipping in a little Elvis Presley in the middle of a Chopin concert at Carnegie Hall?" I replied.

The critics found many music men within the music business to agree with them. The old line, established companies were jealous of the rock 'n' roll upstarts.

Mitch Miller, who ran Columbia Records, led the rock hate campaign. Before rock hit, Miller had had tremendous success in the late forties and early fifties with unreal songs like "Mama Will Bark," featuring Frank Sinatra and Dagmar. He and his moon-June-spoon cohorts feared for their lives when rock arrived. They said rock was nothing but trash—that teen-agers liked it because no one else did.

Miller's attitude was common among older music men. To understand their plight and their venomous attacks on rock, it's necessary to put them in the perspective of the development of the music business in America.

The music business started in the late 1800s when sheet music became the first commercially successful method of distributing a hit song. The middle class of the day enjoyed sitting around the piano, playing and singing the latest ditty. Witmark, Stern, Marks, Harris, and others went into the business of finding songs, publishing them in sheet-music form, and promoting their popularity. These men who printed and distributed the sheets of music controlled the music industry. By the early 1900s these music publishers were selling upwards of two million sheet-music copies of a hit song.

At the same time, popular music progressed from the minstrel show tunes of the 1830s and 1840s to turn-of-the-century vaudeville hits. The black man's music, the Negro minstrels' cakewalk steps, and the ragtime beat were incorporated on the vaudeville stage into a syncopation that made the music both disruptive and exciting.

The music publisher remained in control of popular music until the late 1930s, despite the invention of the phonograph and radio. It wasn't until radio started to play records that the music business took its present form.

In the 1930s record companies brought legal action against radio stations that played their records; they were convinced the public would listen to their records on the radio rather than buy them. The musicians' union tried to legally prevent radio stations from playing records since they were convinced it would put thousands of musicians who played in radio orchestras out of work. The music publishers refused to license radio stations to play the music they published because they feared it would jeopardize sheet-music sales. Suits flew back and forth but nothing was settled.

In the fall of 1939 radio broadcasters formed Broadcast Music, Inc. (BMI) as a method of generating music that could be played on their stations. The American Society of Composers, Authors, and Publishers (ASCAP) had set up stringent membership requirements to keep songwriting and popular music in the hands of its membership. BMI guaranteed that anyone who wrote a song could get it published and licensed and that the songwriter and publisher would be paid in direct relation to the success of the song rather than ASCAP's payment schedule. Before the broadcasters formed BMI, many new songwriters, especially those who wrote country, blues, or other ethnic American pop musics, had been unable to get their music published and licensed because of the strict control Tin Pan Alley had over the music business.

The situation was further aggravated in the late 1940s and

early 1950s by the introduction of Ampex's tape recorder, CBS's long-playing 33.3 RPM albums, RCA's 45 RPM single play records, and the Top 40 radio format. The final straw was rock 'n' roll, a music produced by amateur songwriters who couldn't be controlled by the Tin Pan Alley bigwigs, and sold to the rock audience as a recorded musical performance, not as sheet music.

The fight between the Tin Pan Alley music business and the rock-pop music business came down to a fight between ASCAP and BMI. Each charged the other with monopolistic practices. In 1953, thirty-three members of ASCAP—led by Arthur Schwartz and including Ira Gershwin and Alan Jay Lerner— filed a $150 million antitrust action charging BMI with conspiring to "dominate and control the market for the use and expolitation of musical compositions."

At times ASCAP itself wasn't a party to the suits against BMI. There were groups like The Songwriters of America and The Songwriters Protective Association. This latter outfit was influenced by Billy Rose, an oldline ASCAPer, who said, "Not only are most of the BMI songs junk, but in many cases they are obscene junk pretty much on a level with dirty comic magazines." This from the man who wrote the immortal "Barney Google with his goo, goo, googlie eyes."

By the time ASCAP finally gave up trying to stop BMI and the rock music it licensed, Bing Crosby, Steve Allen, Oscar Hammerstein, Alan Lerner, Dorothy Fields, and Frank Sinatra had had their say against rock 'n' roll.

The message was clear: Stop BMI and rock 'n' roll would stop.

In 1956 the antitrust subcommittee of the House Judiciary Committee was holding hearings on a completely different matter when they became entangled in the ASCAP-BMI controversy. The subcommittee was headed by Representative Emanuel Celler of New York, who said that "rock 'n' roll has its place. There is no question about it. It's given great impetus to talent, particularly among the colored people. It's a natural expression of their emotions . . . " But Celler thought rock catered to bad taste: "The bad taste that is exemplified by the Elvis Presley 'Hound Dog' music, with his animal gyrations which are cer-

179

tainly most distasteful to me, are violative of all that I know to be in good taste."

ASCAP gladly supplied Celler with well-known artists and established music writers and publishers who agreed with him that rock was distasteful and could be stopped very simply: Give the music business back to ASCAP.

The fifties was a time of controversial Congressional investigations—the McCarthy hearings, the Dodd committee hearings on TV violence and sex, the quiz show scandals, the Kefauver hearings, the Jimmy Hoffa investigations. Congress seemed to think that Communists and corruption were everywhere and that even comic books must be censored to protect the American way of life.

To some degree, all these hearings were affected by the politicians' discovery of the power of postwar radio and TV, especially around election time. They got the attention of all America, if they had something scandalous enough to expose. America loved the hearings.

It's my opinion that the congressmen who investigated the quiz shows were riding so high on the publicity they got from it that the payola scandals came as an open invitation for them to continue in the spotlight.

The payola investigations centered around that one word, *payola.* It came out in the investigations that payola had been a common music industry practice for at least one hundred years. The congressmen doing the investigating ignored that; they said rock 'n' roll was the cause of payola. Once more it was Tin Pan Alley against the rockers; old-guard music publisher and ASCAP attitudes against BMI and the new music business.

From the beginning the sheet-music publisher owned the copyrights on the songs he published. The value of those copyrights increased as the song grew popular. The publisher's potential profit was enormous if a song was a hit and justified whatever tactics were necessary to insure the popularity of his songs. So music publishers sent song pluggers to beg, implore, and bribe the leading vaudeville artists to sing their songs. When radio became important, they sent the song pluggers to do the same to get radio orchestra leaders to play their songs. Song pluggers and band pluggers became the record promotion men of the fifties when sheet music and live performances gave way to records and broadcast performances. The promotion men paid off the disc jockey to get the music heard. The system never changed.

In March 1958, *Billboard* sent a reporter to question me about payola. The payola scandals hadn't yet hit the headlines, but there was talk within the industry of rampant payola practices.

"How do you feel about DJ's with interests in other facets of the music business, like publishing and record companies?" asked the reporter over lunch at the Jug.

"What's wrong with it?" I asked. "The matter depends on the individual. If a man knows what's good for him—what side his bread is buttered on—and he's intelligent and honest with himself, then there's nothing wrong with it at all."

By the end of 1959 I was whistling a different tune.

I was always aware of payola as a factor in the music industry. It's the crassest form of promotion, and no more respectable in the record business than it is in any other business —there are always people who expect to have their palms greased. It got out of hand in the late fifties. Otherwise intelligent radio men accepted payoffs. They wouldn't take cash on a street corner, but didn't mind receiving a weekly check for $50 or $100 from a record company in exchange for "listening" to that company's new releases.

One friend, whom I won't identify because he's still in the business, told me how the major record company he worked for handled it.

"Once a year, maybe twice a year, we'd have to pay our dues," he explained. "I would go out with another guy from the company. We took a briefcase with us filled with $25,000 in cash. In each city we rented a suite of rooms at a hotel and invited all the local disc jockeys over for a party.

"They'd come over. As they drank and caroused, we took them one at a time into the next room and handed them our dough. I had a list of the guys' names, how much each was worth. If the guy was Joe Doakes from this particular city, he was worth $500. I handed him $500. If he was less important I gave him $300. If he wasn't too important I gave him $100 or $200.

"We did this in as many cities as we could—until the $25,000 was gone."

Today, payola is a federal offense which carries a possible prison term and a $10,000 fine. But in those days it wasn't illegal. It was *not* against the law. A record company could give a disc jockey $100,000, a list of records with how often to play each one, and it wasn't illegal.

I had my first encounter with payola in late 1959. It was in the middle of "Bandstand." I was leaning against the podium, getting ready to do a commercial. Earlier in the afternoon I'd seen a guy hanging around the studio, but thought nothing of it. He looked like an out-of-town record promo man who was making his big trip to Philadelphia to meet Dick Clark and see "Bandstand." That wasn't an unusual event and Tony usually made sure the visitors didn't get underfoot.

So I was minding my own business when I felt a tug at the back of my jacket. I turned around. The guy had gotten around the podium in the middle of the show, while we were on the air.

I looked at him and frowned.

He motioned for me to lean toward him.

I leaned forward and he moved up next to me to whisper in my ear.

"I have a brand new record," he says.

"Fine, I'll catch you when we get off the air. Now would you mind getting back behind the cameras."

"There's a hundred dollars in it for you," he said.

I had him thrown out.

I was aghast. At that point I was making over half a million dollars a year. I had my own record distributorship, record labels, publishing companies, and management company. And this guy was going to give me $100 to play his record.

## "The Washington *Post* coined the word 'Clarkola'"

In November 1959 investigators for the Special Subcommittee on Legislative Oversight of the Committee on Interstate and Foreign Commerce descended on Philadelphia, beginning a reign of terror that didn't end until the following June.

I was in the bedroom, trying to tie my tie in the mirror, when I realized how nervous I was. "Damn!" I undid the tie and started again, my fingers shaking.

"What's the matter?" Bobbie asked from across the room where she was slipping into her dress.

"It's been a tough day," I said, managing to get the tie knotted properly. Sitting down on the bed I sighed and rubbed my eyes.

"Maybe I should skip tonight."

"Dick, you can't do that!"

"I know, but I wish I could." I stood up, pulled on my loafers, and got into my jacket.

"How bad is it going to be?" asked Bobbie as we got into the car and drove towards downtown Philadelphia.

"I don't know, but I've a feeling that it won't be pleasant. I know for certain that they're going to see me, Bernie Lowe, Georgie Woods, Harry Finfer, Bernie Binnick, and Tony."

"Try to put it out of your mind; you can't let the kids see you this way," said Bobbie as we pulled into the lot behind Bookbinder's restaurant. Weeks before we'd arranged a dinner for contest winners on the show—it was first prize, dinner with Fabian, Frankie Avalon, and Dick Clark.

When Bobbie and I arrived, the winners were waiting for

The winner of a "Date with Fabian" contest poses with us at the lobster tank.

us by the do ... The sight of these excited kids did me a world of good. I returned their smiles, introduced them to Bobbie, and arranged for our table. Just then Fabian and Frankie came in. There were more introductions, we posed for pictures in front of the lobster tank near the door, then went to our table.

All through the meal the thought of the investigation and what it might mean kept coming back to me. It ran through my mind that this might be one of the last nights I'd ever be able to enjoy the exhilaration of success.

Fabe and Frankie knew what was going on, but like the kids they didn't realize how serious a situation it was. I felt like a condemned man eating his last meal.

Fabe pulled me aside as we got ready to leave the restaurant.

"Don't worry, Dick," he said, putting his arm around me. "We're behind you; we know it'll turn out all right."

184

The next morning when I got to the office Bobby Darin was on the phone asking for me.

"Richard, you son of a gun, how are you?"

"Fine, Robert."

"Sure you're okay?"

"Yeah."

"Listen, if those bastards give you any trouble, just let me know," he said. I had to laugh. Bobby was like a bantam cock, he'd take on the whole goddamned world.

"Thanks. I don't think we'd better talk about it on the phone," I said.

"It's like that?"

"I'll tell you about it when I see you."

I'd just rung off with Bobby when I heard a voice from the other room speaking to Marlene.

"Hi," said the voice in a lazy Southern drawl. "I'm Rex Sparger. I'm a Congressional investigator. Id like to see Mr. Clark."

Walking into the outer office I saw a young man in his mid-twenties with a crew cut, gray suit, and black shoes. He was holding a black leather billfold in hand; it was open to display a badge.

Rex and I have since become friends, but that morning I was scared of him and what he represented. Trying not to let it show, I invited him inside and the nightmare began.

I gave Rex the run of the office and agreed to meet him that evening at the Warwick Hotel. All together, there were eight investigators, all on actual expenses rather than per diem. (They later told me they stayed at the Warwick because it had the best smorgasbord in town.)

When I got to Rex's room, a half-dozen investigators were standing and sitting around—some with their feet up, others sitting on the edge of the bed, some sipping Cokes, others smoking cigarettes. It was terrifying. They welcomed me into the room and motioned for me to make myself comfortable. I sat down on the edge of the bed.

For the next hour Rex and another investigator named Ray Cole asked me questions. Had I ever taken payola? No. Did I know anyone who took payola? No. Did I know that payola existed? I'd heard of such things, yes. On and on it went, with them asking me about my business affairs, my income, my friendships, my bank account, what kind of car I had and who'd paid for it.

Finally they finished with me, thanked me politely, and said they'd be in touch.

I had just closed the door and was standing in the hall when I heard one of them say, "That's a hell of a nice guy. Too bad we got to fuck him." Then they all broke up laughing. I left the hotel shaking with fear and outrage.

The investigators proceeded to scare the hell out of me. They were all over the studio and my office. I thought I'd lost my whole career at twenty-nine. I didn't sleep nights worrying about what they might do to me.

Besides me, they interviewed everyone else in the Philadelphia music business. By the end of the first week I realized that I hadn't heard from or seen most of my friends and business associates. The investigators had immobilized the town. No one looked anyone else in the eye; long-standing friendships fell by the wayside. Some of the local disc jockeys left town in the middle of the night.

"If we thought someone was not being honest with us, we were nasty," Rex explained to me later.

On Friday, November 6, the Subcommittee brought up the question of payola in connection with the music industry. In New York all the major record companies made statements as did the radio and TV networks.

At ABC, Leonard Goldenson, president of American Broadcasting–Paramount Pictures, called Ollie Treyz, the head of the TV network, and asked for a complete analysis of every person who had anything to do with music at ABC.

Treyz called me, asking me to come to New York the following Wednesday, November 11, to meet with him.

I walked into the meeting to find a number of network executives there including Leonard Goldenson. We exchanged greetings, Goldenson offered me a chair, and then turned to me.

"Have you ever taken payola?" he said bluntly. There was absolute silence in the room. Everyone looked at me.

"No, I have not," I replied.

"Have you ever made an agreement to play a record for a sum of money?"

"No. I have not."

"Have you ever refused to play a record because you had not received any money?"

"No. I have not."

"As payola is known in the industry, have you ever taken payola in any form?"

"No. I have not."

"Now," said Goldenson, leaning back in his chair and untensing, "I want to get to the question of whether you have any interest in music publishing, recordings, or any other information that would relate to our analysis of the problem."

I told him about my music business interests.

"I would like to have the details of them," he said. "And, in my opinion, if you do have these interests, insofar as our company is concerned, if we are going to consider keeping you on the air, in my opinion, you must divest yourself of these as a matter of company policy. They should have been brought to my attention by you."

"I never brought them to your attention, Mr. Goldenson," I said, "because what I've been doing is nothing that isn't common practice in the industry."

"If that's so, I am not aware of it. You can make up your mind one way or another which way you want to proceed. But you let us know whether you want to divest yourself of all these things, and if so, I would like to know immediately."

"Can I think about it overnight?"

"Yes," he said and the meeting ended.

I hurried back to Philadelphia in time for the afternoon show. When I got to the office I told Tony that I wanted to meet with him that evening to discuss what had gone down at ABC. He seemed strangely reluctant; finally he told me he'd meet with me after dinner and that he would bring his lawyer.

At the meeting were my lawyer, Charles Seton, Tony, and his lawyer. I told Tony that I intended to make a statement to ABC that I had never taken payola. I asked Tony if he would make the statement with me.

Tony asked if he might step into the other room for a moment with his lawyer.

He came back a couple of minutes later, and said, "There are some things that I have done that will be difficult to explain."

I was staggered. I couldn't look Tony in the eye. I didn't really know what to say. Tony's words hung in the air.

"Fine, don't tell me about them," I managed to get out.

In a low voice Tony said, "I intend to resign."

I nodded. He turned and left the room and the house.

Tony resigned on Friday, November, 13, 1959.

The next morning I went to New York again, this time to meet with Charles Seton in his offices. We talked over the situation, then decided to call Tony. We asked him to come to New York and meet with us. Tony agreed.

We were all very formal that day. Tony came in, said hello, and proceeded in a somber voice.

"I don't want to throw Dick a curve," he said.

"Well, if you have any confidential information that would be detrimental to you, we must tell you now that if you tell us we may have to use it against you," said Seton.

"We are all friends in this room," Tony said. "I think it only fair that Dick know that I received . . . monies . . ."

In many ways Tony was like a brother to me. We had sat across from each other in that tiny office, sharing the joys and sorrows that came along as "Bandstand" grew. But in the end I found I really didn't know him. I certainly didn't know he had received money from several record companies in exchange for consultation. I knew of his involvement in the music business; in fact, we were in several ventures together. In the end Tony decided to stick to the music business and get out of TV if that had to be the choice—and the investigation made it so. He kept his share in Swan Records and a couple of publishing companies.

The Monday following Tony's resignation and our weekend meeting in New York, I issued a sworn notarized statement. In it I said that I had never taken or demanded money or property in exchange for airplay, that I never agreed to play records on the air for money, that I did have an interest in some records played on the show because of my activities in the record industry, but that I was divesting myself of all such interests.

I admitted getting during 1958 a fur stole for Bobbie from Lou Bedel of Era and Dore Records, which I later gave Lou a $300 check for, only to learn later that it cost $1,000. On my birthday in November 1958, while Lou and his wife and Bobbie and I were out for a social evening, he gave Bobbie a necklace and me a ring. We were reluctant to accept these. However we kept them because it was embarrassing to do otherwise. Although Bobbie wore the necklace, I never wore the ring. I found out from Lou that the ring and necklace together cost $3,400 and were charged to one of his companies as a promotion expense.

After conferences with my lawyer, ABC issued a statement on Wednesday, November 18.

> Because of great public interest in certain areas of television programming, the American Broadcasting Co. is thoroughly investigating its own programs with particular emphasis on those which feature disc jockeys.
>
> While American Broadcasting Co. employs many disc jockeys on its various owned stations, it features only one such personality, Dick Clark, on its television network.
>
> With particular reference to the Dick Clark programs, which are the best known in their field, we have examined all evidence available to us concerning these programs and their production organizations, and have concluded that Dick Clark has neither solicited nor accepted any personal considerations, money or otherwise, to have any performer appear, or to play any records, on any of his programs.
>
> To avoid any potential conflict of interests and to insure impartiality and objectivity in the free selection of music on its programs, American Broadcasting Co. has instituted a policy whereby performers and others who select and play records will be required to divest themselves of all interests in the recording, music publishing, and allied fields.
>
> Dick Clark has volunteered to divest himself of such interests. We are satisfied that American Broadcasting Co. has been apprised of all pertinent details relating to the various Dick Clark programs and his related activities.

We have concluded our investigation with renewed faith and confidence in Dick Clark's integrity.

ABC and I went directly to the TV audience with our statements, but I knew that the ordeal wouldn't end until I was either called to Washington to testify or I wasn't. In December 1959 the answer came. I was subpoenaed to appear before the Committee on February 9, 1960.

That night I had a terrible dream. I awoke in a cold sweat, wondering if it'd been a wise move to name my son Richard Clark. They almost had me believing I was the Baby Face Nelson of the music world.


The judgment of rock 'n' roll was carried out by congressmen who hadn't the faintest idea of what the music business was about. These men had hardly heard a rock 'n' roll record, listened to a rock radio station, seen "American Bandstand," or been to a record hop. But they had evidence that some disc jockeys were being paid off to play certain records. This evidence, their ignorance of the business, and their prejudice against rock convinced them that only by bribery could this terrible music get on the public airwaves.

To them I personified this corrupt business. They saw me as a twenty-nine-year-old rock 'n' roll TV disc jockey from Philadelphia who played immoral music for kids doing vulgar dances in a TV studio. They discovered I made half a million dollars a year from this enterprise. They also were aware I was the only disc jockey known to all their constituents; going after me got them headlines.

Although their function was to investigate possible legislative oversights and then recommend new laws, their attitude was that there was something criminal about the record business—an attitude fostered by the press and in sympathy with much adult thinking of the time. Because of this attitude my name was dragged into the mud, and I was attacked from all sides.

The Washington *Post* coined the word "Clarkola." Rumors circulated that Anita Bryant's husband, a handsome Miami disc jockey named Bob Green, had been chosen to replace me. The advice column I did for *This Week* magazine was cancelled. Fearful that they'd be tainted by the payola scandals, they reneged on my contract. I sued them and won—the money became a trust fund for Dickie—but I couldn't persuade them to let me have the column back.

At the time I used a public relations firm in New York run by two guys named Barkis and Shalit (the same Gene Shalit who is now the NBC "Today Show" critic). When I was called to testify in Washington, they dropped my account. I was told by others that they had done this out of fear that the publicity would hurt their business. I have a very low opinion of Shalit for what he did to me. But come to think of it, it's exactly what I did to Jerry Lee Lewis.

A few weeks after my subpoena arrived, my lawyer, Charles Seton, called from New York.

"Call me right away," he said somewhat cryptically. He was convinced my phone was tapped, so we'd worked out a system. When he wanted to talk with me, he'd call me, then I'd go down to the corner and call him back from the phone booth at Pop Singer's.

"Chuck, what's up?" I asked from the booth.

"May be some trouble. I'm worried about Hogan, the New York DA. He's started his own investigation. I think the Federal investigators are feeding him information. He could subpoena you, too." It was obvious to me that now Hogan, too, wanted to jump on the publicity bandwagon.

"Oh, my God!"

"He can't serve you in Philadelphia, but he may try it when you come in to do your Saturday night show."

For the next six months I sneaked in and out of New York City. Ed McAdam drove me up by car. When we got to the Lincoln Tunnel I would lie down in the backseat, pulling a blanket over myself. I'd stay there until we got to the stage entrance of the Little Theater. Once Ed gave me the all-clear sign, I dashed out of the car into the theater. Then we locked the theater doors while we did the broadcast. I felt like a damned fugitive.

The big magazines were after me, too. Bobbie and I came home one evening to find a police car in front of the house.

There was a cop at our front door. My first thought was that something had happened to Dickie.

"What is it, officer, what's wrong!" I shouted as I got to the door.

"A little trouble. You're Mr. Clark?"

"Yes, is our son all right?!"

"Oh, yes sir, he's asleep in his room. Please, come in the house."

In the living room our baby-sitter was on the couch, sobbing. A police medical officer was bending over her. He stood up as we walked in.

"Good evening, Mr. Clark, Mrs. Clark." He turned to the cop at the door. "See that she gets home."

Bobbie went to the sitter and comforted her.

"What's happened?" I said.

"Well, she's very upset, but from what I can gather, it seems as if a couple of reporters from a weekly newsmagazine forced their way into the house for a look around. They went through the house, taking pictures, opening drawers, and looking in closets. She got hysterical, started screaming, and they left."

*Life* magazine wasn't any more pleasant. They ran a story on me that began with a choice bit of yellow journalism: "Back in September 1958 a roly-poly Tulsa boy named Billy Jay Killion came home from high school and wanted to watch Dick Clark's television program, 'American Bandstand.' His mother, who didn't particularly care for rock 'n' roll music, was all set to watch a different program, so she told Billy no. He seethed the whole night long. Then in the morning Billy took out a rifle and shot his mother dead."

# "Payola and Other Deceptive Practices"

On Wednesday, January 27, 1960, a week before the public hearings began, Tony Mamarella was called to Washington to testify in a secret executive session before the Subcommittee.

For two days they grilled Tony about "American Bandstand," about me, and about how he could have accepted money without me knowing it. The congressmen then went off to digest what Tony had told them. Because his testimony was heard in executive session, it wasn't immediately released to the public. In fact, the Subcommittee waited until the day I took the stand, nearly four months later, to put Tony's testimony in the public record.

On Monday, February 8, the public hearings into "Payola and Other Deceptive Practices in the Broadcasting Fields" began at the New House Office Building in Washington. The Subcommittee's chairman was Oren Harris of Arkansas. Harris had a straightforward approach; he set out like a dog after a bone to get something and he got it. The Subcommittee members were John Moss of California, whom I didn't like because he often got led astray by misinformation; John B. Bennett of Michigan and Steve Derounian of New York, whom I thought were fools; Peter Mack of Illinois; Walter Rogers of Texas; John Flynt of Georgia; William Springer of Illinois, and Samuel L. Devine of Ohio.

These men were hot. The Subcommittee had been through the vicuña coat scandal involving Bernard Goldfine and President Eisenhower's closest assistant, Sherman Adams; and the

Charlie Van Doren quiz show scandals. Now they were after Dick Clark and the rock 'n' roll music business.

Oren Harris opened the hearings that Monday in February. Speaking with a soft, easy Arkansas drawl, he said, "At its hearings in November 1959, the Subcommittee learned from Max Hess, owner of the Hess Brothers Department Store, of Allentown, Pennsylvania, about numerous secret payments made to obtain plugs for that store, or its wares, on radio and television. Hess testified that this 'is a common practice.'

"Since that time, the Subcommittee has been flooded with complaints from all parts of the country about . . . practices, whereby the selection of material sent over the airwaves has been influenced by undisclosed economic inducements. When this happens, we are told, the public interest suffers in many ways. The quality of broadcast programs declines when the choice of program materials is made not in the public interest, but in the interest of those who are willing to pay to obtain exposure of their records. The public is misled as to the popularity of the records played."

The Subcommittee then went back into executive session to hear Boston disc jockey Norm Prescott's testimony. Prescott said "bribery, payola, has become the prime function of this business to get the record on the air at any cost."

In the early days of the hearings, much of the questioning was done by Robert Lishman, the Chief Counsel. He faced Prescott as Harris and the Subcommittee listened.

"Are you familiar with the fact that at one time there was a record company in California, the Crystallite Record Co., which issued one million shares of stock, which it distributed free of charge to disc jockeys who would accept it?" asked Lishman.

"Yes. . . . They sent it to me. I sent it back to them. I think it has since gone up to ten million shares," said Prescott.

"And this was done, was it not, on the theory that the disc jockeys would favor the records of that company because they would share in the company's profits?"

"Yes, sir."

"Did you not recently receive a letter from this company, suggesting that disc jockeys should get rid of the stock or throw it away, so that the company would not be accused of payola?"

"Yes. It said something of the fact that in view of the recent investigations into payola, it may be embarrassing to any stockholder in this company as well as to us to be a participant in the corporation, and we suggest that you forget that you own stock, and we will forget we issued stock, and see you later. . . . The Crystallite idea, Mr. Chairman, was formed about four years ago. It personally was very laughable and ludicrous to me, because to be one of ten million stockholders in a company just was an obviously funny premise. But it functioned, I guess, for about four years. They had a hit record somewhere along the line. I think it was called 'Pink Shoelaces,' which your children may remember. . . ."

Before Prescott left the stand he told the Subcommittee: "Then, of course, the most important thing, and I think this is probably the toughest problem, is that radio itself is responsible for exposing whatever it exposes, and if it does not expose what is obviously rank or bad music, then these companies cannot continue to function. And let us face it.

"Mr. Harris, you can go into the record business tomorrow, sir, for $150, with a chance of making $100,000. It is as simple as that. All you need are four musicians at a cost of $200—"

"Is that a proposition?" Chairman Harris asked Prescott, a bemused expression on his face.

"No. All you need is the musicians, a singer for $100—there is a total outlay of maybe $250. And $1,500, if you want to go a little bit further, for payola, and you are in the ring.

"But anybody can go into the record business. They record songs in cellars, in telephone booths, it doesn't make any difference—wherever there is a tape machine and a plug.

"As long as you can do these things, and stations—and I do not understand why they are willing to expose these things, or they allow it to be exposed—they just keep the level of the music, the basic level of the music down.

"The thing that bothers me is you begin to wonder what is going to happen to the kids of today when they grow up—they are going to have a heck of a musical education and heritage to pass on to their children," concluded Prescott.

Before Prescott stepped down he and Subcommittee member

John Bennett had a short conversation.

"Well, do you think without payola that a lot of this so-called junk music, rock 'n' roll stuff, which appeals to the teen-agers would not be played, or do you think that kind of thing would be played anyway, regardless of the payola?" asked Bennett.

"Never get on the air," said Prescott.

"Do you think payola is responsible for it?"

"Yes; it keeps it on the air, because it fills pockets."

"Do you consider payola a form of bribery then?" asked Chairman Harris.

"I think it is a form of moral or immoral bribery, yes sir," replied Prescott.

Prescott admitted taking payments of $9,955.08 from Boston record distributors, including one distributor who made payments on Prescott's Mercury station wagon and then helped him finance his new Buick.

After lunch that Monday Dave Maynard, a disc jockey for WBZ in Boston, admitted a record distributor had helped pay for his 1957 Mercury station wagon and his 1959 Buick. Maynard also got $6,817.16 in payments from local Boston record distributors. Maynard said he took the money for playing untested discs at record hops and for listening to the records to give his opinion of their potential. He said he never took money to actually play any of the records on the air.

Another WBZ jock, Alan Dary, was next. He admitted he got Christmas gifts including money, a hi-fi, and liquor, and that one of the station's advertisers carpeted the master bedroom at his house for free in exchange for helping them plan an ad campaign.

The next morning Lester Lanin was the first witness. He told how he'd agreed to play a charity concert in Boston for $1,000 —well below his usual fee—and that he'd been stiffed for $600 of the thousand by the local distributor who was supposed to pay him.

"That balance is still unpaid?" Lishman asked him.

"The balance is. That is why I am here. I have no other reason to be here than that," replied Lanin.

The gallery broke into laughter. Chairman Harris ushered

Lanin off the stand, telling him he hoped he didn't think the Subcommittee was going to collect his debts for him.

Later in the day Joe Finan, a disc jockey at KYW in Cleveland, admitted getting checks from Mainline Cleveland, Inc., the local RCA-Victor distributor.

"RCA Victor was having a great deal of difficulty in supplying the market with commercial product. They were depending primarily on the sales of Elvis Presley records and they were having extreme difficulty with their standard artists, such as The Ames Brothers and Dinah Shore, in selling their product," said Finan. He got $1,300 in cash from Mainline Cleveland. Shortly after he was hired by KYW an RCA color TV was sent to his home completely unsolicited. He also got $200 a month from Hugo and Luigi who headed the artist and repertoire department at RCA and money from other companies, including Mercury Records, United Artists Records, and Decca Records.

Finan's testimony countered Prescott's earlier assertion that payola went hand in hand with rock 'n' roll. Finan was paid off by major companies who weren't recording in phone booths and who, in the case of RCA, were concerned with selling standard artists in the face of rock 'n' roll. This was payola to play nonrock.

The Subcommittee turned their attention to the Second Annual Disc Jockey Convention held in Miami by Storz Broadcasting.

In the early fifties Todd Storz at WTIX in New Orleans and Gordon McLendon at KLIF in Dallas developed the Top 40 format of radio, where currently popular records are played again and again and the radio personality was nothing more than a "disc jockey" who put the records on the turntable. Next to a used car dealer or a politician, this type of disc jockey had to be the world's least valuable animal. They were all named Johnny Rabbitt or Johnny Holiday, had red jackets with an embroidered design of the station call letters and a microphone on the breast pocket, and when they weren't on the air were usually found on the station's front lawn forming human pyramids for promotional photos. With a few rare exceptions, this Top 40 format of radio made the radio announcer a fairly anonymous,

197

easily replaced portion of the overall station format. Storz and McLendon proved it was the records people tuned in to hear and hear again.

In March 1958 Storz held a convention one weekend at a hotel in Kansas City for radio and record people. It was the first industry get-together of its kind and well attended by the important forces in music and radio.

At that convention, Mitch Miller, then head of artist and repertoire for Columbia Records, gave a speech, telling the radio men that they'd "abdicated" the choice of records they played to the "eight-to-fourteen-year-olds; to the preshave crowd that makes up 12 percent of the country's population and zero percent of its buying power, once you eliminate the ponytail ribbons, popsicles, and peanut brittle."

The disc jockeys must have slept through Miller's address if the convention Storz held the following May in Miami was any indication. The convention, at the Americana Hotel in Miami Beach, was a free-for-all the likes of which will never be seen again. It spotlighted just how out of hand the payola thing had gotten among the new breed of fifties disc jockeys who worked the Top 40 format across the country. From all over the country they flew in for their share of the "bribes, booze, and broads" as the newspapers described it.

One promotion man who is a friend of mine says, "I flew in a young 'lady of the night' from Philadelphia. I paid her plane fare to the convention. She spent three and a half days there and drove back to Philly in a brand new Lincoln Continental convertible she bought with the money she made."

The Subcommittee called Edward Eicher, special service director of the Americana Hotel, to the stand at the afternoon session. The Americana was served a subpoena that "required the production of certain records pertaining to the second annual pop disc jockey convention . . . sponsored by the Storz Stations."

Eicher told the Subcommittee that 2,000 to 2,500 disc jockeys arrived for the convention. He produced records that nineteen record companies had participated in the good times. Among them were eight major companies who picked up tabs—Capitol

Records spent $12,357.15 on a cocktail party; Dot Records had a banquet for $14,950; Columbia Records entertained to the tune of $9,415.39.

A press release circulated by RCA Victor Records was produced.

### RCA VICTOR PLANS SPECIAL "MILLIONAIRE" PROMOTION FOR MIAMI DJ CONVENTION

New York—RCA Victor is planning a special promotion to make the Nation's disc jockeys richer and happier in the forthcoming Miami disc jockey convention, it was reported by George L. Parkhill, manager popular advertising and promotion.

Every DJ upon arrival and registration at the Miami convention will receive an envelope from RCA Victor containing auction stage money in the amount of $1 million. Through his own ingenuity each DJ is free to increase (or decrease) his money through Saturday, May 30.

On that day at poolside at the Americana Hotel at 5:00 P.M. sharp, RCA Victor will hold an auction at which the DJ's will be able to bid for five prizes with the auction money they have accumulated. Prizes to be auctioned are a Studebaker Lark, a trip to Europe for two (via Sabena Airlines), $500 worth of Botany clothes, an RCA Victor color TV set, and an RCA Victor deluxe stereo set.

RCA Victor, throughout the convention will hold open house at their suite in the Hotel Americana, where RCA Victor will make it easy for the disc jockeys to augment their million-dollar funds. Each time a disc jockey is served in the RCA Victor hospitality suite, he will receive $5,000 in stage money. Victor will also sponsor the luncheon on Friday, May 29. At Saturday night's banquet, May 30, two RCA Victor artists, Caterina Valente and Lou Monte, will be among the entertainers.

It was now obvious that major record companies were involved in trying to influence the disc jockey, at least as much as any of those hateful independent rock 'n' roll record companies, although the Subcommittee ignored the point.

Eicher revealed that Pat Boone, his wife, and former Tennessee Governor Frank Clement and his wife were at the convention. Eicher said all four of them had their hotel tabs picked up by a record company. The Subcommittee didn't follow this up too closely.

Instead, Subcommittee member Rogers asked Eicher about a barbecue and breakfast hosted by Roulette Records.

"As I recall," said Eicher, "there were some 2,000 bottles of alcoholic beverages consumed . . . during that eight-hour recording session by Count Basie. . . . At midnight, when they started this session, they served a buffet-type barbecue, and that is the figure of $4,000 you see. And concluding the next morning, they served scrambled eggs and coffee, and Danish pastry. . . ." Eicher said that in all, Roulette picked up a $15,415 tab for the all-night wingding. Questioned closely about the affair, Eicher told the Subcommittee that the mayor of Miami and many local politicians showed up for the all-night barbecue, another point that was not pursued.

Eicher ended his testimony by explaining that former Governor Frank Clement had come to the convention to speak on "the importance of the disc jockey in today's way of life."

Next on the stand was Stan Richards, a former disc jockey at WILD in Boston. Richards said he got gifts at Christmas ("Perry Como once sent me a box of cheese which smelled up the house for three months.") and $6,225 from Boston record distributors between 1957 and 1959. The congressmen seemed to overlook Richards being on the take like everybody else when he said he'd fought a campaign against junk music and rock 'n' roll and that he would never say Fabian was great or a gasser because "for my money" Frank Sinatra is the greatest.

"I looked for the established stars—Perry Como, Pat Boone, Frank Sinatra, Kay Starr, Peggy Lee—anybody that was an entertainer," he told the Subcommittee. Adding, "When I saw their name on a label, I took time to listen to the record. I always played one side of that record, because none of these people ever made a bad record.

"But when you say a record by Ookie Ook, who has got three minutes to listen to that? unless, I suppose, someone came into you and gave you a gratuity."

"Without the gratuities, then, probably only the best music

would get played," observed Subcommittee member Peter Mack.

Richards agreed. "There is no question about it in my mind, that the country will now enjoy—it will still be popular music, which will reflect the taste of Americans, but it will be of a better quality."

On Wednesday, the Subcommittee called Samuel Clark, president of AM-Par Records, which was owned by ABC. In the course of his testimony, Sam said that Am-Par gave me a salad bowl one Christmas, a Salton hot tray the next, and an Osterizer the third. Am-Par had also assigned the copyright of "Don't Gamble with Love" and several other songs to publishing companies that I owned.

When the Subcommittee met on the Friday of the following week, Earl Kintner, chairman of the Federal Trade Commission, took the stand to report what his department was doing in regard to payola. There was a lot of bowing, scraping, and ass-kissing going on, all very ceremonial, with Kintner accompanied by eight other government muckie-mucks who were counsel to him in some way or another.

Kintner reported that the FTC had been fighting payola under the FTC's legal right to stop deceptive acts such as concealment of payment in order to have a record played—"since the listeners are misled into believing that the recordings played are selected strictly on their merits or public popularity," he said.

From out of nowhere, in the middle of Kintner's testimony, Subcommittee member John Bennett started to talk about me, outlining in detail various business interests I had.

Chairman Harris cut Bennett off. " . . . . The gentleman is spreading it all on the record at this moment before the case is fully developed. I think we ought to let the whole matter come out in the proper order."

"Mr. Chairman," said Bennett, "I just want to be careful about the facts. It has been published in the newspapers. Some of it, I admit, has not, but it is information that has come to me, and frankly, I am quite concerned about the fact that the Subcommittee has not yet called Clark. He is the outstanding disc jockey in this business. We have called a lot of peanut disc jockeys here for a couple of weeks. This man is obviously very seriously involved in payola. . . . I think his activities pinpoint more than any other thing the evils of payola."

I got the picture of the kind of reception I could expect when I took the stand.

After Bennett finished his outburst, and Kintner left with his entourage, the Subcommittee created something of a sensation by announcing that John C. Doerfer, chairman of the Federal Communications Commission, the man in charge of licensing radio stations, had taken rides to Florida on George Storer's private plane. Storer was a powerful communications pioneer who had thirteen broadcast licenses. Doerfer had also been an overnight guest on Storer's yacht. Doerfer said he couldn't see anything wrong with his actions. The Subcommittee tore him to shreds.

The Subcommittee next met on April 25. George Paxton, the owner of Coed Records and a former bandleader, was called. One of Coed's big hits was "16 Candles" by The Crests. Chief Counsel Lishman put Paxton through a wringer, trying to use him to show how powerful I was in the music business. He wanted Paxton to admit that Paxton gave me 50 percent of the copyright to "16 Candles" because I put pressure on Paxton. Paxton denied this. Lishman also probed to discover that ten to fifteen thousand copies of "16 Candles" were pressed by Mallard, my pressing company.

"I personally dislike most of the music today, if you want to know the truth," said Paxton at one point.

"You dislike it?" repeated Subcommittee member John Moss.

"Yes."

"I do, too."

"But I can't do anything about it because—"

"I do not have any prejudice against a little bit of rhythm," said Moss, interrupting Paxton. "I used to play drum when I went to school. I never heard of so many singers who cannot sing."

"That I have to agree with you 100 percent," said Paxton.

"You mean that would have occurred without payola?"

"I think so. I think the youth of today—"

Again Moss interrupted him, saying, "They use all the tricks in the world to put these characters forward and make them able to sound as if they can get a noise out."

"I think the emotion of the youth called for it, desired it, wanted it. I don't think anything could have stopped it."

"Well, we disagree," said Moss, announcing that "The good music did not require the support, the good music did not require the payment of payola." He turned to Paxton and said, "Let me give you another fairly reasonable example. One of my children is a teen-ager, one is immediately preteen. They listen to these programs when I am not home. They have an allowance which permits them to buy just a few recordings. So they buy this—"

"Trash," Paxton filled in helpfully.

"Trash. And they won't play it more than once or twice after they buy it. They buy it because it has been pushed on them."

"But they are also hearing 'The Sound of Music.' Why don't they buy that?" asked Paxton.

"After a while of that, after a few years of that, I find my youngsters not wanting to buy—"

"They are growing a little older."

"They are buying better music now. They are on a program of developing a library of the next step, the Broadway hits, the shows."

"They change."

"But they bought this, not because they liked it, but because it was the popularly pushed item by the disc jockeys who set the tone for the kids."

"You certainly have a point."

"Then one of the biggest effects on, or impact on, these youngsters is from Mr. Dick Clark."

"I would agree with that. Don't get me wrong. I am not here to protect Dick Clark."

"If you ever got home early you have heard this raucous sound in the middle of the afternoon."

"I make it but I don't listen to it," said Paxton.

"I try not to, but sometimes I have difficulty avoiding it. But I think that is why you are getting it."

"It would be a horrible state of affairs if all of a sudden everyone were to, shall we say, play good music—"

Again Moss interrupted him, asking quizzically, "It would be horrible?"

"No," said Paxton, "It would be great, but it would be horrible if no one went out to buy it."

The next day Paul Ackerman, the music editor of *Billboard*, was called to testify. Ackerman made a statement about the music business, what it was, and where it came from. It was the kind of introduction to the music industry the Subcommittee should have had months before when they first started the investigation.

Ackerman noted that "historically, payola is an outgrowth of a music business tradition—song plugging" and that it had been going on for some time. He explained the shifting patterns of the business's economic structure away from the sheet-music publisher's to the record companies. Then he made the point that always seemed to be at the root of the Subcommittee's misunderstanding about rock 'n' roll.

"Today, Tin Pan Alley is a nationwide rather than a Broadway concept," he read from a prepared statement. "Song hits and record hits come from virtually every state of the Union."

He repored that 1959 had been a banner year for the record industry with $450–480 million in sales. As for the concept that a record could be pushed on the public by buying airplay for it, he tried to explain the basic axiom of the business, that special something in certain records which makes them appeal to lots of people.

"If the record doesn't have some commercial appeal in the first place, no amount of exposure will help it. But granted that it has something of the groove, then there is a relationship between exposure and sales," he told them.

After Ackerman finished, the Subcommittee called Bernard Goldstein, vice president of Computech, Inc., of New York City. Goldstein arrived with half a dozen suitcases, stuffed with 300 pounds of information.

Computech was an "electronic data processing" organization I hired to analyze the record plays on "American Bandstand" from August 5, 1957, to November 30, 1959. I spent $6,000 creating the biggest red herring I could find—something that would shift the Subcommittee's attention away from my scalp.

On some 15,000 file cards I had entered the name and play date of every record played on "Bandstand." In those days I was the only guy in the world that kept lists of the records played. For some reason I'd kept them from the first day I took over the show. Instead of burying them, which I could have done, I supplied Computech with the 15,000 file cards and let them go at it.

Within 10 minutes, Goldstein was in trouble with the Subcommittee. Moss asked him who owned the "Bandstand" theme song. Goldstein said he had no idea. Moss started mashing up Goldstein, asking questions Goldstein couldn't answer. He called Goldstein's survey "statistical gymnastics."

The point was that Computech took my file cards and demonstrated that I didn't play records I had an interest in any more than I played records I had no interest in. An immaculately dressed businessman, Goldstein was as neat and precise in his statistical research as he was in his dress. He knew what he was talking about, but he'd say things that would send the congressmen's heads spinning: "I am sorry if I appear obstinate, but I must assert this, when consideration of public popularity is introduced, because it is very germane. We have in boldface had figures stated in this report that on the average he has played an interest song more than he has played, on the average, a noninterest song. That is a very firm statement here, and would not back up the statement you made. However, when we bring in the independent variable of public popularity, the popularity score, and use this to measure the validity of the number of plays that a given record has received, we then can make—we can draw the conclusion that the analysis establishes that the playing of interest records was consistent with the popularity of these records based upon independent and authoritative popularity ratings."

"Now you have me really confused," said Subcommittee member Moss.

The Subcommittee asked Goldstein who Computech was and why the Subcommittee should listen to all this. Goldstein explained that Computech did similar work for the U.S. Government.

A nice touch, I thought.

After Goldstein was taken off the stand, a succession of chief mathematical statisicians from various Government branches tried to explain the survey.

The confusion mounted.

Eventually the survey was turned around to prove the exact opposite of what Computech and I said it proved. The result was an argument that lasted for several days and wasted a good deal of the time they might otherwise have spent flailing my poor carcass.

With only about a week to go before I took the stand, Harry Finfer, manager of Universal Record Distributing in Philadelphia, and one of my partners in Jamie Records, was called. Harry was a nervous man with black slicked-back hair, and his mustache quivered as he spoke in rapid bursts. I'm sure that to the congressmen he fit the role of the dark, sinister record man. He admitted paying payola to Tom Donahue, Lloyd "Fatman" Smith, Joe Niagra, Hy Lit, and others.

Among the next witnesses to be called was George Goldner, president of Gone Records.

Goldner said he gave my publishing companies four copyrights, among them "Could This Be Magic?" by The Dubs. My name came up, Goldner saying that when I took over "Bandstand" "the feeling in the industry was that Dick Clark was going to become a very powerful personality in the business."

"And you had better all be friends?" asked Subcommittee member Moss.

"No, he wasn't the type of person to say, 'If you are not my friend, to heck with you,' it was nothing like that."

"No," said Moss. "I think he is far more mercenary than to put it to anything that approaches a relationship, purely of friendliness or compassion."

At 10 A.M., Thursday, April 28, the Subcommittee met in executive session to talk to Bernie Lowe and Harry Chipetz. They were questioned closely about their business activities with me.

At one point in his testimony, Harry said he usually visited me once a week, like every other distributor and promo man in Philadelphia, to play new records for me.

Looking up at Harry, Moss said, "Does he hold a levee there every week? Is it a custom that comes from the past, for the absolute monarch to hold levees for lesser subjects?" Moss then started to use the word "Clarkola" and I knew it wasn't going to be easy.

A few days later I got notice that I was expected in Washington to start testifying on May 2.

# 17

## "I want to make it clear immediately that I have never taken payola"

I walked into the Caucus Room of the Old House Office Building just before ten on Friday morning, May 2, 1960. The night before, my parents, Bobbie, and I had come to Washington on the train and they accompanied me to the hearing room. Before they took their seats in the public gallery, I stopped to kiss Bobbie and hug my mother and father, then walked forward to take my place at a chair and small wooden table set in an isolated position in the middle of the room. A dozen photographers pressed forward from the right of the gallery, with their flashbulbs popping and shutters clicking.

On a raised platform several yards in front of me were the tables and chairs at which the Subcommittee sat looking down at me. Directly behind me was my attorney and behind him at the back of the room was the public gallery. It was a very intimidating atmosphere.

At precisely ten o'clock the doors behind me opened to let spectators into the public gallery. A few minutes later the members of the Subcommittee came into the room through their private entrance at the back of the dais. With smiles and nods from the Subcommittee members, the photographers let loose with another barrage.

Taking his seat at the center table directly in front of me, Chairman Harris hit his gavel to begin the hearing. He told the photographers to step back and the public in the gallery to keep still. Then he looked at me.

"Are you Mr. Dick Clark?"

"Yes, sir."

"Mr. Clark, will you be sworn?" I stood up and he continued. "Do you solemnly swear the testimony you give to this Subcommittee to be the truth, the whole truth, and nothing but the truth, so help you God?"

"I do."

Inviting me to take my seat again, Harris said, "Do you have a statement that you wish to present to the Subcommittee at the outset?"

I said I did. He let me proceed.

"Mr. Chairman and gentlemen," I began, hoping my voice wouldn't betray how terrified I felt. "I feel that I have been convicted, condemned, and denounced even before I had an opportunity to tell my story. Further, there has been printed in the press what appears to me to be a prejudgment of my case. For these reasons, I respectfully request that I be given the opportunity to read this statement without interruption.

"My name is Dick Clark. I reside in Wallingford, Pennsylvania. I am a radio, television, and motion picture performer, and, until last winter, I was active in the record and music publishing industries.

"I want to make it clear, immediately, that I have never taken payola. In brief, I have never agreed to play a record or have an artist perform on a radio or television program in return for a payment in cash or any other consideration."

Tracing my professional life from my first days in radio, I listed my thirty-three corporations, how much I owned of each, and the businesses they were formed to handle.

"From the time that your staff interviewed me it was clear from their questions that they wanted to find out whether I used my corporate music and record interests as a consideration for playing their records on my shows.

"I told your staff that the answer to this question was no. Let me state again under oath that the answer is no. However, I want to make it equally clear that although my record interests were set up to operate in a normal competitive manner, I have no doubt but that some of the copyrights received by my publishing firms and some of the records owned, distributed, or pressed by the companies in which I had an interest were given to my firms at least in part because of the fact that I was a network television performer.

"However, the conflict between my position as a performer and my record interests never clearly presented itself to me until this committee raised questions of payola and conflicts of interest. At the lengthy session on November 11 with ABC officials we discussed this question in great detail. Although, as I have said, I was not conscious of any improper conduct, the more we discussed and analyzed my own situation, the clearer it became that I should remove any basis for an inference or a conclusion that my outside activities and interests would influence my judgment and activities on the air. This, as I have said, has now been achieved. I can now program my shows, pick my records, and select performers free of any fear that somebody might think that I am 'playing the angles.' "

Going into detail, I explained my publishing interests, how I had helped write "At the Hop," that Bobbie and I had inadvisedly taken jewelry and a fur coat from Lou Bedell, and that I never leaned on anybody to use my pressing plant to press their records.

I made it clear that I didn't keep any money due artists who appeared on "Bandstand"—a constant rumor in the press during the investigation. There wasn't enough money to pay all the artists, so I set up a system to pay as many of them as possible. The rest were paid by their record company—I gave the artist a check, the record company gave me a check, and the artist gave his check to the record company, resulting in a free appearance by the artist on the show. It was the normal procedure in TV at the time.

My next point was the Computech survey. I reminded the Subcommittee that I paid to have the project done before they or their investigators requested it. I said I did the survey in good faith and hoped they took it as such no matter how they chose to interpret its findings.

Once more I maintained that a hit was in the record's grooves, that no amount of airplay could turn a dud into a hit. I finished by telling the Subcommittee how outraged I was that Lishman had said that many persons interviewed by the investigators were "reluctant to talk for fear of reprisals in the

*Left:* On the witness stand at the payola hearings.
*Right:* My parents and Bobbie listen in the visitors' gallery as I testify at the payola hearings. From left to right, my father, my mother, Bobbie, and an unidentified observer.

"IF IT'S NOT IN THE GROOVES, YOU CAN'T MAKE A RECORD A HIT!"
I set out to prove this indisputable music business axiom when Congress embarked on its payola hearings. I sent myself a certified letter on November 24, 1959, in which I stated I would play "You Hold the Future," by Tommy Sands, "until I am called to Washington." I detailed why the supersaturation airplay of this record, by a recognized hit-maker of the day, would not make this record a hit.

The record was a bomb. My attorney never allowed me to show the congressmen my "proof."

Tommy Sands asked me several years later, "Why did you keep playing that turkey?"

My letter remained sealed for almost sixteen years. Tommy and I opened it together in early September 1975. *No amount of airplay can turn a "stiff" into a "hit"* . . . it's a lesson the congressmen never did learn!

form of being denied future opportunity of having their records aired or their talents displayed on this or other broadcast programs."

I spoke for a half-hour. When I finished reading my statement, I pushed it away from me and looked up at the Subcommittee.

Chairman Harris said he felt I was not being singled out as an example, that it had taken so long to get me to the stand because they wanted to complete their investigation before calling me. He turned to Lishman, asking if he had any questions.

Lishman grilled me, gradually unveiling my entire financial structure, how much I earned, where the money came from, and who signed the checks.

Congressman Derounian took over from Lishman. He went around in circles about whether the statement I made to ABC that I hadn't taken payola was what he termed "a Christian Dior" affidavit since it was not the statement other disc jockeys were required to sign, but one tailored to suit ABC and my needs.

"Mr. Clark, did you ever play Elvis Presley records on your network program?" he asked.

"Yes, indeed."

"How many times would you say you played these?"

"I have no idea."

"Did you play them frequently?"

"Not as frequently as you might expect, because he is a very fortunate man, like Perry Como and Pat Boone and some other recognized artists, and his records are played quite frequently over many different outlets."

"Why would you not play them if you played popular songs?"

"I don't mean to intimate that I didn't play them."

"But you did not play them with the frequency that you played other records?"

"That is quite possible."

"And Elvis, being an outstanding artist, probably did not have to give any payola to get his records played; is that not so?"

"I don't know what your inference is."

"Let me put it this way, did you play his records as often as you played Duane Eddy's records in which you had an interest?"

"No, sir."

"All I can say, Mr. Clark, is that you say you did not get any payola, but you got an awful lot of royola," said Derounian, looking down at some papers in front of him.

"Do you have any further response?" asked Chairman Harris.

I had my copy of the Computech survey with me. Looking through it, I said, "I have a Presley record here, Mr. Derounian, that was played twenty-four times, which I think is substantial."

"How many times did you play Duane Eddy? Nobody heard of him until you played him," Derounian shot back.

"The intimation, then, is that he would never have had a hit record. Here is a Duane Eddy record that was fairly large; it only got eight plays, but that was unusual, to say the least— 'Some Kind of Earthquake.' 'Forty Miles of Bad Road,' it got thirty-three plays compared with the twenty-four plays for Elvis Presley. I don't think that is too far out of line."

"It is quite a meteoric rise for someone who was not heard of before you played him," said Derounian, ignoring what I'd just said.

"Mr. Derounian, there are countless thousands of people I have dealt with in the past few years that were never heard of; that is part of the reason that I have been very lucky and successful; they never had an avenue to be shown or even known by the public. Two of the biggest stars in the country right now are two young men who would probably never have been heard of. And I had no direct financial interest in them or their careers or what-have-you. This has happened to countless hundreds of artists I have dealt with who have become very, very big stars, including, if I may name a few, some who are now used in every major television show in the country that before couldn't even be seen on a network television show."

"Mr. Clark, you mentioned that you did not see anything wrong in all these business interests of yours. Why did you divest yourself of so many last fall?"

"Because I had to make a choice of whether I wanted to remain as a television performer or go into the music business.

213

I preferred television. There was no other choice available to me.

"May I inject in the record—you talked about a very good friend of mine, Duane Eddy, who, when he heard I was going to leave, wanted to cancel a tour and come with me. It was a very personal thing."

"You made him, and now he wants to do something for you. That is between the two of you."

"May I also just mention the names of a few people that I am credited with having some effect on their popularity—and they didn't record for any of my companies.

"One of the biggest stars in the country is Bobby Darin. And he made some appearances on my program quite some time back. And he still comes back and does something when he has a chance.

"Connie Francis is probably the nation's number-one vocalist. She appeared on my first Saturday night show. I played her first record some forty times—I think it shows in the record—I never made a penny from it.

"There are two boys, Fabian and Frankie Avalon, for years I have been walking around with people saying, 'What kind of dough are you making out of Avalon and Fabian?' It gets to be a running gag, and the investigators were surprised to find I didn't have any arrangement with them."

"They do not sing very well either," said Derounian.

Chairman Harris called time out for lunch.

As I walked up the aisle to join Bobbie and my parents, a woman came up to me, smiled, and handed me a folded scrap of paper. Once I was outside in the hall, I opened it. It said, "Don't worry, Dick, we are with you, a fan." It was like a bad movie.

In the afternoon Lishman came at me with questions that moved my interrogation into the twilight zone. A studious-looking mole of a man, it was obvious he took great delight in his job.

"Frank Sinatra has popular records, doesn't he?" asked Lishman.

"Occasionally, yes," I said.

There was a burst of giggles from the gallery.

"Well," said Lishman, ignoring the murmuring, "don't you

214

think in the period August 5, 1957, to November 30, 1959, that he moved some popular records?"

"Mr. Lishman, Mr. Sinatra's audience is slightly different from mine."

"Well, do you know that you didn't play him once during that period?"

"Yes, I am quite aware of that," I said. I was flabbergasted. Before I could stop myself, I added, "As I didn't play any Ezio Pinza."

Lishman asked me the same question about Perry Como and Frankie Lane. All I could tell him was that they weren't my audience's favorites. He didn't understand.

"We will come to Bing Crosby," he said. "Now, during this period he has produced some popular records, hasn't he?"

"He is probably the biggest record seller there ever was," I said.

"Yes, sir," said Lishman, nodding his head. "How many of Bing Crosby did you play during that time?"

"I have no idea."

"One—'White Christmas,'"—said Lishman with triumph in his voice.

The gallery broke into unrestrained laughter.

Lishman motioned to one of the guards at the side of the room. A door opened and three giant, wall-sized charts were wheeled in. I couldn't imagine what he was up to, until I got a close look at the charts. There, facing me, were diagrams with dozens of names and corporations interconnected with solid and broken lines. It was mad; everybody I ever met was on the charts at one place or another. There were people listed on the charts who had the same names as people I knew, but were the wrong people. There were companies that I'd owned and other companies that I'd never heard of.

At that point Chairman Harris suggested they wrap it up for the day and that I come back Monday. I asked if I'd be finished on Monday in time to scoot back to Philadelphia to do "Bandstand." He doubted it.

On Monday morning one of the Subcommittee's investigators was called to again confirm that Tony Mamarella and I weren't in cahoots.

I was put back on the stand.

215

Lishman ran down the charts, then produced every contract that I'd ever had with WFIL, ABC, merchandisers, and business partners. Everything but my supermarket receipts. He spent most of the morning introducing these various documents into the record.

At lunchtime my Washington lawyer, Paul Porter, and I were in a private conference room in the building, discussing what line the questioning might take, when there was a knock on the door.

I went over and opened it. Lishman was standing there with his teen-age son. He let the kid skip school so he could meet me and get my autograph. I gave the kid his autograph.

It was at that point that the light suddenly came on in my head. I realized this whole thing was a shuck. This man had been saying terrible things to me in public, really gunning for me, and then he turned up with his kid for an autograph!

Back in the Caucus Room after lunch, Lishman was back at it. He questioned the affidavit I supplied to ABC. Why hadn't I signed the same payola questionnaire that ABC asked all its other disc jockeys to sign? I told him it was because ABC didn't ask me.

Subcommittee member John Moss questioned me next. He wanted to know about copyrights and my publishing companies. We had a tangle that demonstrated his basic misunderstanding of music publishing. He said there was something wrong with my music publishing business if this was the way I ran it. I told him I couldn't have run it otherwise because that was how all music publishing was conducted. It got thick and got us nowhere. Moss then asked about my reasons for wanting to go into business, the Computech survey, and the size of the office Tony and I shared.

Moss asked about the $7,000 American Airlines had paid me.

I explained, "For a period of weeks on the 'Saturday Night Show,' as is rather ordinary, at the end of the program I would say, transportation for our guests was provided by American Airlines—and probably four or five more words which I don't remember. It is called an airline plug."

Underscoring that American paid $7,000 for this, Moss said,

216

"You were accepting a commercial on the program for American Airlines?"

"I don't think it is known in the television industry as a commercial."

"I do not care what it is known as. I can call it 'Clarkola' if I want to, I can give it any name I want to give it," said Moss in a huff.

At that moment Derounian broke in with one of the most astounding conversations that has ever taken place at the taxpayers' expense.

"Now, do you recall a high school boy named Fabian Forte?" he asked.

"Yes, indeed."

". . . who goes under the title of Fabian, because I understand, it is Frenchy and very continental?"

"He is very successful," was all I could think to say to that one.

"Now, he has been described as 'Apollolike in stature, curly-haired with a seductive eye.' Is that a pretty fair description of him?"

"I think if I described him that way he would have a few sharp words for me, but I know him too well."

"Do you know how this boy was discovered by Mr. Marcucci?"

"Yes, I do."

Ignoring my answer, Derounian picked up a piece of paper and said, "Let me read and you tell me whether it is close to the facts:

> One day this Apollolike individual was sitting on his porch in Philadelphia, in fact, it was his front porch, and a Mr. Marcucci took a look at him and said, "I'm going to make a big-time singer out of you."
>
> "Me, a singer?" said Fabian. "I never sang a note in my life."
>
> "That doesn't matter," said Marcucci. "You look like a singer and that is all that counts."
>
> Within a few months Fabian had made several personal appearances on Clark's television programs. Clark played his records incessantly, and before long the youngster had

become a national teen-age celebrity with a half-dozen smash hit records.

In a recent frank interview, Fabian explained how he makes a record. "First, they put me in front of a mike," he said, "and tell me to sing my number. I sing it maybe twenty times, and then the engineers take over. They listen to the tape for hours before deciding what to do. If my voice sounds too weak, they pipe the music through an echo chamber to soup it up. If it sounds drab, they speed up the tape to make it sound happier. If I hit a wrong note, they snip it out and replace it by one taken from another part of the tape. And if they think the record needs more jazzing, they emphasize the accompaniment. By the time they get done with their acrobatics, I can hardly recognize my own voice."

"This comes from an article written by no fly-by-night. It appears in *Red Book* [sic] of March 1960, by Bill Davidson."

I smiled at Derounian and said, "I could have almost told you that before you told me."

"Well, is that an incorrect description of one of your talented young protégés?"

"Yes, I think that is an incorrect description."

"Now, has Mr. Forte ever sung on one of your programs?"

"Many times."

"Actually, not the recording?"

"Yes—not many times, he has appeared."

"I quote further from the article:

To avoid embarrassment, Clark's protégés rarely sing in public. Instead, they silently mouth their words in a technique called lip-sync as one of their records plays offstage. A near-disaster resulted last June when Clark produced a live television spectacular and included Fabian among such seasoned performers as The McGuire Sisters, Fats Domino, and Les Paul and Mary Ford. Each of the stars was required to sing a few bars of 'Mary Had a Little Lamb.' Fabian had to rehearse the nursery rhyme dozens of times."

"That, incidentally, is a lie."

"Do you mean to say that none of these records are jazzed up?

"Excuse me, the last statement, Mr. Derounian, was written for effect; it is an inaccuracy."

"Was it true about the engineers jazzing up the records of Fabian?"

"I have no idea, I was never there."

"I thought you said you heard him sing?"

"Yes."

"Why hasn't he sung more frequently in his own flesh instead of getting these hormone treatments on the record?"

Before I could answer that one, Derounian continued, "You see, Mr. Clark, this may seem funny to some, but to me it is quite serious. The children of the Nation idolize you, as they did Van Doren, and they feel that when you bring a singer up on the program he has real talent. This fellow Bill Davidson, who I am sure knows more about entertainment than I do, seems to think this fellow Fabian had no talent.

"Maybe there is a difference of opinion between you and him, but it is something to bring out and get the facts on the record, because if you are promoting fellows who do not have talent, I will give you my eight-year-old daughter, who can't even carry a tune, and you might even make some money on her. But that is not the purpose of your program, as you stated it, which is to encourage good music and with it the advancement of youth who have talent."

"May I comment on this?" I asked.

"Surely."

"The main purpose of my television show was to entertain and amuse people. Fabian came to me—first of all, despite the tremendous pressures they put on this sixteen-year-old young man—he is good looking, he is an attractive boy, and is probably one of the nicest human beings I have ever met in my own life. He has been subjected to some of the most foul, vicious attacks I have ever seen. That is pretty hard to take. He recognizes his own deficiencies. He is taking steps to correct them. There is no doubt that he is successful.

"I don't want to have the impression given that I have foisted him off on anybody. He was first sent to me as a young boy by his manager, his mentor, as they call them in show business, and he appeared in public without a hit record; nobody had ever heard of this boy before, and there was the most fantastic response you had ever seen. The kids took one look at him and said, 'Oh.' It was fantastic, the response."

I told Derounian this had happened before Fabian had ever had a hit. I said it'd been the same with Elvis Presley and more recently with Bobby Rydell—the kids loved them from the first instant they saw them. Not to be outdone by Derounian's love for newspaper clips, I pointed out that John S. Wilson had said in *The New York Times* that young people have always liked their own music with as much passion as adults have been unable to comprehend it.

But Derounian wasn't to be swayed. He asked me what I thought of John Crosby of the New York *Herald Tribune* as a critic. I told him I didn't know. Derounian produced another sheet of paper from the file on the table in front of him.

"Here is what he said about your Fabian: 'Reeling like a top, snapping his fingers and jerking his eyeballs, with hair like something Medusa had sent back, and a voice that was enormously improved by total unintelligibility.'

"And Mitch Miller—"

"Wishes he had him," I interrupted.

"No."

"Excuse me; I'm sorry."

"He said: 'You would not invite those unwashed kids into your living room to meet your family, why thrust them into the living rooms of your audience?'

"Mr. Clark, I think what you are saying is this: The singer appears on your program physically—and apparently that is your format. You get a big hunk of young man who has got a lot of cheesecake to him and the kids are thrilled by this on the television program, and then you play his records, but you don't have him sing too often. That is the way you sell records and that is a pretty cute way to do it.

"And all I want you to do, if that is the case, is to admit that the singing part of his talent is not the all-important part, but his physical appearance plays a great part in whether or not you are going to let him appear on your show."

"No, that is an unkind thing to say, Mr. Derounian."

"It is not unkind—is it factual or isn't it?"

"No, it is not factual."

"You would then have an ugly person appear on your show?"

"Mr. Derounian, do you want me to say I have had a lot of ugly people appear on my program?"

"Attractive to teen-agers?"

"Mr. Derounian, all things and all different kinds of people are attracted to different types of people. Beauty—"

"Beauty is relative. I know that."

"I think that is a very difficult thing, but we have had all sizes and shapes."

Derounian began questioning about how much money Fabian made, about which I knew nothing, when Subcommittee member John Springer interrupted.

"Mr. Clark, what Mr. Derounian says is in fact true, isn't it —that on your particular program, for some peculiar reason which nobody can analyze, you don't have necessarily the best singers?"

"By whose standards?"

"I am talking about good music standards—any kind."

"By the people who follow what I do, we have the best people on it."

Much to my surprise, Springer had actually seen "Bandstand."

"I have only heard your show once. The thing that struck me when I heard Frankie Avalon on that particular program was that I thought he was singing off-key. I will admit that he was a striking personality, and I could see why there would be a tremendous appeal to young girls, and I will say that he is a perfect gentleman. That is all that I am willing to concede. But I was amazed when he started to sing. When I heard this song, it was something I couldn't understand, because I had thought he was not a good singer. I think he made a striking appearance on your program, and I can see where he has appeal. But I can see also where he is not an accomplished musician. I realize he is only eighteen or nineteen years old."

"Mr. Springer, there is one other interesting thing—the fact that both of those gentlemen record, their records are popular all over the world, in some places where they have never even been seen."

"Then in that instance I must be wrong," said Springer, smiling, and then turned the proceedings back to Derounian who asked me how many of the artists on my show had gold records. When I told him I didn't know for sure he thanked me for being a patient and willing witness.

"Mr. Clark," said Subcommittee member Rogers, "Mr. Fabian is not here, is he?"

"No, he is in California making pictures."

"I thought we could shorten this by letting him sing for us here," he said. To this day I don't know if he was serious or not.

It was 6:10 P.M. when Chairman Harris took the floor.

"Mr. Clark," he said, "I do not intend to detain you further with any questions, except I thought I did have one question I wanted to ask you. . . . What do you do, or how do you bring about the situation that causes all these fine young people in attendance in these shows to squeal so loud at a particular time? Do you have some kind of a cue that you give them to do it? Or is that one of your trade secrets that you do not want to give away?" Harris had a twinkle in his eye and a smile which told me we were coming down the homestretch.

"Mr. Harris, this is a very basic law of nature. Most of the young people who squeal are girls who are young ladies—again I see you are smiling, so—when you and I can explain women, we can explain why these girls squeal. There is no cue; we don't cue them."

"I think I remember when Frank Sinatra was way up they used to have this all the time. There were always reports about how it was brought about, and I just wondered if you did actually bring this on as part of the show?"

"No, this is a young version of applause, and it is a little more vocal, and a little more exciting."

"Mr. Chairman," said Springer, "some months ago I saw this program in New York, and it was the greatest psychological phenomenon I have ever seen in my life. And I can assure you that there were no cues. I was much interested in the whole thing. I would say nine out of ten in the audience were young people, mainly girls. With the appearance of a boy like Frankie Avalon, who is quite a masculine-looking young fellow, and these others that appeared, it just seemed that the minute they appeared, everybody went into this psychological squealing.

"I am a little more educated as a result of that experience as to what these shows are like. But what brought them such popularity is impossible to decipher."

"Perhaps, Mr. Springer, it has been too long since you and I were at that age," said Harris. Then he turned to me. "Mr. Clark, we know of your importance to the broadcast industry, and particularly to the young people of the country. You are obviously a fine young man. You started in this business young and you are attractive to young people. Therefore, your responsibilities with your influence can be great. I am sure you have realized that for a long time."

"I have."

"It is not my purpose to conclude this with any type of lecture. It is not my job; it is not my duty. You have made from your own viewpoint, I think, a very good witness. You have stated very frankly in your statement that you could not speak more truthfully than to say it was not a great pleasure for you to be here. And I can very well understand that. It does not give me any pleasure to have to inquire into matters where questionable public interest and policies are involved.

"It is our duty and responsibility to determine whether or not certain practices that have been exposed are in the public interest, and I do not think that there is any question in your mind or anybody else's mind, from your actions that took place after these things began to develop and unfold, since last summer. I do not think you are the inventor of the system; I do not think you are even the architect of it, apparently. I think you are the product that has taken advantage of a unique opportunity in exposing to the public, to the teen-agers, the young people, the television productions of this country—and I say that in all sincerity, because our mail indicates concern about the children, and television productions."

Harris spoke for several minutes more, telling me that I'd cast a different light for the Subcommittee on the subject of payola, but that it was obvious something had to be done to make such practices illegal. At 6:20 he thanked me for my appearance, excused me, and I left the room.

There were three more days of hearings—May 3 and then

August 30 and 31. On May 3, Leonard Goldenson of ABC was called to testify. He described how ABC and I had come to terms with my divestiture of my music interests, then got raked over the coals on the American Airlines plug situation. Evidence was presented that not only had "Bandstand" accepted money for airline plugs but so had other shows: "Beat the Clock,'" "The Pat Boone Show," "Bourbon Street Beat," "The Donna Reed Show," "77 Sunset Strip," "The Voice of Firestone," and "You Asked for It."

Goldenson had to redescribe our meetings for Subcommittee member Mack who went over earlier testimony to doublecheck some points. After admitting that he was not present on the Friday that I gave my statement, Mack said, "I have the distinct feeling that not only is he the top disc jockey in the country but he seems to have been the 'top dog' in the payola field as well."

The last item entered into the record was a letter presented at the request of Hon. Gerald R. Ford, Jr., of Michigan. It was a letter to Ford from a local promoter who said disc jockeys were promoting shows and doing radio at the same time and that this was another form of payola. Why Ford wanted that in the record, when it was all over, puzzles me. Better late than never, I guess.

A bill was subsequently passed making payola a criminal offense punishable by a $10,000 fine or one year in jail.

Oren Harris made the speech that got the bill passed in the House. Strangely enough, the speech had nothing to do with payola. Harris had gone on a trip to Antarctica with other congressmen. At a press reception in Hawaii en route he was photographed by *Life* magazine. *Life* ran the picture, which seemed to show Harris with a glass in his hand, and under it a caption which said something like "Congressmen drink it up at taxpayers' expense." Harris didn't drink. He hit the roof. He sent investigators to *Life* to get the negative. The negative showed it was the man standing next to Harris who had the drink in his hand.

Harris got up in the House and made a speech about how terrible Time/Life/Fortune were and how they'd done this terrible thing to him. Now maybe Harris knew how I felt when

*Life* ran the story about the kid who shot his mother because she wouldn't let him watch "Bandstand."

When the Government put me out of the music business I estimate I lost more than $8 million. The hearings taught me a lot about politics and business. I learned not just to make money, but to protect my ass at all times.

# "My husband and your wife . . ."

I was in the office one morning, six months after the payola hearings concluded, when the life I'd built for myself in Philadelphia came to an abrupt end. The wife of a close friend called. "Are you aware of what's going on between my husband and your wife?" she asked.

I was shocked. I got off the phone and just sat there, not knowing how to deal with what I'd heard. At first I doubted the whole story; I was in turmoil. Finally, I decided to hire a private detective, and in the next agonizing months I was in for some surprises.

Bobbie had never found the life I led all that fascinating, though she did pay some attention to my career. She opened the house to magazine photographers who wanted to capture us at home. She let me drag homeless rock stars into the house for Thanksgiving dinners. She dressed up in Gay Nineties fashions to pose with me for the cover of the special Christmas record I'd had Chubby Checker make. At Christmas she came down to "Bandstand" to appear on the show.

She was a very bright, personable woman, and she put up with an awful lot—especially when we went out in public. It was like no one knew she existed. Everybody wanted to see and talk to Dick Clark. I was so busy I didn't appreciate how terribly lonely she got.

But I now began to learn a lot about how she dealt with this loneliness even earlier, and my worst fears were confirmed. In late 1959 or early 1960, Bobbie had started seeing a local record man—a man who'd been my friend, or at least pretended to be

226

my friend. This guy was quite a character. On a business level he told people he had an "in" with Dick Clark. Acts came to him, asking if he could use his "in" to get them on "Bandstand."

"Yes," he'd tell them, "but it costs money to get on any of Dick Clark's shows." He charged them, pocketed the money, then came to me, asking me as a favor whether I'd put so-and-so on the show.

That's how I got on Hedda Hopper's blacklist. A Hollywood actor and would-be singer came to Philadelphia to be on the show and paid my "friend" to arrange for his appearance. My friend took the money, but said, "I gave it to Dick Clark." Back in Hollywood, the actor told Hedda he'd paid to be on "Bandstand."

This so-called friend of mine was a shit heel if there ever was one. At a time when everyone wanted to be my friend because of the show, he was one guy I trusted. I remember at the time somebody told me, "Don't worry about it; time wounds all heels." That wasn't much consolation. He hurt me badly. This guy did just about everything to me that you shouldn't do to a friend.

Bobbie's latest relationship confused and troubled me. I realize now that she was desperate. She needed companionship and love. Obviously I had done a lousy job of expressing to her how much I cared for her. Later Bobbie told me she wasn't quite sure that she had loved me, that the marriage probably took place because it was expected of us.

After much soul-searching, Bobbie and I decided to get a divorce. But we agreed not to tell anyone—not her mother, not my parents—for a few months. Christmas was approaching and we didn't want to upset them.

In the spring I took an apartment in downtown Philadelphia. Bobbie and Dickie remained in the house in Wallingford. Bobbie conducted her new romance discreetly by long-distance telephone calls and frequent rendezvous at out-of-the-way places around Philadelphia. When the school term ended in June, she and Dickie moved to Youngstown, Ohio, to start a new life. On November 21, 1961, we were granted a divorce.

Dorothy Kilgallen wrote in her column that I'd left Bobbie to marry Connie Francis.

While this was going on I was making *The Young Doctors.* We shot the film in New York, so every morning Ed McAdam picked me up in a station wagon, drove me to New York for the filming, then drove me back in time for "Bandstand." To keep my mind off Bobbie and what had happened, I started drinking, a foolish answer to an emotional problem, but an answer nonetheless. I'd arrive on the set with a terrible hangover and do my scenes with a splitting headache. I was living on straight vodka; I came as close as I could ever come to being an alcoholic in those months.

During this period I got a call from Connie Francis who was apearing at the Latin Casino in Philadelphia. Connie and I had been friends since I'd played her first record and helped to make it a hit.

"Come over and see my show," she urged me.

"I'd love to. Have you got time afterwards for dinner?"

"Of course," Connie paused for a moment. "Maybe you should find someplace quiet so we don't wind up in Dorothy Kilgallen's column again."

I called my friend Don Battles at the RDA Club and arranged for a private room. After Connie's second show at the Latin Casino we drove over to the RDA Club. As we ate and talked, I realized again that my warm friendship with Connie, though not romantic, was sincere and deep.

"I've heard a lot about your drinking these days," she said toward the end of the meal. "Are you really that bad off . . . falling down in the dark?"

I laughed. "No, it's not that bad yet, but it hasn't been the most pleasant time in my life."

"You may not realize it, Dick, but that marriage you were holding onto was never any great thing of beauty. Everybody around you knew it wasn't working."

I'd heard the same comment from several other friends, I told her so.

"Maybe now's the time you should start listening to your friends before rather than after," she said.

I eventually snapped out of my depression, not only stopping drinking but stopping smoking as well. Connie, Bobby Darin, and a few others did their best to straighten me out and get me sailing along again. Their heart-to-hearts made a great impression on me. I realized, for probably the first time in my life, that I had real friends in the music business.

# "The 'Caravan of Stars' went everywhere"

Rock concerts today are as plentiful and popular as movies and sporting events, but in the late fifties and early sixties rock 'n' roll had little acceptance as a form of live entertainment. In 1959 I put together the first "Dick Clark's Caravan of Stars." It quickly turned into a huge business that has grossed upwards of $5 million a year. Since I went out with those first shows I've promoted hundreds of artists including The Beatles, The Rolling Stones, Led Zeppelin, Chicago, Alice Cooper, the Royal Lippizzaner Horses, the Destruction Derby, Sonny & Cher, The Osmonds, Tony Orlando and Dawn. But no big-name promotions can match the crazy times when I went on the road with the "Caravan of Stars."

The "Caravan of Stars" was put together to appeal to the "American Bandstand" audience. I followed a simple formula: as many acts as I could afford, each doing two or three songs, all backed by the same band with me as the MC. As many as seventeen acts were listed on the bill, though two or three were fictional—"Little Al and his guitar" on the posters was Al Bruneau from the backup band.

The show started at 8:30 P.M. and ended by 11:15 P.M. The kids paid $1.50 a ticket to see quite an amazing lineup of stars, probably more stars doing more hits than any show they've seen since. The show always closed with a white romantic teen idol like Bobby Vee, Fabian, Gene Pitney, or Paul Anka.

The summer tour went out from Memorial Day to Labor Day, sixty to ninety days on the road nonstop (I'd fly back to Philadelphia once a week to tape a week's worth of one-hour "Band-

stand" segments.) The whole show was sold to the local promoter in each city for about $2,500 a night plus a percentage of
the gate. On a good night we cleared $5,000, but in the early days
especially there wasn't a big profit to be made. The acts were
paid very little compared to what they get today. But it was the
only tour in town. There was no place a rock 'n' roll act could
perform short of renting a tuxedo, buying a nightclub act from
two guys in the Brill Building in New York, and trying to break
into the Latin Casino or the Copa.

For fourteen shows a week, the star of the show got about
$1,200. I think we paid Gene Pitney $1,500 a week when he
was a headliner. The Supremes were on one tour, the three
girls and Diana Ross's mom who was along as chaperone got a
total of $600 a week. Many acts didn't make more than $500 a
week. Even then you knew Diana Ross was somebody special.

Once the act got paid their $500 or $600 they divided the
money among themselves, took off 10 percent for their agent,
10 percent for their manager, put some aside to pay their taxes,
paid for their room and board on the tour—they were lucky
if they had $20 a week to play with.

We made deals to get the acts at rock-bottom prices. Roz
Ross and Bill Lee booked the tours. They watched *Billboard*
and the other trade papers. When they saw a new act appear at
the bottom of the charts they listened to the record and checked
a few locations to see if the record was selling. If they thought
the record would eventually get into the Top 20 best sellers in
the country, they put in an offer for the act.

An unknown act on the charts with a first record would be
offered $500 a week—it didn't matter if there were twelve
people of the band.

"We've got a hit," they'd invariably say.

"Yeah," agree Bill or Roz, "but you're not in the Top 20."

"Well, we're gonna be in the Top 20."

"Well, I'll tell you what we'll do. We'll give you $400 a week.
If you make it to the Top 20 we'll gamble with you—we'll pay
you $600 a week if you get into the Top 20. If you get into the
Top 10 we'll give you $650 a week." The acts would take our
offers, gambling that their record would keep moving up.

Among the acts that went out on the early tours were The

Drifters, The Supremes, Bryan Hyland, Bobby Freeman, Mike Clifford, Johnny Tillotson, The Crystals, George McCannon III, Dee Dee Sharp, The Hondells, Lou Christie, Paul Anka, Chubby Checker, Duane Eddy, Linda Scott, Clarence "Frogman" Henry, The Shirelles, The Jive "5", and Jimmy Clanton.

Life on tour was rough. The acts met in the city closest to the first date—we didn't pay transportation for that. They showed up wearing their latest clothes, bright and smiling, and everyone was in good shape.

That first afternoon we had a rehearsal. Each act was backed by the same band, so it didn't take long to run down the numbers. That was the only rehearsal we had; after that every show was a rehearsal.

In the evening we checked into a hotel. Since the acts paid their own hotel bills, we stayed in the cheapest hotels we could find.

In the morning the bus we rented was in front of the hotel ready to take us to the first date. Ed McAdam, veteran of our Philadelphia record hop days, was the tour manager. Ed was the most lovable guy, but he put on his gruff top-sergeant exterior, shouting, as the acts staggered out of the hotel: "Get on the bus, sit over there, and shut up. You, you're late. We'll leave you in the next town if you don't get down in time; we don't wait for anyone." And they moved. Ed was the boss—big bark, no bite, but everyone listened to him.

Out of the hotel came the strangest collection of people, and each of them with pillows, blankets, and anything else that wasn't nailed down under their arms. There was George Hamilton IV, a long lean country boy from North Carolina; Major Lance, who was a boxer and would work out whenever we stopped; The Shirelles, who'd get on the bus, pull down the windows, and shake out their wigs; Dick and DeeDee, two eighteen-year-old kids accompanied by DeeDee's mom. Many of the black guys in those days straightened their hair. To keep it flat, they wore silk stockings pulled tight over the tops of their heads—a headrag—then they wrapped bandanas around their heads. The rest of us were always sloppy. We looked like a band of gypsies. Real classy, walking out of the hotel like that.

We'd pull out onto the highway. Within half an hour the state police would overtake the bus, lights flashing, sirens wailing. The troopers would come aboard and strip the bus—36 pillows, 20 blankets, 50 towels. In later years we made it a rule: no stealing from hotels.

To save money we didn't stop at a hotel every night. The schedule went this way: After our Sunday night show we checked into a hotel. Monday morning at eight Ed rousted everyone out onto the bus. We drove all day Monday to the show. After the show Monday night we slept on the bus, driving all night to the Tuesday show. We got back on the bus after the Tuesday night show and drove until about seven on Wednesday morning. We checked into a hotel, sleeping all day until the show that night. Then back on the bus to sleep all night while we drove to the Thursday night show. We again checked into a hotel on Friday night.

The bus was our home away from home. It held thirty-one people, including equipment and clothes. We had a number of bus drivers, the most memorable being a guy named Clayton Fillyeau, who worked for James Brown before he joined us. Fillyeau was the bus driver and backup drummer. Drums were the one instrument we couldn't do without, so if the drummer dropped dead we had a fill-in.

It took a couple of days for life on the bus to take shape. There were no preassigned seats, but once a seat was established it was your seat. You didn't mess with anybody's seat. The back of the bus was where the rowdies and drunks sat; there'd be drinking, singing, loving going on all night long. The front of the bus was for people who wanted to sleep at night. Some dummies stayed up all night to sing their act over and over to themselves.

Activity on the bus varied. Tommy Roe and Freddy Weller wrote the million seller "Dizzy" as we drove along. DeeDee was the only person who read books; she'd read a new book every day. I bought a newspaper, then we passed it around, but not too many people read it. We pressed our portable radios up against the windows as we drove through towns to hear whether or not the acts' records were being played. We sat and talked. One night I was sitting with the young bass player of the backup group. He told me about the exhilaration he got from travel, the joy he got from performing. I told him I thought he was foolish to follow it as a career—that most of the money was back down the road with the promoter. Sometime later he told me that was the night he decided to be a producer. His name was James William Guercio, the man behind the multimillion-dollar success of the group Chicago.

From time to time there were fights on the bus. Once Dick St. John and DeeDee Sharp got into a fight with DeeDee's mother. Stars, mothers, roadies, the combination of ego made for a memorable mix. Another time Round Robin and Billy Stewart got into an argument and drew pistols on each other. There we were, barreling down the highway, and the two of them were waving guns in the air as the rest of us crouched down in our seats. Ed managed to cool them down and get their guns away from them.

The bus was never clean. Every time we turned a corner, a dozen or so soda bottles and beer cans would roll across the floor. It got so we hated the bus, and scattered the trash around to show how much we hated it.

The acts would pee on the floor if they couldn't wait for a rest stop. The bus driver would get up every now and then and shout down the bus, "Whoever is pissing in the back of the bus, please stop."

One morning he came to me, really irate, and said, "Some asshole back there is still pissing on the floor."

So the next day I made the announcement: "If you gotta go and can't wait until we stop, please piss out the window."

Ah, show biz.

Only one seat on the bus was taken by a nonperformer. He was Bobby "the Book Man." Bobby was the program seller. He was a short, fat black man, an odd-looking little man who always wore a porkpie hat. He never talked to anyone on the bus, just sat there drinking beer and listening to his expensive portable radio. Moments after our arrival in every town we went to, he'd be met by a lovely lady, usually white, who'd pick him up in a nice-looking car. They'd drive away and we wouldn't see him until showtime when he came back full of smiles. We never knew how he did it.

Sleeping on the bus was the worst part of traveling. There

weren't many places where you could sleep other than your seat. Gene Pitney climbed up and got into the luggage rack and slept there. That seemed like a good idea. I tried it one night and my back hurt for a week. We were in Atlanta, Georgia, and I went to see a doctor.

"What kind of mattress do you sleep on?" he asked.

"Mattress! I slept in the luggage rack of a bus!"

"Aren't you that young fellow on television?"

"Yes. I am."

"Can't you afford a mattress?"

Eventually I built a bed out of 2-by-4's with a sheet of canvas between them that I hung across the aisle from one luggage rack to another. It was about two feet wide and like a hammock. I climbed in there and slept. As the tours grew and we had two buses, I had the first four seats in each bus ripped out, replacing them with a foam rubber mattress about three and a half feet wide and six feet long. Five or six of the performers slept in it at one time.

The bus driver was supposed to get his sleep when he wasn't driving. More often than I like to remember, the driver was as exhausted as the rest of us. I woke up one morning to find Arnie Satin of The Dovells driving the bus. Arnie awoke in the middle of the night just in time to see the bus driver doze off and the bus start to swerve off the road. He took over and there we were, lurching down the road with Arnie, who could hardly drive a car, at the wheel. Other times I woke up to find Duane Eddy driving. Duane loved to drive the bus. I'd say, "There goes the insurance money," and go back to sleep.

Because the drummer was the most important man on the tour, he got the privilege of sleeping stretched out on the rear seat. Before I installed the foam mattresses, he was the only man on the bus who could lie down in a prone position to sleep. He had to get the most rest because he worked the hardest. We didn't want him to get sick, so the backseat was his and his alone.

I had just dozed off one night when I was thrown violently out of my seat. I landed on Bobby Vee, who was sleeping on newspapers on the floor of the aisle. The bus swerved back and forth as I tried to get up, finally coming to a halt with a horrible smash.

Getting to my feet I looked down the length of the bus. The driver had fallen asleep and the bus had hit a bridge abutment before it swerved off the road. The left rear quarter was gone, and there was a gaping hole, like a bomb had exploded.

The backseat was empty. What was left of it was peppered with giant pieces of jagged glass. The drummer was gone.

"Oh, my God!" I said. We all just stood there and stared.

I think it was DeeDee who spoke up, "It's all right, he's here!"

We found the drummer in one of the seats, still sleeping soundly. In the middle of the night he'd gotten up to talk to someone and had fallen asleep next to them. The backseat had been empty when the bus hit the abutment.

The hotels we stayed in weren't much better than a night on the bus. They weren't always terrible, but several rooms had only a bare bulb hanging from a wire from the ceiling as lights. Most often they were run-down hotels and motels that were willing to take a mixed group like ours. It didn't matter; we collapsed as soon as we hit the rooms. Occasionally there were groupies, or "Top 40 Fuckers" as we called them. In one hotel there was a knock on my door, I opened it, and there was a teen-age girl wrapped in her mother's fur coat. She smiled at me, then opened the coat. She was stark, bare-assed naked. I shut the door. I heard her proceed down the hall to the next possibility.

Our main concern was survival. We learned to wash out underwear, nylons, and handkerchiefs with Ivory soap, then we pressed them against the tile in the shower and let them stick there till they dried, finally peeling them off the next morning. The biggest single luxury was to hit a town that had a laundromat so we could do our clothes. We'd find a grocery store and buy a couple of eggs and a can of Campbell's soup. Back at the hotel we'd put them in the washbasin, with the little rubber stopper pulled out slightly, and the hot water on. If we left it that way when we got back from the show we had reasonably hardboiled eggs and lukewarm soup.

Under these conditions there wasn't much true romance cropping up. Mostly there were convenience romances. Toward the end of one tour one of The Dovells, a nice middle-class Jewish boy from Philadelphia, announced he was going to take his newfound girl friend, a pretty black girl in The Crystals, home to meet his parents. This was 1959, mind you. But when the tour ended the romance ended.

Johnny Tillotson brought his wife, Lou, along on tour, except nobody knew they were married. He arrived and left the concerts alone. If we saw her in the hotel lobby or during interviews we weren't supposed to recognize her. Like every other teen idol, Johnny didn't want to do anything that would destroy his image as the available young white bachelor.

Next to sleeping, drinking was our favorite pastime. Everybody boozed. We were on this schedule for two to three months, hanging around in locker rooms and vacant theaters, eating in grungy hamburger joints, loaded on the bus at the end of the show stinking and sweating and ready to ride all night. Booze was a great relief. Before the bus pulled out we went to a liquor store and brought three or four jugs of wine. It was a great joy to pass the bottles around, sing, tell jokes, and laugh. We'd drink ourselves into a stupor by the middle of the night, riding along through some godforsaken Midwestern cornfield.

One night some wise guy included the bus driver in the circuit as we passed the bottle around. The driver got as plastered as the rest of us. Then we came into a tiny town, and there we were with this giant bus, the driver weaving it back and forth across the road and stopping whenever he saw a pretty girl. He'd push open the door and invite her aboard, while the rest of us roared with laughter.

Finally the police showed up. One of the girls we picked up got scared and jumped off the bus just as the cops stopped us. She ran into the bushes by the side of the road. The cops got out and started shooting at her. Luckily, their aim wasn't very good. When they came aboard the bus, only my fast talking and guarantee that we were on our way out of town kept us out of jail.

Bobby Sheehan, who was Bobby Soxx in Bobby Soxx and The Blue Jeans, had it down to a science. He carried an extra briefcase filled with booze so no matter where we were, we didn't run dry.

We caught a guy in the back of the bus smoking pot once. This strange aroma came wafting down the aisle. He was thrown off the tour as a dope fiend!

237

The site of the concert could be a high school auditorium, roller-skating rink, burlesque house, or ballroom. In those days there weren't many municipal auditoriums, so we played where we could. Some of the places were in terrible condition—at one show the whole stage collapsed, it fell apart just as we were about to roll on the amplifiers. No one was hurt. At another job I was in the middle of introducing The Shirelles when I took a step back and fell through a trapdoor down eight feet onto a mess of folding chairs.

One of my favorite dates was the Allentown, Pennsylvania, State Fair. We played at a racetrack there. The audience of several thousand sat in the grandstand watching us as we performed on a stage set up in the middle of the track. One leg of the track was between us and the audience. Most of the audience watched us through binoculars. I could see the glint of the glass lenses as they caught the sun during our early show, which started about four in the afternoon.

Freddy Cannon was on the show; he had the number-two spot after Duane Eddy. Freddy kept asking me to let him close the show, just once. Finally I said go ahead.

"Ladies and gentlemen," I said from center stage, my voice booming back at me from the stadium PA system, "we want to close today's show with a very special star. He's one of the most outstanding entertainers in rock 'n' roll. In fact he's outstanding in the wings right now. Ladies and gentlemen, Freddy Cannon!"

Freddy ran out on stage, shaking my hand as he went by. The band struck up "Palisades Park" and he was off. I could see he was thrilled with the closing spot; he was the star of the show. About the third song Freddy got this strange look on his face. I looked at the crowd, the binoculars were looking to the left, away from the stage and Freddy's performance. The track had started a horse race. In fact it was only a couple minutes later that the horses came galloping by, closing the show. Freddy finished the song and came into the wings where I told him I'd never let him forget the day a horse race upstaged him as the closing act.

Whenever we played a high school gym, the first thing we'd do was head for the showers. I can't tell you what a social leveler it was to take a shower with Big D. Irwin, Round Robin, and twenty other guys. When there weren't any dressing rooms, both men and women changed clothes together under the stage.

We carried very primitive amplification gear with us and used the house lighting system. At first we used the house PA systems, but that became a problem. In those days I'd get backstage with these ancient stagehands, venerable members of the International Association of Theatrical and Stage Employees who didn't care about rock 'n' roll. I'd tell them to turn the sound up as far as it can go.

"That's as far as we're gonna take it up," some gray-haired old bastard would snarl back at me.

"That's as loud as you can get it?"

"Yup."

"Great, now take it up another six or seven notches."

"Sure," he'd say. Then, the minute my back was turned, he'd take it back down again.

After a little of that we started carrying our own PA system. In the early days they'd never turn us up loud enough. It was the same in movie theaters. When the first movie I produced, *Jamboree*, was shown I went crazy opening night because I couldn't hear the rock 'n' roll songs. All I could hear were people talking in the theater. It was a long, hard road getting them to turn it up. Now I scream at my kids to turn it down.

At showtime, our grubby organization became a well-oiled machine, if a little the worse for wear. The acts were told that if the audience left their seats to start towards the stage they had to stop performing. It was our house rule. The kids had to get back in their seats before we started the show again. We were responsible for the hall and we wanted to play it again. We were also responsible to the local promoter and local radio station. And I worried about our insurance and our goodwill. If any performer ever incited the audience I'd toss him off the tour.

We never had any real problems with the kids, even during the mid-sixties, when screaming and running the stage became part of the show. We did play some one-nighters in Toronto and Montreal, where Paul Anka was on the bill. Paul was born

*Left:* At the wheel of the "Caravan of Stars" bus. I remember vividly the nights when others on the talent roster took over that function.

*Right:* When Ray Hildebrand suddenly left the "Caravan of Stars" one night, the team of Paul and Paula fell apart. For the next few weeks, I played Paul.

The attendance record at Atlantic City's Steel Pier was broken with one of our rock 'n' roll shows. In the summer of 1960 we presented this lineup.

Wall-to-wall people at the Marine Ballroom of the world-famous Atlantic City Steel Pier.

The "Caravan of Stars" rock 'n' roll shows succeeded so well that we leased a bus fifty-two weeks a year.

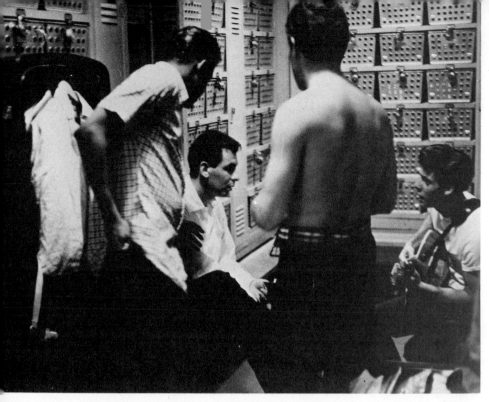

Backstage in a high school locker room, Freddy Cannon (left) and Brian Hyland (right) get ready for a "Caravan of Stars" concert.

Round Robin fascinates an early "Caravan of Stars" audience with "The Slauson."

Freddy Cannon opens our "Caravan of Stars" show.

This high school gym was typical of the places the "Caravan of Stars" played.

in Ottawa and when he played his hometown many years ago, there were reports that the audience threw tomatoes at him. People are strange about their hometown heroes. It didn't stop him from becoming a superstar.

The most important dates on the tour were the tie-in dates. For example, if we were in Las Vegas, the next big date might be Los Angeles. But since it's a major city, we would only play Los Angeles on a weekend. So it was important to get the weekday dates in between the major dates. These were the tie-in dates.

One time I called Roz Ross to fill in my schedule.

"What's the next date?" I asked her, my clipboard in hand.

"Windowrock, Arizona," said Roz.

"What's that?"

"An Indian reservation."

The "Caravan of Stars" went everywhere.

In Indianapolis, thieves broke into the bus and stole all the clothes and equipment we hadn't brought into the hall with us. The robbery was discovered in the middle of the show.

"Get The Orlons to go out into the parking lot and see what's happening," I told Billy Cook, a former "Bandstand" regular, who worked with Ed McAdam as tour manager. The Orlons had already made their appearance so I could spare them.

The next act went out onstage, the show continued, but none of The Orlons returned. I couldn't find Billy so I went out to investigate.

In the parking lot the cops had arrived and had handcuffed the lead singer of The Orlons. They had him in the backseat of their patrol car, a flashlight shining in his face.

"No, no sir, you don't understand," I said. One of the cops grabbed me and swung me around.

"You shut up or you're going right in too," he yelled in my face. Then he shoved me in my shiny mohair suit up against the wall.

"I've got to introduce the next act," I said and ran back into the theater.

A couple minutes later Billy stuck his head out the door to see what was happening. Someone hit him in the face and broke his nose. As I came offstage he came up to me, his hand over his face, blood gushing out between his fingers.

I got the local police station on the phone and told them what was going on. In between running back and forth introducing the acts I managed to get The Orlons out of the cops' grips.

When the show was over we ran onto the bus and got the hell out of town.

Several weeks later the police informed us they'd found all our stuff in a construction site down the street from the hall.

On one tour when we had two buses, I was in the first bus with Ed McAdam and the acts that would open the show. In the second bus, about a half hour behind us, were Bill Lee and Billy Cook with The Crystals, Big D. Irwin, Round Robin, Dick and DeeDee, and a couple other acts. It was about noon, they were coming out of North Carolina into Virginia when their bus broke down. The driver got the bus off to the side of the road, on a green knoll overlooking a roadside tavern.

It was one of those taverns where they serve a lot of beer—there were beer signs all over the outside—and inside it was a greasy spoon with a back room just visible from the front door where the local guys played pool.

Bill Lee and the bus driver, who was black, walked into the tavern to call the bus company. Bill noticed that the guys playing pool had their sleeves rolled up, were overweight, flushed from drinking beer, and staring at him.

The bus driver went to the phone booth to make the call. Then the waitress came from behind the counter up to Bill.

"You all on a freedom bus?" she asks.

Bill didn't know what to say.

He noticed that she was standing at the window staring at the bus. Bill looked out the window in time to see the acts starting to get off the bus, 70 percent of them black, the rest white.

The waitress turned back to Bill. "What are you doing with all those colored people?" she wanted to know.

"It's a rock 'n' roll show, Dick Clark's 'Caravan of Stars.'"

"Go on, you're a freedom bus, freedom riders."

"No, not at all."

Bill noticed that the guys with the pool cues have started eyeing him up and down and were standing near the door muttering to each other.

Bill went over to the bus driver, got him out of the phone booth, and whispered, "I think we ought to get back on the bus to wait for the relief bus."

Back at the top of the hill, Bill told everybody to get back on the bus. Now they'd gotten off the bus because the air conditioning had stopped working.

The Crystals, four black girls in their late teens, told Bill, "Bullshit, we want to stay outside."

Bill turned to Billy Cook. "You ought to try to get these people back on the bus; they're a little uptight down in the tavern."

"We got to use the bathroom," The Crystals started yelling. "If we don't use the bathroom we'll pee right here on the ground."

"No, oh God, please no," Bill cried. He went back into the tavern and negotiated a trip to the bathroom for them.

"They can use that, but they can't come into the restaurant," said the waitress.

After that everybody got back on the bus. About an hour passed and everybody was getting hungry. Bill went down to the tavern again.

"Can I buy some hamburgers?" asked Bill.

"No way," he was told, "we're not cooking no food that goes into *their* mouths."

DeeDee came into the restaurant at that point. She asked if she could cook the food.

"You can cook it, but we don't want to touch it."

DeeDee cooked hamburgers for everybody. Bill paid. They charged him double.

Twenty minutes later two cars pulled up, six guys got out of each car, and the guys from the back room came out of the restaurant with pool cues in their hands. Some of the guys from the cars had ax handles and clubs. In the meantime The Crystals, who had no hold on reality at that point, are singing "My eyes have seen the glory of the coming of the Lord." Then they start yelling at the guys—they're from the North, they have a big hit record, what is this shit.

The guys were walking up the hill to the bus when the Highway Patrol showed up. Three or four patrol cars pulled in. The troopers came over to the bus. One of them yelled for everyone to get back in the bus and close the door. In the meantime the guys with the clubs got back in the cars and drove off.

One cop came on the bus. "You all know better than to cause trouble like this," he said. "What are you doing to this poor restaurant?"

We had trouble another night in South Carolina. There was a large group of tobacco men in the hotel, and a small group of well-oiled white conventioneers accosted one of The Drifters on the way to his room. They started by teasing him, then pushed and shoved him around. The odds didn't look good until several of the white guys on the tour showed up and proceeded to kick the shit out of the tobacco interests.

We finally solved the problem by eliminating the Southeast from the tour schedule.

Every two weeks we had a blowout party. The frustration of being on the bus almost twenty-four hours a day built up until we were all bitching at each other. Before it would boil over we'd have a party to let it all "out."

At these parties we had a show the audience never saw. Before the party I wrote the name of every act on the bill on slips of paper, then went up and down the aisle of the bus and let everybody draw one out of a hat. Each performer had to then secretly prepare an imitation of the act on his or her slip of paper.

I remember Tom Jones coming out wearing one of The Shirelles' wigs and dresses. Round Robin pretending he was Gene Pitney, doing all Gene's sexy shtick. It was a sight that had us roaring, putting each other on about the same act we'd seen night after night.

One of the acts on one tour was Joanne Campbell. Joanne traveled with her secretary, Loretta Martin. I became friendly with Loretta during that tour. It was at the time I was awaiting my divorce from Bobbie. One night I asked Loretta for a date; it was at the Michigan State Fair and The Shirelles had a party after the show. Loretta and I went to the party, but wound up out in the dark by the motel pool, kissing, having a long talk, and generally getting to know each other.

It was a whirlwind romance. It may sound like a bad joke,

247

but when the tour ended we went off for a weekend to Atlantic City. It was a wonderful weekend.

Loretta and I were married in 1962, and in the next few years we had two kids—Duane who's thirteen now, and Cindy who's eleven.

Loretta and I had great times on the bus tours—friends later told me it was the classic bounceback relationship. At the time I was head-over-heels in love with this very lovely lady.

The bus travel affected some performers more than others. Occasionally one would just get crazy from the tour. When the bus stopped in a town, he'd go for a walk and never come back. He probably went straight to the nearest airport, spending most of the money he'd made on the tour for a ticket home.

Ray Hildebrand, the male half of Paul and Paula, was one of the acts who deserted us. His partner, Jill Jackson, came to tell me one morning when we were checking out of a hotel.

"Ray got so tired and miserable he's gone home to Texas," she said. "I don't know what to do."

I thought for a moment. They were a big act, already on all the posters we'd printed.

"No problem. I'll be Paul," I said.

For the rest of the tour I announced religiously "Paul has been taken ill, but he'll be back with us in a day or so. In the meantime Paula and I would like to sing."

Then we'd do their big hit "Hey, Hey Paula" and Jill would perform a medley of "Cottonfields" and "Old Man River."

By the end of the tour most of us were in bad shape, ready for a month's collapse. I was ready to sleep for a week, since at the same time I was making once-a-week flights to Philadelphia for "Bandstand" tapings. Freddy Cannon told me he knew one promoter who booked two or three acts together for a show and sent them around in a laundry truck. They had to stand up, driving from town to town, in the dead of winter. The "Caravan of Stars" was never as bad as that, but it was rugged. I can't picture any of today's rock stars, who complain if the jet seats don't recline enough or the champagne isn't chilled properly, going out on one of the old tours.

But then, I can't picture myself ever being that young again.

248

# "I have a secret wish that 'Bandstand' will go on forever"

I made my first trip to Los Angeles in early 1959 to appear in *Because They're Young,* a movie I'd developed from a book called *Harrison High* and sold to Columbia Pictures. It was an extraordinary experience. Columbia really laid it on; they rented a house for me in Bel Air owned by Mercedes McCambridge, provided a maid, butler, and chauffeur, and gave me a hundred dollars a day in expenses.

In those days the film companies hired a Fabian or Frankie Avalon to appear in a John Wayne picture or stuck Ricky Nelson in a Dean Martin movie to insure teen-age appeal at the box office. *Because They're Young* starred Doug McClure and Tuesday Weld as a couple of high school kids. I played the made-to-order role of a friendly high school teacher.

While I was in Los Angeles a giant rock 'n' roll show called "A Salute to Dick Clark" was presented at the Hollywood Bowl. It was the first rock concert ever produced at the Bowl, which was renowned for its presentation of attractions like the Los Angeles Symphony Orchestra, the Budapest String Quartet, and other longhair events. The concert was a sellout, with 18,600 fans jamming the Bowl to see Bobby Darin, Anita Bryant, Freddy Cannon, Duane Eddy, Annette Funicello, and a host of other stars. The trade paper reports of the show's success proved to Hollywood that rock 'n' rollers and Dick Clark were hot properties.

Before I returned to Philadelphia (and the problems of payola and divorce still to come) I was also the subject of Ralph Edwards' "This Is Your Life" TV show. The premise of

249

the show was that a known personality was lured to a TV studio under some pretense, then Edwards walked out, a large book with the personality's name on it under his arm, and announced, "Dick Clark, *this* is *your* life."

Among those who appeared to agree what a "wonderful" guy I was were Fabian, Connie Francis, Andy Williams, Frankie Avalon, David Seville, Bobbie with Dickie, my mother and father, Roger Clipp and Lew Klein (who were in town for a broadcasters' convention), and Tony Mamarella, who had come to the coast to work with me on *Because They're Young*.

From time to time in the next few years I returned to Los Angeles. The Saturday night show was broadcast from there a couple of times, and I did a return date with my entourage of stars at the Hollywood Bowl. In 1961 I appeared in *The Young Doctors*, the first Arthur Hailey book made into a movie. It starred Frederic March, Ben Gazzara, Eddie Albert, and a newcomer named George Segal.

In his book on the history of rock, British author Nik Cohn observes that California in the early sixties was, as Chuck Berry sang, "The Promised Land." It was the new American wonderland—the home of a free teen world with surfboards and woodies and those gorgeous California girls. Two girls, in fact, for every boy. It was the land where all the kids had cars and dates and friends and nobody was ever left out for long. As Cohn says, California was like a very special high school where it was always summer vacation.

When Tony Mamarella quit as producer of "Bandstand" rather than give up his music business interests, he and Bernie Binnick bought out my share in Swan Records and became partners in the company. Tony and I hadn't spoken during the payola investigations, except for occasional good wishes relayed by intermediary friends, but once the investigations ended we were friends again. He or Bernie would stop by WFIL to leave copies of their latest releases. They continued to have hits with Freddy Cannon, putting out such rock 'n' roll classics as Gabriel and The Angels' "That's Life" and The Rebels' "Wild Weekend," and introduced a number of new artists, among them Frank Slay, who had a brief solo career on Swan after writing hits for Freddy Cannon with Bob Crewe.

In the late fall of 1963 I called the Swan offices to check if Freddy Cannon was in town and available to do "Bandstand." Tony and I worked out the details and were gabbing about this-and-that when he told me Bernie Binnick was in London.

"I just got a package of records from him this morning," Tony told me. "He's picked up a number of masters that are available from EMI for licensing here."

"Anything good?"

"I don't know, I haven't had time to listen to them yet; there must be thirty or thirty-five dubs."

I didn't think anything more about our conversation until a couple of weeks later when Bernie came by the office. Bernie was a lovable guy, but sometimes his manner was quite abrupt. He wasn't in the office more than a minute or two, when he opened his briefcase and began rummaging through it.

"Bernie, sit down, tell me about your trip."

"Great time. Listen, Dick, can you listen to this right now?" he asked, handing me a single.

I took the record and looked at the label. Below the black and silver Swan logo and the "Don't Drop Out" slogan they'd put on all their records, it read "She Loves You" by The Beatles. I flipped the record over; the other side was "I'll Get You" by The Beatles.

"What's the "A" side?"

" 'She Loves You.' It's one of the masters we picked up from EMI. Tony thinks it's a hit so we took it on a four-month option. If we don't sell 50,000 copies EMI gets it back." Bernie stuck his hand back in the case and pulled out a black-and-white glossy photo. "This is what they look like."

"God! Are they kidding?" I handed him back the photo, got up, and put the record on the turntable. It ran 2:18. When it was over I shook my head. "I don't think so, Bernie. It sounds old-fashioned, real mid-fifties, kind of hollow."

"They're a sensation in England."

"Yeah?"

"You wouldn't believe it."

251

"Okay, I tell you what I'll do. I'll add it to the Record Revue this afternoon. Can I borrow that picture?"

Just after 4:30 that afternoon I selected the kids for the Record Revue.

"This first record is 'She Loves You' by The Beatles," I told my reviewers. The record played, the kids danced to it, and when it finished, I questioned each of the three reviewers while the fourth kid tallied up the score.

"It's all right, sort of like the Everly Brothers and Chuck Berry mixed together," said the first reviewer. "I'll give it a 77."

"It's not all that easy to dance to," complained the second reviewer. "I give it a 65."

"It doesn't seem to have anything, but it's sort of catchy," said the third kid. "The best I can give it is a 70."

I turned to the score keeper. "It gets a 73," he said.

"Before we rate the next record, I want to show you a photo of the group," I said, picking up the glossy from the podium and holding it so the cameras could get a tight shot.

Some of the kids snickered, others laughed at the picture of the four shaggy-haired boys from Liverpool. The response was less than enthusiastic.

After the show I called Swan. Bernie got on the phone.

"You saw?"

"Yeah, I told Tony we may have a stiff," said Bernie. "Thanks for giving it a try anyway."

I left the station that afternoon without the faintest idea that the days of good ol' rock 'n' roll were about to become a few scratched film clips, a list of golden oldies, and some cherished memories of growing up in the fifties.


By late 1963 I realized how rapidly times were changing. I knew that "Bandstand" and I would soon be out of date unless I did something about it. ABC wanted to take the show to a once-a-week format during this quiet period before The Beatles broke the next big rock movement. When the network told me their plan, I knew I had to get out of Philadelphia and move to either New York or Los Angeles if I wanted to continue in the entertainment business.

Fabian, Frankie Avalon, Bobby Darin, and many other teen

stars were moving to Los Angeles in the hope of getting into the movies. The Philadelphia music scene was fading, while in Southern California Jan and Dean and The Beach Boys were making fresh, new sounds. When the Saturday night show ended, Deke Heyward moved to Los Angeles to write and produce the first beach party movies, which painted the image of a new teen-age paradise—Annette Funicello and Frankie Avalon making out on the beach in an all-outdoor world where kids devoted their time to "hanging ten" on the biggest wave they could find.

In March 1964 I made the big move to Los Angeles. The "Bandstand" "staff" came with me: Ed McAdam, Chris Betlejeski, my new secretary (Marlene had gotten married), and Charlie O'Donnell, our announcer. We packed up a moving van with our stuff and found we couldn't get everything in. So I rented a U-Haul and Ed McAdam drove from Philadelphia to Los Angeles, dragging the U-Haul which had the "Bandstand" podium, my *Life* magazine collection, and boxes of records and files crammed in it.

The first "Bandstand" office was in the Capitol Records Tower at Hollywood and Vine. Bobby Darin had the office next door to mine. It seemed like old home week.

One afternoon over lunch at Chasen's, Henry Rogers, the head of the prestigious Rogers & Cowan public relations firm, told me I was making a mistake hiding myself away in an office building.

"You know, the way to make progress here is not to have an office like you've got; you don't understand Hollywood. Rent a building, hang out a sign, call it Dick Clark Productions, look like you're in business. It doesn't matter if it's just you and your secretary inside," Henry told me.

Rosalind Ross, who was booking the "Caravan of Stars" tours, found a building on Sunset Boulevard, down the street from Dean Martin's 77 Sunset Strip restaurant, the Schwabs where Lana Turner was discovered, the Whiskey A Go-Go, and the rest of the landmarks that make Sunset Strip world famous. I hung up a very modest sign in lowercase print—*dick clark productions*—and started producing.

Once we were settled we created two of our most successful music TV shows. The first was "Where the Action Is," which became a daily afternoon TV show on ABC during the sixties. "Action" was "Bandstand" out-of-doors—a gang of kids, including dancers and current rock stars, gallivanting around the beach, singing songs, and basking in the California sun.

When "Action" first went on the air, the bikini had just come in. The network censors wouldn't let us show a female navel on TV. We could show a male navel, but not the female variety. One day I got so pissed at the idea of this ban—especially when the show often took place on the beach at Malibu with the kids in swim suits—that I showed up on the set with a pound of nose putty. I had all the girls putty up their navels and take their bikinis down to just above pubic-hair level so it looked like they had stomachs a yard and a half long! It was the most grotesque thing you've ever seen. We taped a number of navelless shows before the little old lady at the network censorship office caught on.

"Happening" was the second show. It featured Paul Revere and The Raiders, one of the biggest teen acts of the late sixties. The most unexpected guest we ever had on the show was then presidential-hopeful Hubert Humphrey, who stopped by to glad-hand Paul and The Raiders in the hopes of picking up a few votes.

Dick Clark Productions has continued to grow. We're still on Sunset Strip, where we produce TV shows, movies, radio shows, concerts, and "Bandstand." I work behind the scenes with most of these projects, producing up to two hundred TV shows a year. In addition, I've expanded my TV hosting chores to include a daytime game show. When I first came to California I did a game show for ABC called "Missing Links." It required that I fly to New York once a week. I've been flying between Los Angeles and New York regularly ever since—I've logged over four million miles in air travel, going to New York for a day or two a week to tape various shows. My current hosting job is on the "$20,000 Pyramid."


Nine years and nine months after we were married, Loretta and I separated. She was the first to realize it wasn't working; it took me a bit longer.

I never in my whole life imagined that I would be married

and divorced twice. To me it's an express admission of failure on my part. I've always had the traditional American male concept of life: I'd find a woman, marry her, raise kids, own a house and car, and we'd grow old gracefully together. It's a source of deep-seated disappointment that that didn't happen.

During my marriage to Bobbie and my marriage to Loretta, eighteen years of my prime life, I never cheated. I don't know why exactly, I think out of respect to my wives and parents. That sounds hokey, but the principle was ground in early, and it stuck. The last few years since Loretta and I parted I've lived a single man's life, but when I examine it, it's centered around one woman. She's Kari Wigton, to whom I'm not married but with whom I spend most of my time.

When I first met Kari she asked me, "How long were you married the first time?"

"Nine years," I said.

"And how long the second time?"

"Nine years."

"That's not bad for a guy with a short attention span."

The other day, in explaining my relationship with her I said, "She's perfect for me. One out of three isn't bad!"

I have good relationships today with Bobbie and Loretta. They are fine ladies, I respect them both, and I hope they still have respect for me. I have three terrific kids. Dickie (now Richard) is a junior in college. He grew up with Bobbie in Ohio so I wasn't able to be with him more than three months a year. He still spends his vacation time with me, and we've grown close. Duane and Cindy are growing up near me; I see them frequently, and we have a pretty normal relationship. All three kids are attractive, healthy, and bright, and I'm very proud of them.


For a couple of years in the late sixties, I lost touch with the music that was happening. It was the one time when I just couldn't figure out the kids. Like most adults in the late sixties, I had a negative attitude toward drugs and many of the kids and what they were going through. I hoped the hell they would grow out of it, which, fortunately, they did.

I put an antidrug message in *Psych-Out,* a picture I made

From left to right, Jack Jones, myself, George Hamilton, and Jackie De-Shannon attending a Hollywood party in the early sixties.

Somewhere along the way I did a movie premiere and talked to a lady whom I did not like, Dorothy Kilgallen.

When I appeared on "This Is Your Life," Ralph Edwards brought on Frankie Avalon as a "surprise" guest.

From left to right, Connie Francis, who was also a personal friend; Ralph Edwards, host of "This Is Your Life"; myself and my first wife, Bobbie. Seated behind us are Andy Grass, my high school chum and best man, and my parents, Julia and Richard Clark.

*Left:* In this scene from *Because They're Young*, I vigorously kiss Victoria Shaw, while standing on two volumes of the Los Angeles Yellow Pages. (*Copyright © 1960 Columbia Pictures Corp. All rights reserved.*)

*Right:* During the filming of *Because They're Young*, Tuesday Weld celebrated her "sweet sixteen" birthday. We were joined on the high school classroom set by Tab Hunter. (*Copyright © 1959 Columbia Pictures Corp. All rights reserved.*)

When "Bandstand" first moved to California, we had a "Welcome to the West" party. From left to right, Dick and Loretta Clark, Johnny Mathis, Sandra Dee Darin and her husband, Bobby.

Pictured here in the early sixties are Rona Barrett, Johnny Mathis, record producer John D'Andrea, and me.

Michael Callan is threatened by Chris Robinson, brandishing a switchblade, in a scene from *Because They're Young*.

Doug McClure and Roberta Shore starred as teen-age lovers in *Because They're Young*, a story that these days seems humorous and naive. (*Copyright © 1959 Columbia Pictures Corp. All rights reserved.*)

From left to right, Ben Gazzara, Frederic March, myself, and Eddie Albert in a highly dramatic scene from *The Young Doctors*, the only good picture I ever made. (*© 1961 United Artists Corporation.*)

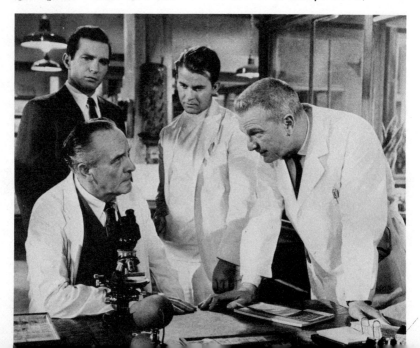

with Jack Nicholson, Bruce Dern, Dean Stockwell, and Susan Strasberg. I insisted that it be in there subliminally because I'd seen the kids in the hippie communities living in awful squalor. In the film you see scenes where it's all wonderful, they're all stoned-out having a great time. Then there's the morning-after scene—the garbage lying around, a roach crawling through the food, a half-eaten orange crawling with maggots. Bruce Dern played a freaked out, self-styled messiah in the film. He and Jack Nicholson had to wear wigs because their hair wasn't long enough. If you saw it today you'd say it was a reasonably accurate view of what was going on then. Originally, we titled the picture *The Love Children,* but the distributors objected—they thought it was a film about bastards.

The late sixties affected each of my friends differently. Bobby Darin became a latter-day hippie. All of a sudden he was wearing jeans and letting his hair grow. He gave up his house and moved into a trailer in the northern part of California. He wasn't a happy guy. He spent all of his money making a movie that was never released.

As a result of rheumatic fever Bobby had a bad heart. He was in the hospital having the first of a series of operations. We were putting together the "Twentieth Anniversary Bandstand" and Bobby and I talked on the phone about the good old days. I told him that my marriage with Loretta wasn't working out. He gave me strength, telling me he thought we were doing the right thing by calling it quits rather than continuing to agonize over something that wasn't meant to be.

The last time I talked to Bobby was shortly before his death. He'd had open heart surgery and developed a rare blood infection. They gave him several blood transfusions, but he couldn't be saved.

I always thought that Bobby had a fear he wasn't going to grow old, that he wouldn't live long. Maybe that's why he went to such extremes—spending money to live high on the hog, dropping out to find himself. I think he always wanted to be like Sinatra. He was misquoted as saying he'd be bigger than Frank Sinatra one day. He wasn't that egotistical. I miss him a lot because he was so good, such a total full-out pro and real friend.

261

My ego is reasonably well developed and I want people to know I'm a smart fellow. I don't give a hoot in hell if I get on a train or plane and nobody says, "Hey, there he is, go get his autograph." Nobody has ever really applauded anything I've done as a performer . . . and I don't expect it. But I would like recognition for having done something other than Clearasil commercials all my life.

I remember an incident some years ago, when I was on the Pennsylvania Railroad making the run into New York. I happened to walk through the bar car. The bartender stood behind the bar, polishing a glass and talking to a customer. They turned to look at me as I went by.

"Hey, I know him. I see him on television," the bartender told the customer as I walked to the end of the car. I opened the door to pass through to the next car when I heard the bartender add: "Yeah, I see him on TV all the time. That's Pat Boone."

After the first day on the network, Tony Mamarella told me we had a problem: nobody knew my name. We didn't have an announcer at the start of the show in those days. I told Tony I didn't want to come on and just say my name. We began to superimpose "Dick Clark" at the bottom of the picture the first time I appeared on the screen each afternoon. After a while the name and the show became synonymous. We do it to this day. I hated hearing people say, "What's that guy's name down in Philadelphia with the records and the kids?"

I lived the image that was expected of me on TV for over twenty years. At times I've almost lived that image in my private life. I have a certain resentment about what I did to myself and what TV did to me. To this day if somebody hears me say, "Oh, shit," they say, "I didn't know you could even *say* that!" The TV role often imposed itself on my private life, but I admit it was a role I created myself.

I'm not really much different from the people who are "my people." I have a lot of affection and regard for the people who watch me on TV; they make it happen for me. The people who know Dick Clark better than anybody else are America's ordinary people. I call them the McDonalds people—there's nothing wrong with that because that's where I like to be. I could

262

never live on the Main Line in Philadelphia or in Beverly Hills —I really like going to motorcycle races and drinking beer. I don't relate to being anything other than what I am. For me, a good time is going to the movies, taking a drive, finding goodies in the supermarket. I can't pretend I'm any different.

Over the years people have asked me what's my secret for staying young—possibly because I've looked about the same to them for twenty years. I've got a variety of answers, depending on the occasion, including, "Have an open mind and a closed refrigerator." The truth is, it's hereditary. My father, who at this writing is almost eighty, looks like he's in his early sixties. I've always looked younger than my age. For a guy approaching his late forties, all I can say is we should all be so lucky. Of course I'm as concerned about middle age as anybody else my age. I watch my weight as best I can, but we all develop such godawful habits as we get older—we pleasure ourselves more and more because we know our time is getting shorter.

As for "Bandstand," it's still my baby. It's like a child I've raised. I don't want to see it grow up and fly away. If I had my own personal say I'd be doing it five days a week, an hour or two a day. I've rarely missed a show. I arrived late for the show once. The train got in from New York in a snowstorm and Tony stood in for me until I got there. When I took vacations or was off the show to make movies or tour, I came up with a system where disc jockeys from various affiliate stations would do the show. None of them would guest-host for more than one afternoon. The wisdom of that was that nobody could learn to do the show in one day and they were all scared the first time out, so I never felt any threat. I don't mind admitting I've clung to "Bandstand." I had laryngitis once, I couldn't even squeak, so I had my friend and the show's announcer, Charlie O'Donnell, do the show while I worked as his sidekick giving sign language. In the flu season, when we did the show live, I'd go on, flu, colds, diarrhea . . . it was alarming when I think I did shows in front of 20 million people and I'd know that I had to leave the podium within 30 seconds or have a terrible accident right there. I'd signal to Tony anxiously, he'd put two records back to back, and I'd dash for the men's room.

I know that someday "Bandstand" will be canceled. I'm trying to prepare myself for its demise. There've been a lot of times when it's come close to being canceled and I've worked hard every year to keep it going. I have a secret wish that "Bandstand" will go on forever. I'm striving now to keep it on for our twenty-fifth anniversary. After that, it will be in the laps of the gods.

Pixie hairdos, two pairs of bobby socks to make the ankles look thick, Peter Pan collars, circle pins, penny loafers—such is the stuff of nostalgia. In the fifties I never imagined that cuffed corduroy pants and high school sweaters would someday elicit a heart-tugging desire for the good old days. Truthfully, I never expected the fifties to be anybody's good old days.

Although we celebrate "Bandstand's" birthday every year, it never seemed to me that nostalgia was anything but people living in the past. A few years ago I had a fellow working for me named Richard Nader. Richard came into my office one morning and said he had a great idea; he wanted to bring back all the old fifties artists we didn't hear anymore, who weren't making records any longer, and package them into a fifties show.

I told Richard I thought it was a dreadful idea.

At that point he said he thought he'd do it himself. He quit and returned to New York, where he organized the first rock 'n' roll revival shows. They did very well. I still wasn't tuned into what he was up to until he called me to ask me to help him out. He'd booked a giant fifties show in Madison Square Garden and one of the main acts had canceled on him. He offered me a considerable amount of money to fly in to introduce the acts. I told him I didn't want to do that; if I wanted to be in that business I'd do it myself. He cajoled me a bit more and I told him I'd do it for old-times' sake.

When I walked out onstage that night at Madison Square Garden the crowd went wild. I was overwhelmed by the reaction. There was love in the air. Back in Los Angeles I couldn't get what had happened out of my head. Eventually I decided to put together my own revival show in Las Vegas.

"Good Ol' Rock 'n' Roll" opened in Las Vegas in July 1974.

The review featured Freddy Cannon, Cornell Gunter and The Coasters, Jackie Wilson, dancers, and nostalgic film clips. We opened at the Las Vegas Hilton and were a sensation. It was extraordinary. Dick Clark the "performer," which I am not, went out onstage and entertained people just by being himself. I got a taste of making people really happy, of feeling that warmth come toward me . . . seeing them applauding, crying, yelling, laughing, and as they left at the end of the show saying to each other, God, that was fun. I realized what memories can do for people. We still present good ol' rock 'n' roll.

At the end of each show I come out to speak to the audience Standing there, alone on the stage, the spotlight on me, I say, "I couldn't have had a nicer past, but I really like my present more. I hope your present is as happy as mine, because tomorrow morning you and I will have to go out there in the world and be happy with ourselves as we are today.

"Let me finish the night with a toast. We've all sort of grown up together . . . so here's to you . . .

> 'Rock 'n' roll is here to stay,
> They said it wouldn't last.
> You've gotta live for today,
> You can't live in the past.
> Those good times won't come 'round again,
> They were fun in many ways,
> But one thing for sure, my friend . . .
> We shared some happy days!' "

# Index

270

273